About This Book

Why is this topic important?

Continuing education and development lie at the very heart of any successful organization. Time and time again, studies show that the best organizations, those that deliver better-than-average return on investment, also happen to be the ones with the highest commitment to training and development. Moreover, training has become a powerful ally in the war for talent. Job seekers frequently cite a strong commitment to development as one of the principal reasons for joining or remaining with an organization.

What can you achieve with this book?

In your hands is a working toolkit, a valuable source of knowledge for the training professional. Offering entirely new content each year, the Pfeiffer Training *Annual* showcases the latest thinking and cutting-edge approaches to training and development, contributed by practicing training professionals, consultants, academics, and subject-matter experts. Turn to the *Annual* for a rich source of ideas and to try out new methods and approaches that others in your profession have found successful.

How is this book organized?

The book is divided into four sections: Experiential Learning Activities (ELAs); Editor's Choice; Inventories, Questionnaires, and Surveys; and Articles and Discussion Resources. All the material can be freely reproduced for training purposes. The ELAs are the mainstay of the *Annual* and cover a broad range of training topics. The activities are presented as complete and ready-to-use training designs; facilitator instructions and all necessary handouts and participant materials are included. Editor's Choice pieces allow us to select material that doesn't fit the other categories and take advantage of "hot topics." The instrument section introduces reliable survey and assessment tools for gathering and sharing data on aspects of personal or team development. The articles section presents the best current thinking about training and organization development. Use these for your own professional development or as lecture resources.

About Pfeiffer

Pfeiffer serves the professional development and hands-on resource needs of training and human resource practitioners and gives them products to do their jobs better. We deliver proven ideas and solutions from experts in HR development and HR management, and we offer effective and customizable tools to improve workplace performance. From novice to seasoned professional, Pfeiffer is the source you can trust to make yourself and your organization more successful.

Essential Knowledge Pfeiffer produces insightful, practical, and comprehensive materials on topics that matter the most to training and HR professionals. Our Essential Knowledge resources translate the expertise of seasoned professionals into practical, how-to guidance on critical workplace issues and problems. These resources are supported by case studies, worksheets, and job aids and are frequently supplemented with CD-ROMs, websites, and other means of making the content easier to read, understand, and use.

Essential Tools Pfeiffer's Essential Tools resources save time and expense by offering proven, ready-to-use materials—including exercises, activities, games, instruments, and assessments—for use during a training or team-learning event. These resources are frequently offered in looseleaf or CD-ROM format to facilitate copying and customization of the material.

Pfeiffer also recognizes the remarkable power of new technologies in expanding the reach and effectiveness of training. While e-hype has often created whizbang solutions in search of a problem, we are dedicated to bringing convenience and enhancements to proven training solutions. All our e-tools comply with rigorous functionality standards. The most appropriate technology wrapped around essential content yields the perfect solution for today's on-the-go trainers and human resource professionals.

Pfeiffer
www.pfeiffer.com

Essential resources for training and HR professionals

The Pfeiffer Annual Series

The Pfeiffer Annuals present each year never-before-published materials contributed by learning professionals and academics and written for trainers, consultants, and human resource and performance-improvement practitioners. As a forum for the sharing of ideas, theories, models, instruments, experiential learning activities, and best and innovative practices, the Annuals are unique. Not least because only in the Pfeiffer Annuals will you find solutions from professionals like you who work in the field as trainers, consultants, facilitators, educators, and human resource and performance-improvement practitioners and whose contributions have been tried and perfected in real-life settings with actual participants and clients to meet real-world needs.

The Pfeiffer Annual: Consulting
Edited by Elaine Biech

The Pfeiffer Annual: Leadership Development
Edited by David Dotlich, Ron Meeks, Peter Cairo, and Stephen Rhinesmith

The Pfeiffer Annual: Management Development
Edited by Robert C. Preziosi

The Pfeiffer Annual: Training
Edited by Elaine Biech

Michael Allen's e-Learning Annual
Edited by Michael Allen

Call for Papers

How would you like to be published in the *Pfeiffer Training* or *Consulting Annual*? Possible topics for submissions include group and team building, organization development, leadership, problem solving, presentation and communication skills, consulting and facilitation, and training-the-trainer. Contributions may be in one of the following three formats:

- Experiential Learning Activities

- Inventories, Questionnaires, and Surveys

- Articles and Discussion Resources

To receive a copy of the submission packet, which explains the requirements and will help you determine format, language, and style to use, contact editor Elaine Biech at Pfeifferannual@aol.com or by calling 757-588-3939.

Elaine Biech, EDITOR

The *2009*
Pfeiffer
ANNUAL

TRAINING

Pfeiffer
A Wiley Imprint
www.pfeiffer.com

Contents

**Talent Management Topics

Editor's Choice

Inventories, Questionnaires, and Surveys

Articles and Discussion Resources

Preface

The 2008 Training and Consulting *Annuals* were the first to focus on a specific theme, that of "change." The themed *Annuals* were so successful with our readers and our authors alike that we decided to present a theme for this year. The 2009 theme is "talent management."

The *Training Annual* presents eight talent management submissions, and the *Consulting Annual* provides you with ten talent management submissions. Both *Annuals* continue to present our other popular topics: team building, leadership, communication, problem solving, and so forth. The talent management theme is an added bonus to concentrate some of our great contributors' talents in one year. Please let us know what you think of the idea of the topic-focused *Annuals*.

Why talent management? Organizations throughout the world are finding it difficult to hire the talent required to conduct business. The competition for talent is keen. To be successful, organizations of the 21st Century must have a clear vision; understand the competencies required to achieve the organizational vision; and acquire and retain a talent pool of people who possess the required competencies.

Strong forces are hampering many organizations' ability to attract and retain the talent required to meet the organizations' strategic vision. Some of these forces include:

1. A critical talent shortage that has been fueled by the retirement of the Baby Boomers. Estimates as high as 50 and 60 percent of the managers in some companies will be eligible to retire in the next five years.

2. The challenge of attracting, retaining, and engaging critical talent. U.S. organizations have not kept up with hiring and retention tactics that are attractive to a diverse population. In addition, employee loyalty and the value of tenure are decreasing.

3. Short supply of some talent such as scientists, engineers, and technicians. Highly skilled, techno-savvy individuals are always in demand, but a tighter supply is expected.

4. The lack of transferring critical knowledge throughout the organization. Most organizations' knowledge management efforts have been heralded by a few forward-looking souls, but fallen on deaf ears and languished by the wayside.

5. A need to develop a global workforce. Again, most organizations have ignored the seriousness of this issue, an imperative in a global business world.

What is talent management? The meaning of talent management has grown and changed over the past dozen years from a narrow focus to a broad and integrated plan. Talent management processes are treated as a whole system of interrelated aspects that provide the assurance that an organization will be able to strategically leverage its talent. The integration provides organizations with the ability to attract, develop, promote, engage, and retain talent to meet its strategic imperative. Organizations are starting to structure talent management goals that are directly connected to their business strategy.

The aspects that make up the definition of talent management may vary from organization to organization. They may include some of the following: recruiting talent, retaining talent, developing the workforce, planning for high-potential employees and leadership development, addressing performance management, implementing knowledge management systems, providing feedback and metrics, conducting annual workforce planning, forecasting employee placement and succession planning, supporting mentoring and coaching, offering career planning, conducting job analysis, measuring employee engagement, strategizing for replacement planning, investing in diversity efforts, and managing culture and value expectations. Organizations may combine several of these under one heading. Most organizations create a process in which human resources is a player, but may share the lead.

As you can see, many elements make up the broad theme of talent management. Many organizations have claimed for years that their people are "their greatest asset." Few demonstrate it. A strategic talent management plan must work in tandem with the business strategy in order for today's organizations to succeed. A well-designed talent management strategy will result in a workforce that goes beyond simply completing the job. It generates a workforce that is committed to improving the overall performance of the organization. Many organizations have a huge task ahead of them. They will face keen competition for the workers that are available. We hope that the ELAs, articles, and inventory that address talent management will fill a need for you.

The *2009 Pfeiffer Training Annual* includes a wonderful array of tools to help you with talent management. You'll want to check out the two diversity ELAs— by Dennis Gilbert and M.K. Key. The ELA for interviewing by Peter Garber is also useful for those of you wrapped up in your talent management efforts. Talent management articles are presented by well-known author Jean Barbazette; long-time contributor Homer Johnson; Ajay Pangarkar and Teresa Kirkwood; Richard Rees, Allen Minor, and Paul Gionfriddo; and Yusra Visser and Ryan Watkins.

The 2009 *Consulting Annual* also includes talent management tools. Check out the ELA by long-time contributor Bob Preziosi. Two talent management ELAs are by authors you know: Thiagi and Len and Jeanette Goodstein. We are excited to have Nancy Kristiansen as a first-time author. Check her ELA out; it's creative and one you'll want to try. Talent management articles are presented by two former authors, Andy Beaulieu and Mohandas Nair, well-known Julie O'Mara and Alan Richter, and Ajay Pangarkar and Teresa Kirkwood. The *Consulting Annual* also has an inventory by James Moseley, Sacip Toker, and Ann Chow.

This year the famed Marshall Goldsmith joins us as a contributor. We have one of his articles in each *Annual*. Thumb through the table of contents in each volume. I think you will be pleasantly surprised about the large number of experienced authors who have contributed for 2009. And you will be delighted with the exciting new ELAs, articles, and inventories you'll be able to use.

What Are the Annuals?

The *Annual* series consists of practical materials written for trainers, consultants, and performance-improvement technologists. We know the materials are practical, because they are written by the same practitioners that use the materials.

The *Pfeiffer Annual: Training* focuses on skill building and knowledge enhancement and also includes articles that enhance the skills and professional development of trainers. The *Pfeiffer Annual: Consulting* focuses on intervention techniques and organizational systems. It also includes skill building for the professional consultant. You can read more about the differences between the two volumes in the section that follows this preface, "The Difference Between Training and Consulting: Which Annual to Use."

The *Annuals* have been an inspirational source for experiential learning activities, resource for instruments, and reference for cutting-edge for thirty-seven years. Whether you are a trainer, a consultant, a facilitator, or a bit of all, you will find tools and resources that provide you with the basics and challenge (and we hope inspire) you to use new techniques and models.

Annual Loyalty

The Pfeiffer *Annual* series has many loyal subscribers. There are several reasons for this loyalty. In addition to the wide variety of topics and implementation levels, the *Annuals* provide materials that are applicable to varying circumstances. You will find instruments for individuals, teams, and organizations; experiential learning activities to round out workshops, team building, or consulting assignments; ideas and contemporary solutions for managing human capital; and articles that increase your own knowledge base, to use as reference materials in your writing, or as a source of ideas for your training or consulting assignments.

Many of our readers have been loyal customers for a dozen or more years. If you are one of them, we thank you. And we encourage each of you to give back to the profession by submitting a sample of your work to share with your colleagues.

The *Annuals* owe most of their success, though, to the fact that they are immediately ready to use. All of the materials may be duplicated for educational and training purposes. If you need to adapt or modify the materials to tailor them for your audience's needs, go right ahead. We only request that the credit statement found on the copyright page (and on each reproducible page) be retained on all copies. Our liberal copyright policy makes it easy and fast for you to use the materials to do your job. However, if you intend to reproduce the materials in publications for sale or if you wish to reproduce more than one hundred copies of any one item, please contact us for prior written permission.

If you are a new *Annual* user, welcome! If you like what you see in the 2009 edition, you may want to consider subscribing to a standing order. By doing so, you are guaranteed to receive your copy each year straight off the press and receive a discount off the cover price. And if you want to go back and have the entire series for your use, then the *Pfeiffer Library*—which contains content from the very first edition to the present day—is available on CD-ROM. You can find information on the *Pfeiffer Library* at www.pfeiffer.com.

I often refer to many of my *Annuals* from the 1980s. They include several classic activities that have become a mainstay in my team-building designs. But most of all, the *Annuals* have been a valuable resource for over thirty-five years because the materials come from professionals like you who work in the field as trainers, consultants, facilitators, educators, and performance-improvement technologists, whose contributions have been tried and perfected in real-life settings with actual participants and clients to meet real-world needs.

To this end, we encourage you to submit materials to be considered for publication. We are interested in receiving experiential learning activities; inventories, questionnaires, and surveys; and articles and discussion resources. Contact the Pfeiffer Editorial Department at the address listed on the copyright page for copies of our guidelines for contributors or contact me directly at Box 8249, Norfolk, VA 23503, or by email at pfeifferannual@aol.com. We welcome your comments, ideas, and contributions.

Acknowledgments

Thank you to the dedicated, friendly, thoughtful people at Pfeiffer who produced the *2009 Pfeiffer Annuals:* Kathleen Dolan Davies, Lisa Shannon, Marisa Kelley, Dawn Kilgore, Susan Rachmeler, and Rebecca Taff. Thank you to Lorraine Kohart of ebb associates inc, who assisted our authors with the many submission details and who ensured that we met all the deadlines.

Most important, thank you to our contributors, who have once again shared their ideas, techniques, and materials so that trainers and consultants everywhere may benefit. Won't you consider joining the ranks of these prestigious professionals?

Elaine Biech
Editor
July 2008

The Difference Between Training and Consulting

Which Annual to Use?

Two volumes of the *Pfeiffer Annuals*—training and consulting—are resources for two different but closely related professions. Each *Annual* serves as a collection of tools and support materials used by the professionals in their respective arenas. The volumes include activities, articles, and instruments used by individuals in the training and consulting fields. The training volume is written with the trainer in mind, and the consulting volume is written with the consultant in mind.

How can you differentiate between the two volumes? Let's begin by defining each profession.

A *trainer* can be defined as anyone who is responsible for designing and delivering knowledge to adult learners and may include an internal HRD professional employed by an organization or an external practitioner who contracts with an organization to design and conduct training programs. Generally, the trainer is a subject-matter expert who is expected to transfer knowledge so that the trainee can know or do something new. A *consultant* is someone who provides unique assistance or advice (based on what the consultant knows or has experienced) to someone else, usually known as "the client." The consultant may not necessarily be a subject-matter expert in all situations. Often the consultant is an expert at using specific tools to extract, coordinate, resolve, organize, expedite, or implement an organizational situation.

The lines between the consulting and training professions have blurred in the past few years. First, the names and titles have blurred. For example, some external trainers call themselves "training consultants" as a way of distinguishing themselves from internal trainers. Some organizations now have internal consultants who usually reside in the training department. Second, the roles have blurred. While a consultant has always been expected to deliver measurable results, now trainers are expected to do so as well. Both are expected to improve performance; both are expected to contribute to the bottom line. Facilitation was at one time thought to be a consultant skill; today trainers are expected to use facilitation skills to train. Training one-on-one was a trainer skill; today consultants train executives one-on-one and call it "coaching." The introduction of the "performance technologist," whose role is one of combined trainer and consultant, is a perfect example of a new profession that has evolved due to the need for trainers to use more "consulting" techniques in their work. The "performance consultant" is a new role supported by the American Society for Training and Development (ASTD). ASTD has shifted its focus from training to performance improvement.

As you can see, the roles and goals of training and consulting are not nearly as specific as they once may have been. However, when you step back and examine the two professions from a big-picture perspective, you can more easily differentiate between the two. Maintaining a big-picture focus will also help you determine which *Pfeiffer Annual* to turn to as your first resource.

Both volumes cover the same general topics: communication, teamwork, problem solving, and leadership. However, depending on your requirement and purpose—a training or consulting need—you will use each in different situations. You will select the *Annual* based on *how you will interact with the topic, not on what the topic might be.* Let's take a topic such as teamwork, for example. If you are searching for a lecturette that teaches the advantages of teamwork, a workshop activity that demonstrates the skill of making decisions in a team, or a handout that discusses team stages, look to the Training *Annual.* On the other hand, if you are conducting a team-building session for a dysfunctional team, helping to form a new team, or trying to understand the dynamics of an executive team, you will look to the Consulting *Annual.*

The Training Annual

The materials in the Training volume focus on skill building and knowledge enhancement as well as on the professional development of trainers. They generally focus on controlled events: a training program, a conference presentation, a classroom setting. Look to the Training *Annual* to find ways to improve a training session for 10 to 1,000 people and anything else that falls in the human resource development category:

- Specific experiential learning activities that can be built into a training program;

- Techniques to improve training: debriefing exercises, conducting role plays, managing time;

- Topical lecturettes;

- Ideas to improve a boring training program;

- Icebreakers and energizers for a training session;

- Surveys that can be used in a classroom;

- Ideas for moving an organization from training to performance; and

- Ways to improve your skills as a trainer.

The Consulting Annual

The materials in the Consulting volume focus on intervention techniques and organizational systems as well as the professional development of consultants. They generally focus on "tools" that you can have available just in case: concepts about organizations and their development (or demise) and about more global situations. Look to the Consulting *Annual* to find ways to improve consulting activities from team building and executive coaching to organization development and strategic planning:

- Skills for working with executives;

- Techniques for solving problems, effecting change, and gathering data;

- Team-building tools, techniques, and tactics;

- Facilitation ideas and methods;

- Processes to examine for improving an organization's effectiveness;

- Surveys that can be used organizationally; and

- Ways to improve your effectiveness as a consultant.

Summary

Even though the professions and the work are closely related and at times interchangeable, there is a difference. Use the following table to help you determine which *Annual* you should scan first for help. Remember, however, there is some blending of the two and either *Annual* may have your answer. It depends . . .

Element	Training	Consulting
Topics	Teams, Communication, Problem Solving	Teams, Communication, Problem Solving
Topic Focus	Individual, Department	Corporate, Global
Purpose	Skill Building, Knowledge Transfer	Coaching, Strategic Planning, Building Teams
Recipient	Individuals, Departments	Usually More Organizational
Organizational Level	All Workforce Members	Usually Closer to the Top
Delivery Profile	Workshops, Presentations	Intervention, Implementation
Atmosphere	Structured	Unstructured
Time Frame	Defined	Undefined
Organizational Cost	Moderate	High
Change Effort	Low to Moderate	Moderate to High
Setting	Usually a Classroom	Anywhere
Professional Experience	Entry Level, Novice	Proficient, Master Level
Risk Level	Low	High
Professional Needs	Activities, Resources	Tools, Theory
Application	Individual Skills	Usually Organizational System

When you get right down to it, we are all trainers and consultants. The skills may cross over. A great trainer is also a skilled consultant. And a great consultant is also a skilled trainer. The topics may be the same, but how you implement them may be vastly different. Which *Annual* to use? Remember to think about your purpose in terms of the big picture: consulting or training.

As you can see, we have both covered.

Introduction

to *The 2009 Pfeiffer Annual: Training*

The 2009 Pfeiffer Annual: Training is a collection of practical and useful materials for professionals in the broad area described as human resource development (HRD). The materials are written by and for professionals, including trainers, organization-development and organization-effectiveness consultants, performance-improvement technologists, facilitators, educators, instructional designers, and others.

Each *Annual* has three main sections: Experiential Learning Activities; Inventories, Questionnaires, and Surveys; and Articles and Discussion Resources. A fourth section, Editor's Choice, has been reserved for those unique contributions that do not fit neatly into one of the three main sections, but are valuable as identified by the editorial staff. Each published submission is classified in one of the following categories: Individual Development, Communication, Problem Solving, Groups, Teams, Consulting, Training, and Facilitating, Leadership, and Organizations. Within each category, pieces are further classified into logical subcategories, which are identified in the introductions to the three sections.

The Training and Consulting *Annuals* for 2009 have a slightly different focus from past years. Both focus on the topic of *talent management*, a topic that permeates our organizations and pervades all that we do as professionals in the learning and consulting arena.

The series continues to provide an opportunity for HRD professionals who wish to share their experiences, their viewpoints, and their processes with their colleagues. To that end, Pfeiffer publishes guidelines for potential authors. These guidelines are available from the Pfeiffer Editorial Department at Jossey-Bass, Inc., in San Francisco, California.

Materials are selected for the *Annuals* based on the quality of the ideas, applicability to real-world concerns, relevance to current HRD issues, clarity of presentation, and ability to enhance our readers' professional development. In addition, we choose experiential learning activities that will create a high degree of enthusiasm among the participants and add enjoyment to the learning process. As in the past several years, the contents of each *Annual* span a wide range of subject matter, reflecting the range of interests of our readers.

Our contributor list includes a wide selection of experts in the field: in-house practitioners, consultants, and academically based professionals. A list of contributors to the *Annual* can be found at the end of the volume, including their names, affiliations, addresses, telephone numbers, facsimile numbers, and email addresses. Readers will find this list useful if they wish to locate the authors of specific pieces for feedback, comments, or questions. Further information on each contributor is presented in a brief biographical sketch that appears at the conclusion of each article. We publish this information to encourage "networking," which continues to be a valuable mainstay in the field of human resource development.

We are pleased with the high quality of material that is submitted for publication each year and often regret that we have page limitations. In addition, just as we cannot publish every manuscript we receive, you may find that not all published works are equally useful to you. Therefore, we encourage and invite ideas, materials, and suggestions that will help us to make subsequent *Annuals* as useful as possible to all of our readers.

Introduction
to the Experiential Learning
Activities Section

Experiential learning activities ensure that lasting learning occurs. They should be selected with a specific learning objective in mind. These objectives are based on the participants' needs and the facilitator's skills. Although the experiential learning activities presented here all vary in goals, group size, time required, and process, they all incorporate one important element: questions that ensure learning has occurred. This discussion, led by the facilitator, assists participants to process the activity, to internalize the learning, and to relate it to their day-to-day situations. It is this element that creates the unique learning experience and learning opportunity that only an experiential learning activity can bring to the group process.

Readers have used the *Annuals'* experiential learning activities for years to enhance their training and consulting events. Each learning experience is complete and includes all lecturettes, handout content, and other written material necessary to facilitate the activity. In addition, many include variations of the design that the facilitator might find useful. If the activity does not fit perfectly with your objective, within your time frame, or to your group size, we encourage you to adapt the activity by adding your own variations. You will find additional experiential learning activities listed in the "Experiential Learning Activities Categories" chart that immediately follows this introduction.

The 2009 Pfeiffer Annual: Training includes thirteen activities, in the following categories:

Individual Development: Diversity

> **Popular Choices: Discovering Workplace Generational Diversity, by Dennis E. Gilbert
> **Humanity Training: Exploring Stereotyping, by M.K. Key

** Talent Management Topics

Individual Development: Life/Career Planning

What I Like About My Job or Career: Using an Appreciative Approach, by Marty C. Yopp and Michael Kroth

**First Impressions: Interviewing, by Peter R. Garber

Communication: Feedback

The Challenge: Sculpting Communication, by Devora Zack

Problem Solving: Generating Alternatives

Rope Trick: Solving the Unsolvable, by Richard T. Whelan

Problem Solving: Information Sharing

Posters: Looking at What You Already Know, by Dawn J. Mahoney

Groups: Competition/Collaboration

Hidden Agenda: Learning the Benefits of Cooperation, by Lorraine L. Ukens

Teams: How Groups Work

Incredible Ball Pass: Integrating the Team, by Ronald Roberts

Consulting, Training, and Facilitating: Facilitating: Opening

23, What Do You See? Experiencing Energizers, by Dave Arch

Consulting, Training, and Facilitating: Facilitating: Skills

From Mundane to Ah Ha! Using Training Objects, by Linda S. Eck Mills

Leadership: Styles and Skills

The Real Focus: Strategizing Leadership Behavior, by Mohandas Nair

Organizations: Change Management

Signs of Change: Identifying and Overcoming Roadblocks, by Travis L. Russ

To further assist you in selecting appropriate ELAs, we provide the following grid that summarizes category, time required, group size, and risk factor for each ELA.

** Talent Management Topics

Category	ELA Title	Page	Time Required	Group Size	Risk Factor
Individual Development: Diversity	Popular Choices: Discovering Workplace Generational Diversity	13	Approximately 2 hours	Even number from 6 to 30 or more	Moderate
Individual Development: Diversity	Humanity Training: Exploring Stereotyping	25	45 to 60 minutes	Any even number	Moderate
Individual Development: Life-Career Planning	What I Like About My Job or Career: Using an Appreciative Approach	31	1 hour, 45 minutes	Any size, in groups of 3	Low
Individual Development: Life-Career Planning	First Impressions: Interviewing	37	90 minutes	Any	Low
Communication: Feedback	The Challenge: Sculpting Communication	45	65 minutes	10 to 20, in two even teams	Moderate
Problem Solving: Generating Alternatives	Rope Trick: Solving the Unsolvable	51	20 to 30 minutes	Up to 30	Low
Problem Solving: Information Sharing	Posters: Looking at What You Already Know	55	30 to 45 minutes	10 to 20 from the same organization	Low
Groups: Competition/ Collaboration	Hidden Agenda: Learning the Benefits of Cooperation	61	90 minutes	Groups of 4 to 7	Moderate
Teams: How Groups Work	Incredible Ball Pass: Integrating the Team	73	Approximately 90 minutes	10 to 150 participants	Low to Moderate
Consulting, Training, and Facilitating: Opening	23, What Do You See? Experiencing Energizers	81	5 minutes each	Any	Low
Consulting, Training, and Facilitating: Skills	From Mundane to Ah Ha! Using Training Objects	97	Approximately 2 hours	8 to 20 trainers	Low
Leadership: Styles and Skills	The Real Focus: Strategizing Leadership Behavior	105	Approximately 2 hours	Up to 15 leaders	Moderate
Organizations: Change Management	Signs of Change: Identifying and Overcoming Roadblocks	111	90 minutes	4 to 28	Moderate

Experiential Learning Activities Categories

Note that numbering system was discontinued beginning with the 2004 *Annuals*.

Popular Choices
Discovering Workplace Generational Diversity

Activity Summary

An activity that promotes a deeper understanding of life experiences as a result of societal changes, cultural differences, and technological advances.

Goals

- To create awareness of differences in work motivation based on variances in age.

- To help participants discover the need for shared goals and outcomes while setting aside age diversity.

- To create awareness of the need for group cohesiveness while embracing age or generational diversity in the workplace.

Group Size

This activity works best with an even number of participants. A single trio can be utilized to accommodate an odd number of participants. It is most appropriate for groups of at least six people and can accommodate group sizes up to thirty or more, depending on the facilitator's comfort level.

Time Required

Approximately 2 hours.

Materials

- One copy of the Popular Choices Questionnaire for each participant.

- One copy of the Popular Choices Partner Questions for each participant.

- One index card for each participant.

- Pen or pencil for each participant.

- Several pages of newsprint or a whiteboard for the facilitator.

- Markers.

Physical Setting

Participants should have a writing surface and enough space to form pairs for breakout discussions without interfering with one another.

Facilitating Risk Rating

Moderate. Use care to avoid creating circumstances in which age or cultural differences are exploited. Emphasis should be placed on discovering and embracing differences.

Process

1. Introduce the activity by discussing the possible effects that differences in age and generation have in the workplace. Say that they sometimes can hinder optimum performance and serve as a catalyst for communication breakdown and dysfunctional teams. Say that often opinions about age are based on learning experiences and values formed during childhood or young adult lives. Write participants' thoughts on these issues on the flip chart. Some possible discussion items might include:

   - Consider age differences that may span twenty or thirty years. How would a twenty-five-year-old manager work effectively with a fifty-year-old worker (or vice-versa)?

   - During young adult or teenage years, what were your in-school or out-of-school activities? It is likely a person who is now fifty-five or sixty years of age had very different after-school activities than someone who is in his or her early twenties and just entering the workforce.

   - How has technology changed our cultural values or workplace motivation?

- Considering what we've been discussing, what differences in workplace motivation or cultural values may exist between employees? (5 minutes.)

2. Hand out the Popular Choices Questionnaire and pens or pencils and ask participants to individually complete it. Explain that they should read every question and every possible answer. In some cases, more than one choice may apply, but they should choose the answer that *most closely matches* their own feelings toward the statement or question. Emphasize that no scoring will apply and that there are no right or wrong answers. (20 minutes.)

3. Once participants have completed the questionnaire, break the group into two subgroups. Care should be used during this step to not create discomfort within the group. It is strongly recommended that you avoid asking people to disclose their ages. Consider creating the subgroups in the following manner:

   Explain to the group that the goal is to split the group into two equal-sized subgroups, newer workers in one group and those with more years in the workforce in another group. Explain that the objective is to help participants discover differences, but not to make anyone feel uncomfortable or to discover anyone's exact age.

   Take the current year and subtract 22 (approximately one-half of a working career). (Example: 2009 minus 22 = 1987) You may consider doing this on newsprint to demonstrate your objective.

   Ask the group to stand and those who started in the workforce before 1987 go to one side of the room and those who started in 1987 or later go to the other side. Explain that this year is approximate and that the exact year is not important. Reinforce that the idea is to create two equal-sized groups. Often participants will help make this separation into two groups easier by observing each group's size and moving to the "appropriate" side with limited instructions. *Note:* Avoid selecting specific individuals to move to one side or the other; allow the participants to choose for themselves. If the group is not significantly diverse, you can narrow (or broaden) the calculation (Example: 2009 minus 15 = 1994) to establish more balance in the two subgroups. Give the groups some sort of identifier, but use care if calling them "younger group" and "older group." Consider identifying groups as Group 1 and Group 2. (10 minutes.)

4. Have participants individually select one question from each of the three categories on the Popular Choices Questionnaire for discussion with a partner. This should represent the question that the participant finds most interesting. Hand out index cards and ask them to write the numbers of the three questions they are going to discuss on the index cards, along with a group identifier (Group 1 or Group 2). For example: Group 1, Questions 2, 12, 27.
(5 minutes.)

5. Ask participants to select discussion partners from the other group. Optionally, you can match partners or use a count-off method to pair participants. Ask the pairs to find places to hold their discussions.

6. Have pairs take turns discussing the reasons for and their reactions to the questions they chose in the first category. After both participants have discussed their feelings about their questions from the first category, then both should discuss their chosen question and reactions to the second category, and finally the third category. Tell participants that it is important that they take turns. Each participant should reflect on his or her reaction to the partner's question or statement, even if he or she did not choose the same question for discussion.
(20 minutes.)

7. While the paired participants are discussing their reactions to the questionnaire, collect the index cards from the participants and tally the responses for each group. This can be posted on newsprint with one newsprint sheet for each group and the numbers 1 through 30 written on the newsprint. Tally each "vote" beside the representative number. This can serve as a visual aid to the participants during the popular choices and large group debriefing.

8. Following the pairs discussions, hand out the Popular Choices Partner Questions and have participants ask their partners the questions on the sheet and record their partners' reactions to the questions.
(5 to 10 minutes.)

9. Reassemble the large group and lead the discussion by comparing and contrasting the "popular" questions on the sheet with those identified by the participants from the index cards tallied in Step 7. Create a visual example and display it on a whiteboard or newsprint. Discuss with the

group why these choices may have been the most popular, using the following questions:

- What factors in this group may have led to this outcome?

- What do you find interesting about the most commonly chosen question(s)?

- Why are there similarities (or differences) between Group 1 and Group 2?

- What conclusions can you draw about workplace culture considering the outcome of the "voting"?

(10 to 15 minutes.)

10. Debrief the entire experience by asking for reactions from the subgroups, utilizing these questions:

- Considering this activity and discussions, how do you feel?

- What did you notice during your discussions with your partners?

- What did you learn about those in the other group?

- What role has technology played in our differences?

- Would the outcomes change if the participants were paired differently?

- How can you apply what you have learned to your workplace environment?

(25 minutes.)

11. Conclude the activity by suggesting that understanding the existence and relevance of age diversity in our workplaces can increase group cohesiveness. Groups with a more thorough understanding may also see improvements in motivation, innovation, and productivity. Embracing differences may lead to an improvement in organization culture.

(5 to 10 minutes.)

Variations

- The questionnaire can be modified by changing some of the questions or answers as you deem appropriate. For example, even within one country there may be differences in culture, depending on economic conditions or geographic locations. Organizations with a strong population from rural communities may have experienced different young adult activities than those living in more urban areas. Those living in different locations may also have experienced different activities.

- You may choose to note that the categorical questions have the following correlations:

  - Category 1: Free time/play time/general attitude

  - Category 2: Parental observations/parental guidance

  - Category 3: General perceptions

  This can serve as optional discussion at your discretion, as participants may be curious about the grouping or categories of questions.

Submitted by Dennis E. Gilbert.

Dennis E. Gilbert *is the president of Appreciative Strategies, LLC, a human performance improvement training and consulting business. He combines his expertise in private for-profit business management with his experience in the non-profit educational sector to deliver outstanding results through training and consultation. An accomplished executive, consultant, and trainer, he delivers exceptional human performance improvement solutions to businesses and organizations. His focus is on leadership development, communications, and group dynamics.*

Popular Choices Questionnaire

Category 1

1. My after-school activities were
   a. Playing a sanctioned sport
   b. Playing outside with a friend(s)
   c. Doing homework
   d. Helping mom or dad with meals or chores

2. Playing with friends meant
   a. Tag, jump rope, neighborhood football
   b. Watching TV
   c. Online chat
   d. Video games

3. When we rode our bicycles
   a. We had to put on our helmets
   b. A three-speed banana seat bike was cool
   c. My bicycle was a single speed with foot (petal-activated) brakes
   d. No one I knew had a bicycle

4. When I was a teenager, watching television meant
   a. Turning on the LCD panel in my bedroom
   b. Lying on the couch flicking the remote control
   c. Getting up to change the channel of our then state-of-the-art color TV
   d. Wiggling the "rabbit-ear" antenna on our black-and-white TV

5. As a teenager listening to music meant
   a. AM/FM radio
   b. Playing 33 LP albums or 45 rpm records
   c. Listening to CDs or watching MTV
   d. No music was allowed

6. If the television didn't work we
   a. Went to the set in the other room
   b. Waited for the weather to clear
   c. Called a repair man
   d. Went online and bought a new one

7. If I don't like my boss
    a.   I'm thankful to still have a job
    b.   I tell him or her off and go tell his/her boss
    c.   I walk off the job at break and do not return
    d.   I find a new job

8. I want to work for a company that
    a.   Pays reasonable wages and is close to home
    b.   Values the environment
    c.   Pays well and most of all is fun
    d.   Pays the best, as I will not work there long anyway

9. In the workplace I should be permitted to
    a.   Listen to music (headphones, MP3, etc.)
    b.   Wear whatever clothes I want
    c.   Talk to friends and socialize
    d.   Take breaks as often and as long as I want

10. If I accept a job for $X.XX per hour or $X,XXX annual salary I will
    a.   Give my effort comparable to the rate of pay
    b.   Give 100 percent regardless, because I accepted the pay
    c.   It doesn't matter; it is just a job
    d.   Quit immediately if I find a job paying more money

Category 2

11. As a child, getting in trouble at school meant
    a.   Getting a "time out" to sit quietly
    b.   A note sent home to my parent(s)
    c.   Getting spanked with a paddle
    d.   Writing one hundred times "I will not _____ "

12. My childhood school-day mornings meant
    a.   Breakfast and a ride on the school bus
    b.   Jumping out of bed, no breakfast, and getting in the car
    c.   Walking to school every day, regardless of weather
    d.   Being ready early with no rushing around

13. My childhood chores were
    a.   Cutting firewood
    b.   Taking out the garbage
    c.   Cutting the grass
    d.   What is a chore?

14. Doing dishes as a teenager meant
    a. Throwing away a paper plate
    b. Filling the sink with hot water
    c. Rinsing a plate and putting it in the dishwasher
    d. What dishes?

15. As a child during the school week my bedtime was
    a. Around 8 or 9 P.M.
    b. Before 10 P.M.
    c. Midnight
    d. As late as I wanted

16. As a teenager before I started driving
    a. I expected my parents to drive me anywhere I wanted
    b. I often carpooled with other kids' parents
    c. Walking, biking, or taking the bus was common transportation
    d. I rang for the chauffeur

17. As a teenager I remember on Sunday
    a. We visited family
    b. We went to church
    c. No shopping stores were open
    d. It was a day of rest

18. As a child I remember my parents made coffee
    a. With a percolator type pot on the stove
    b. With an electric percolator pot
    c. In a "Mr. Coffee" or other coffeemaker
    d. Went to Starbucks, the convenience store, or other coffee store

19. When I was a kid playing outside, I drank
    a. Bottled water
    b. From a garden hose or spigot
    c. A juice box
    d. From a bucket at a hand-dug well

20. As a young child when I rode in the family car
    a. I was strapped in a car seat
    b. I was free to play in the back seat
    c. There were not any seat belts
    d. We didn't have a car

Category 3

21. As a young adult when using the telephone
    a.   We made sure no one was on the party line
    b.   We had to be patient as we spun the rotary dial
    c.   We used the one in the other room
    d.   We flipped open our cell phones

22. I remember the "delivery man" bringing
    a.   Milk and eggs, placed in a small insulated galvanized box outside
    b.   Pizza!
    c.   Anything we ordered online, and he/she drove a brown truck
    d.   Frozen foods

23. Blue jeans meant
    a.   Durable, stiff, denim
    b.   Stonewashed, pre-washed
    c.   Hip hugger
    d.   Levis, Wrangler, or Jordache

24. The sneakers my parents bought me probably cost
    a. $10 or less
    b. $10 to $30
    c. $30 to $75
    d. $100 or more

25. As a teenager a notebook meant
    a.   A canvas/cardboard three-ring binder
    b.   A plastic/cardboard three-ring binder
    c.   A Trapper Keeper®
    d.   A personal computer with 15-inch screen in my backpack

26. When I was a young adult, mailing an ordinary letter probably cost
    a.   10 cents or less
    b.   11 to 20 cents
    c.   About 25 to 30 cents
    d.   More than 33 cents

27. In high school sneaking some fun communication to a classmate meant
    a.   Writing a note and asking someone else to pass it
    b.   Sending an email to someone across the room in the computer lab
    c.   Sending a text message from my cell phone
    d.   Whispering when the teacher wasn't looking

28. In grade school when I bought my lunch
   a.   I used coins from my plastic wallet that I squeezed and the center opened
   b.   I used bills and coins
   c.   My parents set up an account
   d.   I put it on a credit card

29. As a teenager I drank soda, soft drinks, pop
   a.   From a glass bottle
   b.   From an aluminum can
   c.   From a 16-ounce plastic bottle
   d.   From a 20- or 24-ounce plastic bottle

30. The letters TXS mean
   a.   A model of a Toyota car
   b.   Thanks
   c.   Thermal cross winds
   d.   A vacation spot

Popular Choices Partner Questions

Instructions: Share your reactions to the questions or statements with your partner. Consider workplace culture, motivation, or generational diversity as you respond. Record your partner's reactions in the space provided.

1. Which statement or question from the questionnaire did you find the most interesting?

2. Given no obstacles, what workplace perception or value would you like to change as it relates to age or generation gaps?

3. What did you discover or learn from this exercise?

Humanity Training
Exploring Stereotyping

Activity Summary

A short experiential diversity activity that explores group stereotyping between pairs.

Goals

- To experience the harmful effects of stereotypes and what it feels like to be limited by a label.

- To examine and question one's assumptions about groups.

- To learn to appreciate and seek out differences among people.

Group Size

Any "even" number of participants, as many as the room will allow, seated in pairs.

Time Required

45 to 60 minutes, depending on group size and discussion.

Materials

- One Humanity Training handout for each participant.

- One copy of the Humanity Training Lecturette for the facilitator.

- One pencil or pen for each participant.

- Flip chart and markers.

Physical Setting

Tables and chairs for initial seating. A room large enough for participants to pair off and be seated for discussion.

Facilitating Risk Rating

Moderate.

Process

1. Explain that they are going to examine the groups that they belong to and the assumptions people make about these groups. Give a copy of the Humanity Training handout and a pen or pencil to each participant.

2. Using yourself as an example, name some groups or categories that you belong to. For example. "I am a white female, with a Ph.D., over fifty, divorced, and I am from the South."

3. To stimulate their thinking, ask for examples of groups or group categories. You may suggest a few to get started. Expect to hear some of these:

   - Skin color.

   - Hair color.

   - Gender.

   - National origin.

   - Race.

   - Age.

   - Socioeconomic level.

   - Geography.

   - Sexual preference.

   - Religion.

   - Disability.

   - Ancestry.

   - Marital status.

   - Medical condition.

- Pregnancy.

- Education level.

- Job type.

- (The sky's the limit.)

4. Ask participants to silently list ten categories they belong to in the left-hand column of their handouts.
   (10 minutes.)

5. Ask participants to list the assumptions in the second column that others make about them because of their membership in each group category. Again, use yourself as an example, for example, "I am blond, so I must be _____." Tell them they have about 5 minutes for this step.
   (5 minutes.)

6. When everyone has finished (or nearly so), ask them to stand up, look across the room, and pick a partner who is least like them—or at least seems very different.

7. When the pairs sort out, ask them to be seated. Have them take turns presenting their answers and asking their partners to add assumptions that they know are held about membership in each group.
   (10 minutes.)

8. Reconvene the whole group and process the activity, using the following questions:

- How easy was it to identify the assumptions that others hold?

- What was your reaction to seeing how others might view you for being a member of a particular grouping?

- Did some of these differences make you feel uncomfortable or even embarrassed?

- Did you ever feel inferior or that your status was less than others'?

- Do you feel misjudged? Are you misjudging other people?

- Were the assumptions that others hold negative or positive? Were they true for you?

- How would it feel to come to work if you focused on how others are judging you?

- How can our organization counter any common stereotypes? (10 to 20 minutes.)

9. Finish the exercise with the Humanity Training Lecturette on stereotyping. (Or you may wish to use some of your own materials.)

10. Close by writing the following quotes on the flip chart and discussing each briefly with the group:

    "I know the difference between each sort and type, but we are more alike, my friend, than we are unalike." (Maya Angelou)

    "It is not the differences that divide us; it is our judgments about them that do." (Margaret Wheatley)

Variation

- Eliminate the pairing and work with the group as a whole.

Reference

Gardenswartz, L., Rowe, A., Digh, P., & Bennett, M.F. (2003). *The global diversity desk reference: Managing an international workforce.* San Francisco, CA: Pfeiffer.

Submitted by M.K. Key.

M.K. Key, Ph.D., *a licensed clinical-community psychologist, is a writer, teacher, and consultant who has published extensively. Her most recent books include* Managing Change: Innovative Solutions for People-Based Organizations *(1999) and* Corporate Celebration: Play, Purpose, and Profit at Work *(1998). Prior to forming Key Associates in 1997, she was vice president of the Center for Continuous Improvement with Quorum Health Resources, Inc. There she managed a national learning institute with a curriculum in quality that educated thousands of people across the country.*

Humanity Training

Group Categories	Assumptions/Stereotypes
1.	
2.	
3.	
4.	
5.	
6.	
7.	
8.	
9.	
10.	

Humanity Training Lecturette

Stereotype means a "fixed image," whether positive or negative. They are oversimplified generalizations about the characteristics of all members of a group, usually untrue when applied to an individual. Stereotypes exist in any way you can categorize people. These stereotypes are easily acquired by osmosis and are very resilient to change. We are all victims and perpetrators of stereotypical thinking—as we are putting people in boxes, they are doing the same to us.

It is a normal human response to simplify a complex world by categorizing and using labels—short-hand identifiers. But think about the discrimination and losses that come from these biases. The cumulative effect of a repeated image is belittling and harmful. Stereotyping can lead to prejudice and discrimination, and, eventually, isolation, and persecution.

The challenge is in surfacing and examining these biases. They are blind spots that impact our workforce. It is important to question them, so that they do not control your decisions and interactions with other people. Any over-generalization about a person's group is limiting, because we fail to see the unique person and his or her talents.

People are more than their categories, as we have just seen. We should be looking for the unique person, the common ground in being human, not wishing to assimilate but appreciate. To acknowledge differences and take steps to make them discussable and valuable.

Diversity is not about THEM; it is about US. WE.

What I Like About My Job or Career
Using an Appreciative Approach

Activity Summary

Using an appreciative inquiry approach to discuss jobs, careers, or professions and outline personal plans to focus on those positive qualities.

Goals

- To offer participants an opportunity to examine their jobs, careers, or professions from a positive perspective.

- To help participants align their future careers with what they find positive rather than negative.

Group Size

Any size, in groups of three.

Time Required

Minimum of 1 hour and 45 minutes, or longer with more time for discussion and reflection.

Materials

- One set of the three What I Like About My Job or Career worksheets for each participant.

- Pens or pencils for participants.

- Whiteboard or flip chart.

- Markers.

Physical Setting

A room large enough for the participants to have comfortable discussion and reflection, both individually and in groups of three.

Facilitating Risk Rating

Low.

Process

1. Open by saying that this will be a short exercise to help participants begin to look at what is positive in their work lives and to think about what they can do to make their jobs, careers, or professions an even more positive experience. Say that they will be working from an affirming perspective, drawing from appreciative inquiry approaches. Indicate that this is only a starting point and an outline for further reflection and planning.
   (5 minutes.)

2. Hand out the three worksheets and pens or pencils and ask participants to complete the Self-Discovery worksheet independently.
   (10 minutes.)

3. Ask participants to find two other persons with whom they will share the results and insights they learned from completing the worksheet. Tell them they will have about 15 minutes. Have each group be seated together away from other groups to facilitate discussion.
   (20 minutes.)

4. After the small groups have discussed their answers for about 15 minutes, ask the entire group to share what they have learned about themselves. Record significant insights on the whiteboard or flip chart.
   (15 minutes.)

5. Ask participants to individually complete the Aspirations worksheet.
   (15 minutes.)

6. After about 15 minutes, have participants discuss their answers with their partners. Ask group members to work in their groups to revise their answers until they come up with statements that they can make a personal commitment to achieve.
   (15 minutes.)

7. Ask participants to complete the Planning worksheet.
   (15 minutes.)

8. After 15 minutes, bring the entire group together. Ask them to describe any particularly significant insights about themselves or the process. Ask them how they will use this information in the future. Remind them that this activity was only the beginning of the reflective process and that they should consider spending further time to deepen their self-understanding and commitment. Answer questions and adjourn.
   (10 minutes.)

Trainer's Note

AI involves a cycle of (1) discovery, which entails seeking out the best things; (2) dreaming, which looks at what might be; (3) designing, developing possibility plans of the ideal end state; and (4) destiny, strengthening capabilities and processes (Cooperrider & Whitney, 2000).

Reference

Cooperrider, D.L., & Whitney, D. (2000). A positive revolution in change: Appreciative inquiry. In D.L. Cooperrider, P.F. Sorenson, D. Whitney, & Y.T.F. (Eds.), *Appreciative inquiry: Rethinking human organization toward a positive theory of change* (pp. 3–27). Champaign, IL: Stipes.

Submitted by Marty C. Yopp and Michael Kroth.

Marty C. Yopp, Ed.D., *serves as the director of the University of Idaho Center for Economic Education. She is a professor of business education and adult/organizational learning and leadership at the University of Idaho and has published in numerous journals on topics including the successful program planning and design of adult education programs and effective training and development activities. Her experience has been diverse, including working for five years as the assistant to United States Supreme Court Justice William O. Douglas.*

Michael Kroth, Ph.D., *is the author of* The Manager as Motivator *and the co-author of* Transforming Work: The Five Keys to Achieving Trust, Commitment, and Passion in the Workplace. *He is an assistant professor at the University of Idaho in adult/organizational learning and leadership. He is the leadership field editor for ASTD's* In-Practice *online newsletter, a member of the National Speakers Association, and a past member of the ASTD International Program Advisory Committee.*

What I Like About My Job or Career: Self-Discovery

Instructions: After reflecting on each question, answer it as completely and in as much depth as possible. You will be discussing your answers within your small group and also with the larger group. Use the back of the page for extra writing room.

Describe what attracted you to your job, career, or profession.

Looking at your entire work experience, describe a time when you felt the most alive, excited, and engaged.

What made you feel so alive?

What did you like about what you were doing?

What did you do especially well that made you feel good about your work?

How did you grow and change as a result of this experience?

Who else was significant in making this such a peak experience, and why was this significant?

What is the most important thing that your job, career, or profession has contributed to your life?

In your work, what are you being called on to become?

What three wishes do you have that would make your job, career, or profession more alive, exciting, and engaging?

What I Like About My Job or Career: Aspirations

Instructions: Taking into account the best experiences you listed on the Self-Discovery worksheet and your wishes for your future work, answer the following questions as completely and in as much depth as possible. You will be discussing your answers with the others in your small group and within the larger group.

Given the insights you had and the earlier discussion, what are the best parts of your job, career, or profession?

Given the insights you had earlier, describe in the *present* tense what your job, career, or profession would be if you could wave a magic wand and make it so. (Be sure to use present tense verbs: "I am," "It is," "They are," and so on.) Don't be afraid to write something that is a stretch from your current situation, but do stay grounded in what is possible. Be sure that the end-state you describe would be something you would find highly desirable.

What I Like About My Job or Career: Planning

Instructions: Consider the commitment you just made when working with your small group and consider the types of actions you can take to achieve your aspirations. Answer the following questions:

What are all the ways I might achieve the aspirations to which I have committed? (Use your imagination! Don't be limited by your present circumstances.)

What capabilities will I have to develop in order to achieve the aspirations to which I have committed?

What relationships will I need to expand or deepen in order to achieve the aspirations to which I have committed?

What else might I need to do in order to achieve the aspirations to which I have committed?

What would be the most important steps or activities I will have to undertake to achieve the aspirations to which I have committed?

1.

2.

3.

4.

5.

First Impressions
Interviewing

Activity Summary

An activity that helps participants learn some factors that influence both job candidates and interviewers.

Goals

- To help participants better understand how first impressions influence both participants during an interview.

- To make participants more aware of the influence of first impressions on results.

- To help participants be more successful during employment interviews, regardless of which role they play.

Group Size

Any group size.

Setting

A room in which participants can break into groups for discussion or all face the facilitator.

Time Required

90 minutes.

Materials

- One copy of First Impressions: Job Candidate for each participant.

- One copy of First Impressions: Potential Employer for each participant.

- Flip chart and markers.

Facilitating Risk Rating

Low.

Process

1. Introduce the activity by explaining that, while participating, they will learn what a job interview is like from the perspectives of both an interviewer and an interviewee.

2. Ask participants what their objectives are when either acting as an interviewer or when seeking a new job. Write their answers on the flip chart. Emphasize the importance of making a good first impression, no matter which role you play, and remind them that the interviewer has an especially important responsibility for the success of the interaction in a job market in which talented candidates are becoming harder to find. (5 minutes.)

3. Ask participants to share some of their own experiences in a job interview and how they felt at the time. After a brief discussion, give each person a copy of the First Impressions: Job Candidate handout. Explain that the items listed on the handout are things that people tend to practice during successful interviews, but may not be conscious of doing. Explain that using the tips that are provided can help interviewees make better first impressions. Read each of the tips aloud and encourage participants to discuss them. Ask for specific examples of ways that participants could have used each tip during a job interviews in the past. Jot ideas on the flip chart. (15 minutes.)

4. After wrapping up discussion of the interviewee's role, give participants the First Impressions: Potential Employer handout and ask them to discuss how they could have used these tips when interviewing a job candidate. Ask participants which of these tips they feel are most important for future interviews they will have with job candidates. List these on the flip chart for discussion. Ask participants which they feel are least important and why. (15 minutes.)

5. Ask participants to break into pairs to create brief role plays that demonstrate how each of the tips could be utilized in an actual job interview, practicing first in pairs and then presenting to the whole group. (30 minutes.)

6. After the presentations, say that there are two important perspectives during a job interview and that focusing only on evaluating the candidate and not trying to make a good impression as a prospective employer may cause them to lose the job candidates they really want to hire.

7. Debrief with these questions:

   - What is the most important thing you've learned about interviewing in this session?

   - How will what you have learned change the ways in which you interview job candidates in the future?

   - How would you behave differently if you were a candidate for a job?

   - What will you do differently in the future, whichever role you are playing?
   (15 minutes.)

8. Conclude the activity by reminding participants that everyone should leave a job interview with a good impression of the other person for the process to be successful.

Submitted by Peter R. Garber.

Peter R. Garber *has been a contributing author to Pfeiffer* Annuals *for more than ten years. He is the author of over twenty human resource and business books, including his most recent,* Designing Effective Employee Reward Programs. *Mr. Garber has been employed by PPG Industries in Pittsburgh in human resources for the past twenty-eight years.*

First Impressions: Job Candidate

First impressions are important for both the candidate and the potential employer during the interview. As the old saying goes, "You never have a second chance to make a good first impression!" Studies have shown that both the candidate and the potential employer make important decisions concerning acceptance or rejection of one another within the first few seconds of an interview. Thus, getting off to a good start is obviously critically important.

If you are the candidate, your objective should be to receive a job offer or at least be invited back for another interview. Not making a strong first impression will make achieving this ultimate objective more difficult, if not impossible. Some of the first impressions that the interviewer might formulate about you in these critical first moments include:

1. *Ability:* One of the foremost questions on an interviewer's mind is, "Can this person do the job?" You should do everything you can to convince the interviewer that you have the ability to be successful in the position. Tell the interviewer why you believe you have the ability to perform the job and how your past experiences and education have qualified you for the position.

2. *Adaptability:* The interviewer will also be judging you on your ability to adapt to his or her organization. The interviewer will be paying attention to how well you follow the structure of his or her interview. So let the interviewer structure the interview and follow his or her lead.

3. *Attitude:* This is an extremely important first impression and can overshadow all others. Present a positive attitude from the first instant. Anything less can overshadow other qualities you possess.

4. *Compatibility:* Organizations often have many very qualified candidates to select from. Often it comes down to who they believe would be most compatible with the organization. Learning as much as you can about the organization and position prior to the interview will allow you to make a stronger impression.

5. *Confidence:* Organizations want to hire candidates who have confidence in themselves and their abilities. Begin with a confident handshake and greeting and project confidence throughout the interview. Remember that it is not only about what you say but about how you say it. Pay attention to your body language. Your words may sound confident, but your body language may be giving a different impression.

6. *Interest:* Interviewers don't want to waste their time with candidates who are not interested in their organizations. Let the interviewer know that you are interested. Pay close attention during the interview, ask questions, be responsive, as well as telling the interviewer that you want the job.

7. *Motivation:* Make sure that the interviewer understands just how motivated you are to be successful in the position. Point out how you have succeeded in the past and how your high level of motivation will enable you to be successful in this position.

8. *Openness:* Being open about yourself and your background from the very beginning of the interview will allow the interviewer to learn as much as possible about you in a relatively short time.

9. *Potential:* An interview is really about assessing potential. Make it clear that you have great potential. Convince the interviewer not only that you can successfully perform the job for which you are interviewing, but that you can hold more responsible positions in the future as well.

10. *Sincerity:* If the interviewer does not feel that you are sincere, the chances of being hired are far less. Sincerity can't be faked. If you are not sincerely interested in the position, you shouldn't spend either your or the interviewer's time.

Think of the interview as an opportunity to introduce yourself to your new employer. Think about the first impressions you want to make and find ways to get them across to the interviewer.

May you always make a great first impression and land the job you really want.

First Impressions: Potential Employer

First impressions are important during the interviewing process for both the candidate and the potential employer. As the old saying goes, "You never have a second chance to make a good first impression!" Studies have shown that both the candidate and the potential employer make important decisions concerning acceptance or rejection of one another within the first few seconds of an interview. Thus, getting off to a good start is obviously critically important.

If you are the potential employer, your goal should be to make a positive impression on the candidate so that he or she will want to work for your organization. To achieve this objective, you must be aware of some of the thoughts that are likely to go through a job candidate's mind during the interview. Making a positive impression on the candidate from the first moment sets the stage. Often candidates make up their minds from the interview whether they would like to join an organization or not. Their decisions can be based on impressions or feelings they experience during the interview.

The following are some of the first impressions that the interviewee might formulate about you and your organization in these critical first moments:

1. *Advancement opportunities:* Every job candidate hopes to move ahead in his or her career. Make sure you explain the opportunities that exist for the candidate. Give examples of how others may have risen through the ranks from this position.

2. *Career growth:* Career growth also involves personal development. Job candidates want to hear about opportunities to grow both personally and professionally. Be sure to share information about any programs or opportunities that exist for career growth.

3. *Organizational culture:* A job candidate is always very interested in the culture of the organization he or she may join, including principles, values, and ethics. Try to give the candidate some idea of how he or she will fit into the organizational culture. Spend some time reflecting on your organization's culture and how it supports new employees, particularly in the early part of their careers.

4. *Promise:* Job candidates want to know what promises there may be in the form of a commitment to some tangible benefit such as salary or promotion. This aspect might also simply involve the future of the organization, as well as his or her future there.

5. *Job security:* Job security means not only having a job today but having one in the future. Share any plans for growth or expansion or other career opportunities that may exist in the organization.

6. *Reputation:* Candidates want to work for organizations that are respected. Share any awards, distinctions, accomplishments, and so forth, that the organization has achieved. Remember that you are selling the organization's credentials to the candidate.

7. *Professionalism:* How you conduct yourself during the interview will make a big impression on the candidate about your organization. Remember that you represent the entire professional image of your organization.

8. *Responsibility:* Candidates want to know how much responsibility they will have on the job and how soon they will be given this responsibility. Be sure to assure the candidate that he or she won't be assigned too much responsibility too soon.

9. *Receptiveness:* Being receptive to a candidate is important. You don't want candidates to feel they do not have a chance of being hired—particularly if this isn't the case. If you have an interest in a candidate, be sure to let him or her know. Even if you think that you are not interested, be receptive to hearing about the person's background and experiences. Keeping an open mind is important, as you may hear something that could change your mind.

10. *Image:* Image is often everything to a job candidate. The corporate image you help to project will be an important part of a candidate's decision about whether to accept an employment offer. Pay attention to the literature you provide, written correspondence, and personal interactions to ensure that you are presenting a professional image.

The first impression you present to candidates for employment can be the most important step in your recruiting process. Competition for the best candidates is getting tougher and tougher every year. Getting off to a positive start can be the determining factor for attracting the talent you need in your organization. The first impressions you give can make the difference between your top choices coming to work for you or for your competition.

The Challenge
Sculpting Communication

Activity Summary

An upbeat and creative team communication challenge.

Goals

- To overcome communication barriers for successful goal achievement.

- To strengthen and reinforce teamwork.

- To engage participants in a task combining kinesthetic, visual, and auditory learning styles.

Group Size

Ideal for 10 to 20 participants in two teams with 5 to 10 members each. (Activity can be modified for various group sizes by using additional pairs.)

Time Required

65 minutes.

Materials

- Two digital cameras.

- Challenge Observer Guides for observers.

- Pens or pencils for participants.

- A stopwatch or timer.

Physical Setting

Two adjoining rooms or physical spaces (a room and a spacious hallway or two outdoor areas in close proximity) such that teams cannot see or easily hear the other teams. Comfortable seating.

Facilitating Risk Rating

Moderate.

Process

1. Say that the activity they are about to participate in is about communication. Split participants into two equal-sized teams. Ask for one volunteer from each team to take the role of Observer. If there are an odd number of participants, solicit three Observers. The third Observer can "float" between teams. Assign or otherwise identify one additional participant per team to assume the role of Communicator (to be further defined shortly). Provide Communicators with cameras.

2. Provide Observers with Challenge Observer Guides and pens or pencils. Instruct Observers to disengage from participating actively in The Challenge; they are to take a silent role, separating a bit physically from the central group. Explain that they may not assist the group verbally or physically during The Challenge. Say that, following The Challenge, Observers will lead teams in discussion regarding the team's behaviors and interactions. (5 minutes.)

3. Assign teams to separate activity areas. Tell teams to configure themselves in a "living sculpture" actively including all members *except the Observer and Communicator*. Say that the sculptures should be designed to create a symbolic image of positive group communication. Communicators are to visit the other teams and photograph the other teams in sculpture form and then bring the camera back to their own teams' venues. (5 minutes.)

4. Tell each team to attempt to replicate the other team's sculpture, using the following guidelines:

   - Only the Communicator may view the photo.

   - Participants may only ask the Communicator questions that can be answered by yes and no.

- A team member may not ask more than one question at a time and must not ask two in a row.

- Participants may not speak to one another.

- Communicators can only answer "yes" or "no."
(15 minutes.)

5. Tell participants that when a team believes they can accurately depict the other team's sculpture, they are to create it themselves and ask their Communicator to take their photo. They are only allowed one opportunity to replicate the sculpture. The original and final photos will be compared for accuracy by the team being depicted.
(10 minutes.)

6. Give teams a few minutes to compare the first and second photos of each structure and to discuss their accuracy, what's missing, and why that may be.
(10 minutes.)

7. Have the Observers lead teammates in an interactive discussion of the entire experience, including:

- Highlights from the Observer Guide notes.

- Whether the symbolic representation of ideal communication was realized during the activity. If so, how? If not, why not?

- What behaviors helped or hindered success.

- The impact of assumptions made by team members.

- How the team responded and adapted to communication restrictions.

- How feedback or lack of feedback contributed to the results.

- Tell them to reflect on their subjective experiences.
(10 minutes.)

8. Lead a concluding discussion. Include some of the following questions, along with relevant links to participants' current work life challenges.

- How did participants manage barriers and frustration?

- What is the impact of collaboration in the face of challenge?

- How is this activity a metaphor for communication and feedback challenges on the job?

- What lessons can be applied from this activity to improve workplace communication?
(10 minutes.)

Variations

- If the digital cameras used can be downloaded to an available AV system and viewed by all participants on a large screen, this creates an additional dimension to the challenge, enabling both teams to view, enjoy, and discuss both sets of "before" and "after" photos. However, this is not a necessary requirement for a successful activity.

- If there is a particular challenge facing a team engaged in this activity (for example, significant organizational change), the symbolic sculptures can instead depict some aspect of that challenge (for example, a well-managed change initiative). Theprocessing questions during the debriefing can be adapted to draw out how the challenge is a metaphor for the group's particular situation.

Submitted by Devora Zack.

Devora Zack *is president of Only Connect Consulting, Inc. (OCC), a leadership development firm with twelve years of delivering innovative, award-winning programs. She is a consultant, coach, and facilitator for over seventy-five clients, including Deloitte, Enterprise Rent-A-Car, America Online, the U.S. Treasury, HBCU, and the U.S. Department of Education. She is visiting faculty at Cornell University and program director for the prestigious Presidential Management Fellowship Orientation. Zack received her MBA from Cornell University as a merit scholar and her BA from the University of Pennsylvania. She holds certifications in neuro-linguistic programming and the* Myers-Briggs Type Indicator. *Her memberships include Phi Beta Kappa and Mensa.*

The Challenge Observer Guide

Instructions: Use this form to write what you observe about team behaviors. What did you notice about:

Stated ground rules, plan of approach, and/or goals of the team, if any?

Behaviors that contributed to or hindered team success?

The result of assumptions that participants made?

How collaboration was established given communication constrictions?

Team responses throughout the task?

Behaviors/challenges that were similar to workplace communication?

Additional observations and reflections:

Rope Trick
Solving the Unsolvable

Activity Summary

A simple magic trick that will start a discussion on ways to solve seemingly unsolvable problems participants may have.

Goals

- To use a memorable format to achieve maximum results.

- To allow the participants to brainstorm some new methods of solving problems.

Group Size

Up to 30 participants who can clearly view the "trick."

Time Required

20 to 30 minutes.

Materials

- Three pieces (9 inches, 24 inches, and 40 inches) of white rope (about the thickness of a clothesline). Wrap the ends of each piece with bright-colored adhesive tape to allow the participants to better view the "trick."

- Flip chart and markers.

Physical Setting

Seating for participants facing the front so they have a clear view of your hands while performing the "trick."

Facilitating Risk Rating

Low.

Process

1. State that Mark Twain once observed, "It is better to keep your mouth shut and appear stupid than to open it and remove all doubt." Have participants brainstorm some "unsolvable" problems they may be having in the workplace. Write a few on the flip chart. Say that you are about to demonstrate how a seemingly unsolvable problem can be solved.

2. Show the participants the three pieces of rope and say you will make the ropes all the same length as a "visual demonstration of solving an impossible problem." (Never call it a "trick.")

3. Let one or two participants examine the ropes so they know they are real, solid, and do not stretch when pulled.

4. Hold up your left hand chest high, with the back of your hand facing the participants. Take the ropes back and place them in your left hand, the smallest rope closest to your wrist, followed by the middle-length piece, and then the longest piece. (See the diagram.)

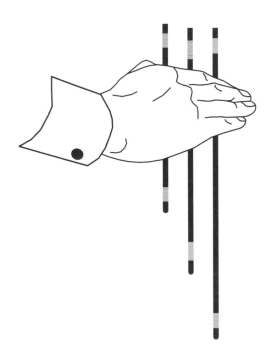

5. Tell them you are now going to stretch the ropes so all are the same length. Slowly look around at the participants for their reactions, and ask, "Do you think this can be done?" Let a few people answer (they will doubt your ability). Nod as you listen to them, but do not respond. Continue by saying, "Remember that there are many ways to solve seemingly impossible problems."

6. With the participants looking at the back of your left hand and watching, use your right hand to take the lower end of the short rope and *seemingly* place it to the right of the longest piece. As you do this, quickly and carefully (so no one sees) slip the end *behind* the long piece so it settles between the middle piece and the long piece. The adhesive tape makes all the ends look alike, so no one will notice which end is which.

7. Slowly bring up the lower end of the middle piece and place it to the right of the upper long piece. Do this again with the lower end of the long piece, placing it to the right of the other ropes. What the participants will see is the illustration in the top half of the diagram.

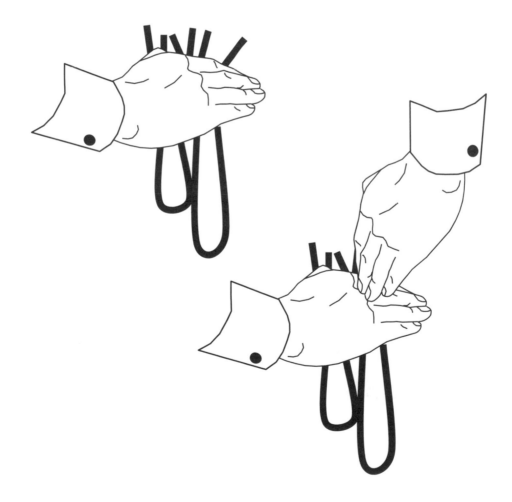

8. Now carefully (so all can see) take the three rope ends closest to your fingertips (as shown in the bottom half of diagram) and pull them away with your right hand, holding the other three ends with your left hand. What the participants will see is that all three ropes appear to be the same length. They will not know you are pulling both ends of the long piece and one end of the middle piece, leaving both ends of the short piece in your left hand.

9. Everyone will react with a bit of amazement. At that point, quickly let the ropes drop out of your hand, so no one can see what you actually did. You may then pick up the ropes and let those who examined the ropes earlier examine them again to prove they cannot be stretched. (It is very important *NEVER* to tell anyone how you performed this "trick.")

10. Expect participants to ask how you did it. Simply say, "I did what I said I would do, although you thought it could not be done."

11. Process by asking them to think back to the "impossible" tasks or problems they listed earlier or others they may have experienced in their workplace and what types of solutions they have tried to solve them. Ask for ideas from the group about how to solve the problems. List their ideas on the flip chart for later discussion.

12. To wrap up, ask participants what they have learned from this activity and lead them to the conclusion that most problems have a solution—even if they seem to be in the realm of magic.

Trainer's Note

Practice this trick on your own or with friends a few times so you become comfortable with it. It is easy and fun to do.

Submitted by Richard T. Whelan.

Richard T. Whelan, M.A., *is a comprehensive human resource coordinator, certified mental health counselor, and a published freelance writer. He designs, develops, and delivers human resource and technical workshops for businesses, organizations, and agencies in the public and private sectors, both nationally and internationally.*

Posters
Looking at What You Already Know

Activity Summary

Attendees draw on existing product knowledge to complete new product content posters.

Goals

- To learn enough about a new product to be able to describe it to a customer.

- To recognize that much is already known about a new product, as it is likely to be built on other products that participants already know and use every day.

Group Size

10 to 20 participants from the same organization who are responsible for introducing new products/services.

Time Required

30 to 45 minutes.

Materials

- Enough laminated posters, each containing basic product information for one existing company product, for each pair of participants. Posters should be at least 24 inches by 36 inches. (See the Sample Poster.)

- A collection of laminated product information cards (each the size of a 4 by 6 index card) that describe features of various new products or services the company is about to introduce. Benefit cards should be printed in a large font, laminated, and cut apart. (See the Sample Benefits List.)

- Masking tape for each pair.

Physical Setting

A room large enough for attendees to move around easily. Sufficient wall space for product posters.

Facilitating Risk Rating

Low.

Preparation

Prior to the session, create and post laminated product information posters around the room and prepare and place the laminated new product information benefit cards face down on a separate table. Each poster should display items common to several existing company products or services and across new products you are introducing. See the Sample Poster and Sample Benefits List for an idea of how this works.

Process

1. Lead a large group review of the basic product information listed on each of the posters. Participants should be familiar with the existing products described.
   (5 minutes per poster.)

2. Introduce a new product by pointing out familiar features that are the same as for older products, what is new, and what has changed for the new product. Tell them they will be creating product posters to introduce new products.
   (5 minutes.)

3. Place participants in pairs and give each pair a new product to "sponsor." Assign each pair one of the product posters and some masking tape. Tell them that, at your signal, they will proceed to the table and begin selecting the new product cards they need to make a poster for their new products. They will use the existing information on the poster and apply new information from product cards to their posters. Tell them to attach the appropriate product cards to their posters with tape until their posters accurately describe the new product.
   (15 minutes.)

4. Ask pairs to take turns debriefing the rest of the group on their assigned new products, referring to similarities and differences with the existing products on the posters.
   (10 minutes.)

5. Process the activity by asking the following questions:

   - What did you discover about the new product(s)/service(s) while completing your assignment?

   - What caused you to be successful (or more successful) at understanding the new products?

   - Now that you've spent time discussing the new products, on a scale from 1 to 10, indicate your level of confidence of your ability to explain them to a customer.
     (10 minutes.)

Variations

- Benefit cards could be distributed to the participants like playing cards, instead of having them face down on a table.

- Distribute the same benefit cards to the participants for application to all of the posters. As they read through the various product information summaries, they could apply the appropriate cards to each poster.

Submitted by Dawn J. Mahoney.

Dawn J. Mahoney *is presently a learning facilitator at Humana One and past president of her local ASTD chapter. Mahoney has been designing and delivering training sessions for over twelve years and considers providing this activity a way of giving back to the profession and honoring the people who've been there to assist during her career.*

Sample Poster

Insurance Plan 1

Preventive Care

Dental Benefit

Term Life Insurance

Standard Physician

Networks

Pharmacy Network

Sample Benefits List

In Network Deductible: $1500/$2000; $2600/$5000

In Network Deductible: $500/$1000; $2500/$5000

Rx Co-Payments: $10, $30, $50, 25 percent

$0 Rx Buy-Up

$75 ER Co-Payment

$500 Rx Deductible

Office Visit Co-Payment Rider Available

Maternity Rider Available

$25/$40 Office Visit Co-Payments

Four Office Visits

$5,000,000 Lifetime Max. Buy-Up

$2,000,000 Lifetime Max. Buy-Up

Integrated with Medical Deductible

Hidden Agenda
Learning the Benefits of Cooperation

Activity Summary

A cooperative-competition activity that requires teams to share information in order to solve a logic problem while working against one another to be the first to complete the assignment.

Goals

- To explore the effects of cooperation and competition on performance.

- To examine the process of logical analysis and problem solving.

- To use deductive reasoning for solving problems.

Group Size

Three relatively equal-sized groups of 4 to 7 people each.

Time Required

90 minutes.

Materials

- One copy of each of the following handouts for each participant:

  - Hidden Agenda Problem

  - Hidden Agenda Worksheet

  - Hidden Agenda Master Information Sheet

  - Hidden Agenda Solution

- One copy of Hidden Agenda Information Sheet 1 for each member of Team 1.

- One copy of Hidden Agenda Information Sheet 2 for each member of Team 2.

- One copy of Hidden Agenda Information Sheet 3 for each member of Team 3.

- A pencil for each participant.

- A flip chart and felt-tipped markers.

- Masking tape.

- A clock or timer.

Physical Setting

A separate table should be available for each of the three teams to work without disturbing one another. There should be additional room available for participants to move about and mingle freely. Wall space is required for posting flip-chart sheets.

Facilitating Risk Rating

Moderate.

Process

1. Introduce the session by explaining that the participants will be working in teams to solve a logic problem.

2. Divide the participants into three relatively even groups of four to seven members each. Assign numbers to three teams, using the designations 1, 2, or 3.

3. Distribute copies of the Hidden Agenda Problem to all participants. Read the information aloud while the participants follow along.

4. Distribute a copy of the Hidden Agenda Information Sheet 1 to each member of Team 1, a copy of Information Sheet 2 to each member of Team 2, and a copy of Information Sheet 3 to each member of Team 3. Provide each participant with a pencil.

5. Distribute one copy of the Hidden Agenda Worksheet to each team member. Direct the team members to complete their worksheets by analyzing

the clues given on their group's Information Sheet. Explain that solving logic problems involves using information, whether directly or indirectly. Say that, because the information is often sketchy, it is necessary to draw some inferences based on the facts that are provided.

6. Emphasize that the teams are in competition to be the first to finish. Each team is to present its worksheet to you when it is complete. Tell the participants that you will give a warning 5 minutes before the 30-minute time limit ends.
(10 minutes.)

7. Time the activity for 30 minutes, giving the participants a 5-minute warning. Collect any worksheets completed prior to the end of the period, writing on the sheet the sequence in which it was received (1, 2, or 3). When time expires, ask the teams to stop working and return any remaining worksheets.
(30 minutes.)

8. Distribute copies of the Hidden Agenda Master Information Sheet to all participants. Explain that all teams received information items 1 through 10. However, each team received two items that were exclusive to that group. These items are designated by an asterisk and appear at the end of the list. Allow several minutes for participants to review the information.

9. Ask the following questions of each team:

   • Did your team figure out all sixteen items of information? If not, why not?

   • What process did your team use to share information? Was it effective? Why or why not?

   • How willing was your team to share information with the other groups? Why did you refuse to share/share freely? How did your actions affect the outcome of the activity?
   (10 minutes.)

10. Distribute copies of the Hidden Agenda Solution to all participants. Review the answers by referring to the Suggested Reasoning section. Ask each team to count the number of correct answers they had and record these on a flip-chart sheet. Determine the winning team; if there is a tie, declare the first team who completed the worksheet with the highest number of correct answers as the winner.

11. Ask the following questions of each team:

- What was your team's approach to completing the worksheet, that is, solving the problem? Was it effective? Why or why not?

- How well did team members use deductive reasoning to solve the problem? What factors may have contributed to this?

- How did the time pressure affect your team's ability to solve the problem?

- What kind of roles (e.g., leader, recorder, negotiator, and so forth) emerged during the activity? How did this occur?

    (10 minutes.)

12. Lead a final debriefing, using the following questions:

- What roles do cooperation and competition play in teamwork? How do they affect overall team performance?

- In what ways is what you did in this activity related to the issue of solving problems in your workplace?

- In what ways can you apply what you have learned to your own work environment?

- Record their answers on flip-chart sheets and post them.

    (15 minutes.)

Submitted by Lorraine L. Ukens.

Lorraine L. Ukens, *owner of Team-ing With Success (www.team-ing.com), is a performance improvement consultant who specializes in team building and experiential learning. She is the author of sixteen training activity books and games. Ukens has a bachelor's degree in psychology and a master's degree in human resource development from Towson University in Maryland, where she also taught as an adjunct faculty for eight years prior to her move South.*

Hidden Agenda Problem

It has come to the attention of the State Department that secret information is being passed between agents of two foreign countries. To stay better informed of events that may be influenced by these exchanges, it is crucial to domestic security to learn more about the meetings that will take place between the agents.

The Department knows the code name (each has a color OR a letter) of the agents who are involved, but does not know which agent will meet with which one. It also needs to uncover the exact date, time, and place for each meeting. It is known that the meetings are scheduled to begin on the eighth of the month and that the remaining meetings will occur every four days in various locations.

Three teams of State Department agents have been chosen to solve the problem. The members of the group that is able to determine the solution first will be assigned to prominent positions and receive substantial bonuses.

You are a member of one of these teams, and your group has worked hard to gather information. You just learned that your colleagues on other teams may have some information you were unable to obtain, and vice versa. Because only one team will be rewarded, you are anxious to be the first to solve the problem.

Examine the Information Sheet you have been given and begin to unravel the mystery. Determine the AGENTS, DATE, TIME, and LOCATION for each meeting. Your team also must decide how to handle any exchange of information with other teams. If no team completes the solution within 30 minutes, the team with the most correct information will be chosen as the winner.

Hidden Agenda Information Sheet 1

- The meeting at 2:00 was arranged by Agent White.

- The meeting Agent Brown has planned is for the eighth.

- Agent B's meeting is scheduled for 6:00.

- The meeting in the park will take place at noon.

- The bookstore meeting is scheduled later in the month than the meeting Agent Black has arranged.

- Agent A is scheduled to meet someone on the twentieth.

- Agent Black will be leaving the country on the eighteenth.

- Agent Green and Agent B are scheduled to meet with one another.

- Agent D will be meeting at 4:00.

- Agent White is not meeting with anyone on the twelfth.

- The meeting in the bookstore is scheduled eight days after Agent C's meeting.

- Agent Black's meeting is scheduled to take place before the date that Agent B will meet.

Hidden Agenda Information Sheet 2

- The meeting at 2:00 was arranged by Agent White.

- The meeting Agent Brown has planned is for the eighth.

- Agent B's meeting is scheduled for 6:00.

- The meeting at the museum will take place at 4:00.

- The bookstore meeting is scheduled later in the month than the meeting Agent Black has arranged.

- Agent A is scheduled to meet someone on the twentieth.

- Agent Black will be leaving the country on the eighteenth.

- Agent Black and Agent D are scheduled to meet with one another.

- Agent D will be meeting at 4:00.

- Agent White is not meeting with anyone on the twelfth.

- The meeting in the bookstore is scheduled eight days after Agent C's meeting.

- Agent Black's meeting is scheduled to take place before the date that Agent B will meet.

The 2009 Pfeiffer Annual: Training.

Hidden Agenda Information Sheet 3

- The meeting at 2:00 was arranged by Agent White.

- The meeting Agent Brown has planned is for the eighth.

- Agent B's meeting is scheduled for 6:00.

- The meeting at the zoo will take place at 2:00.

- The bookstore meeting is scheduled later in the month than the meeting Agent Black has arranged.

- Agent A is scheduled to meet someone on the twentieth.

- Agent Black will be leaving the country on the eighteenth.

- Agent Brown and Agent C are scheduled to meet with one another.

- Agent D will be meeting at 4:00.

- Agent White is not meeting with anyone on the twelfth.

- The meeting in the bookstore is scheduled eight days after Agent C's meeting.

- Agent Black's meeting is scheduled to take place before the date that Agent B will meet.

Hidden Agenda Worksheet

Team Number:

Agents	Date	Time	Location

Hidden Agenda Master Information Sheet

1. The meeting at 2:00 was arranged by Agent White.

2. The meeting Agent Brown has planned is for the eighth.

3. Agent B's meeting is scheduled for 6:00.

4. The bookstore meeting is scheduled later in the month than the meeting Agent Black has arranged.

5. Agent A is scheduled to meet someone on the twentieth.

6. Agent Black will be leaving the country on the eighteenth.

7. Agent D will be meeting at 4:00.

8. Agent White is not meeting with anyone on the twelfth.

9. The meeting in the bookstore is scheduled eight days after Agent C's meeting.

10. Agent Black's meeting is scheduled to take place before the date that Agent B will meet.

11. The meeting in the park will take place at Noon. *(Team 1)

12. Agent Green and Agent B are scheduled to meet with one another. *(Team 1)

13. The meeting at the museum will take place at 4:00. *(Team 2)

14. Agent Black and Agent D are scheduled to meet with one another. *(Team 2)

15. The meeting at the zoo will take place at 2:00. *(Team 3)

16. Agent Brown and Agent C are scheduled to meet with one another. *(Team 3)

---

*This information has been provided only to the team indicated.

Hidden Agenda Solution

Agents		Date	Time	Location
A	White	20th	2:00	Zoo
B	Green	16th	6:00	Bookstore
C	Brown	8th	12:00	Park
D	Black	12th	4:00	Museum

Suggested Reasoning Process

Determine the pairs of agents first (12, 14, 16); this necessitated teams sharing information. Next, find all data directly related to these pairs (1, 2, 3, 5, 7). Deductive reasoning is required to determine what is possible and what is not. To complete the third section that contains all but one piece, use 11 to get the location. With this complete, the remaining information provides clues to the other answers. Everyone has 4 to complete the second section. Specific teams have 15 to complete the first section. The date in the last section can be completed by the process of elimination and confirmed by remaining indirect information (4, 6, 8, 10). A and White (12, 14, 16) account for all others. Other answers can be found in the following:

20th (5)

2:00 (1)

Zoo (15)

B and Green (12)

16th (9)

6:00 (3)

Bookstore (9)

C and Brown (16)

8th (2)

12:00 (11)

Park (11)

D and Black (14)

12th (4, 6, 8, 10)

4:00 (7)

Museum (13)

Incredible Ball Pass
Integrating the Team

Activity Summary

A lively activity in which participants experience how teamwork can improve performance and efficiency.

Goal

To help participants to experience increases in performance and process efficiency by learning about and gaining mastery in the area of systems thinking and large/small team integration.

Group Size

10 to 150.

Time Required

Approximately 90 minutes for 5 rounds.

Materials

- Ten to fifteen different balls or other objects of various sizes and colors, such as tennis balls, Koosh® balls, Ping-Pong balls, heavy sponge balls (Nerf® balls are too light), rubber playground balls, socks rolled up in a ball, towels tied in a knot, a ball of silver foil, a ball of rubber bands, etc. Ideally, balls or objects will be of different shapes, sizes, and colors. Since participants will be throwing all items, all balls or objects should be relatively small to medium-sized and soft enough to avoid injury.

- Stop watch or regular watch with a second hand.

- At least five tables with chairs for participants.

- A whistle or some other loud distinctive tone to start and stop the activity.

- Flip chart and markers.

Physical Setting

Tables and chairs that can be moved easily, arranged in an irregular pattern, alternating longer and shorter rows (avoid symmetrical patterns such as a square or a circle) that seat six to eight participants at a table (four to six participants per table can also work).

Facilitating Risk Rating

Low to Moderate.

Process

1. State the purpose of the activity (learning about teamwork) and randomly throw various balls or other objects to participants at each table. If there are twenty or fewer participants, you may wish to have three or four balls or objects per table. If it is a large group, you may have fewer objects at a ratio of one object for every four to five participants.

2. Tell participants that before the first round is over, every participant at every table must actually hold, at least momentarily, every object at his or her table *as well as objects at other tables* as quickly as possible. In addition, each participant who starts with an object must also end the game physically holding that same object.

3. Tell them that there will be a series of three to five rounds for which some of the rules change. State that each round will start when you blow the whistle. Ask them to take care when tossing (no throwing or pelting) any item to other participants, ensuring that they have the receiver's attention. Remind participants that they are to pass all items so that everyone in the entire group touches and actually holds every object for at least a moment unless you instruct them otherwise during later rounds.

4. Announce the rules as follows (and post them, if desired):

   - All participants must remain seated and cannot move their chairs unless you say so. If participants are sitting at a table facing out, they must turn their chairs around to face the middle of the table with their legs under the table before the game begins.

- At the beginning of the game, participants who have objects in their hands must hold them up in the air so that all can see where they are located before the activity can begin.

- During any round, in the event that anyone drops an object, the clock keeps running. Participants must stand up quickly, pick up the dropped item, return to their seats, sit down in their exact same space, and start throwing items again (from the exact point at which it fell in the first place). The penalty is that more time accumulates.

- The round is not over until all participants who had an object at the beginning of the game have touched all the objects and have the identical object that they started with, at which time they are to hold the item up in the air for you to see.

  (5 minutes.)

5. Answer any questions participants may have.
   (5 minutes.)

6. Be sure everyone is seated and that those with objects are holding them in the air. Begin Round 1 by sounding the whistle. As play slows and participants begin to have their original objects again, remind them to hold their objects in the air for you. The first round might take from a minute and a half to four minutes, depending on the size of the group. Write the score in seconds elapsed on a big flip chart for all to see, like this: 2 minutes and 40 seconds = 160 seconds.

   Note: There is no strategy in this first round. In fact you want to make sure that you start relatively quickly so that they don't have too much time to think and plan. If by some chance the team starts planning, you may say, "We are under a serious production schedule, we have one minute until we start."

   Anticipate total chaos. Just keep shouting, "Make sure that everyone at every table touches every item." If all goes well, the objects and everything else will be flying through the air in total chaos as the entire system of communication and teamwork breaks down completely.
   (10 minutes).

7. Debrief Round 1 with these questions:

   - What happened during this round? Why was there such chaos?

   - How were you acting as a team?

- Who were you communicating with?

- What kind of strategy did you have as a team? How much planning was there ahead of time?
(10 minutes.)

8. Tell them to take a few minutes to plan together for what they might do to make this activity more effective and discuss how to improve their next effort. After a few minutes, if no one takes charge, ask for suggestions from individuals as to how to improve. Don't hesitate to ask one of them to get up and show you how to make the changes happen.
(7 minutes.)

9. State that it is time for Round 2 and ask everyone to make sure that they have all their original items back in their hands. State that the rules are the same. Blow the whistle to begin Round 2. Note that in this round the teams will try to create an orderly pattern of passing objects from one table to the next. They will still have numerous points of process breakdown in which their best plans to pass all the items from table to table are not implemented properly.
(7 minutes.)

10. Blow the whistle to end Round 2 once all participants have their original items back. Write the time on the flip chart and announce it with great fanfare, stating what a great job they did. Ask them to give themselves a round of applause. Comment on any really crazy or wild things that happened during this round.
(5 minutes.)

11. Debrief Round 2 with these questions:

- How did your process improvements work? How did you shorten your time? (Await their excited answers, and reinforce what a great job they did.)

- How did you improve (or create) teamwork this time?

- How much did it help to have a leader emerge and show you clearly how to perform this task?

- To what degree did having a clearly defined strategy help improve the process?

- Why were you able to execute the strategy so much better this time?
(10 minutes.)

12. State that it is time for Round 3. Tell them that they are now becoming experts at passing the balls and other objects, but that the boss still wants further improvements and cuts in production time. Tell them that they need to change the rules and the process of how they perform this task to improve the time. Continue by saying that, in this round, all the same rules apply except that participants may now rearrange themselves and their chairs and move them anywhere they want before the round begins, as long as they are around at least one table.

   Note: The ideal solution is to place all the chairs in one big circle around a single table for ease and flow in movement of the objects. However, should the teams not come up with this solution, which happens occasionally, you can either just let them go with whatever solution they decide on or coach them to get them one right if time is limited.

13. Blow the whistle to begin Round 3. Once all the objects have returned to their original owners, blow the whistle to end the round and post their time. Make sure you help them to recognize and appreciate how much they have improved from beginning to end. Use percentage of improvement by saying something like: "Wow, your team went from 180 seconds in the first round to 20 seconds in this last round, that is an 900 percent improvement overall. Wouldn't your boss be happy with a small fraction of that!" (5 minutes.)

14. Debrief Round 3 with these questions:

   • Why did you improve so dramatically this time? (The most important reason you are looking for is that they simplified the process!)

   • How did simplifying the process affect the task as hand?

   • Did you actually achieve the same objectives?

   • What have you learned here that you can take back to the workplace?

   • How can you implement what you learned?
   (10 minutes.)

15. Summarize by stating that this activity was basically a study in task and process management. Emphasize that, to the degree that you step back and study what your objectives are for any project, plan with incredible accuracy how you are going to achieve these objectives, and meticulously lay out in detail how you are going to implement and execute your plan, your team will improve its efficiency dramatically.

16. Allow the participants to try another round or make a repeated effort to improve if they ask for the opportunity. You may wish to use these additional debriefing questions:

- What was the secret for process improvement in this round over the last round?

- How have you improved in communication, teamwork, and leadership this round?

- What has made the difference in your ability to execute?

- From the first to the last round, in what ways did you improve your ability to implement your plan? What steps were necessary to make sure that everyone in the group did exactly what you needed him or her to do?

- How has this exercise helped you to improve your ability to plan strategically and execute flawlessly?

- How has the overall group improved from the first round to this final round?

(10 minutes.)

Trainer's Note

This is not a competition between teams but an attempt to get one team to improve performance by integrating their big team/small team functions, planning strategically and executing properly, taking leadership risks, thinking creatively, and learning new problem-solving techniques. Participants will have to play three to five rounds in order to improve their performance significantly.

Variations

- If necessary, balls can be numbered with a marker to create unique identifies.

- If further rounds are desired, the rules can be changed by offering more options for streamlining processes. Some optional rule changes that will dramatically affect the performance of a team are as follows:

  - Before a round starts, participants may rearrange themselves any way they wish, but must be sitting in their chairs.

  - Participants may place the balls or objects anywhere they wish before a round starts and do not have to have possession of them.

- When a round starts, participants may get out of their chairs and move around.

- The round is over when everyone has merely touched all the items and it is no longer necessary to actually have items back in people's possession.

- You may ask for completely out-of-the-box creative solutions. These may include:

  - Have a few participants run around the circle carrying one ball or object each.

  - Place all the items in the middle of the group on a table in one pile.

  - Create a double circle and concentrate efforts.

Submitted by Ronald Roberts.

Ronald Roberts *is president of Action Centered Training and ACT Games. He has invented over fifty games and holds six patents. Roberts uses these games to teach executives, managers, line staff, government and military, students, learning disabled and gifted students, as well as teachers about communication, teamwork, leadership, conflict management, stress reduction, strategic planning, change management, process improvement and many other soft skills. He has his master's degree in counseling psychology and teaches at Penn State University. Roberts has appeared on CNN Live, ABC, and NBC's "Today" show and the NBC affiliate in Arizona. He has also won the prestigious Dr. Toy and Parent's Choice awards.*

23, What Do You See?
Experiencing Energizers

Activity Summary

Twenty-three slides that can be used as icebreakers or energizers for training events.

Goal

To provide easy riddles that can be used as energizers, icebreakers, or in group competition.

Group Size

Any.

Time Required

Less than 5 minutes each.

Materials

- PowerPoint slides or transparencies of the energizers.

- Projector and screen.

- 23, What Do You See? Answer Key.

- (Optional) Bubble gum or other small prizes.

Physical Setting

Any.

Facilitating Risk Rating

Low.

Preparation

Transfer the energizing questions you want to use to PowerPoint slides or transparencies. You could also write out the questions and use them as handouts if desired.

Process

1. At any point in your training session when you believe participants need an energizer, call a 23, What Do You See? break.

2. Post one of the questions and have table teams (or other designated teams) compete for the first (or most) correct answer(s).

3. Each time, display one of the questions and have teams shout the answer. (5 minutes.)

4. If desired, award bubble gum or another small prize to the winners.

Variations

- List ten of the questions and give them to different teams as a competitive team-building activity.

- Use the questions to pair people for an activity. Give one person the question and a different person the answer.

Submitted by Dave Arch.

Dave Arch *is president of Dave Arch and Associates, Inc. (http://davearch.sandler.com), an authorized licensee of the Sandler Sales Institute. He is a best-selling author, internationally recognized speaker and conference presenter, and serves as the National Training Consultant for the Sandler Sales Institute and its 170 franchisees. Drawing on twenty-five years of training experience and a twelve-year background in personal and family counseling, Dave's sales training workshops are featured annually at national conferences. He has authored a dozen resource books currently used throughout the training industry.*

23. What Do You See? Puzzles

1.

What is it that you see in water that never gets wet?

2.

When it's light, I'm dark; when it's dark, I'm gone; when I'm gone for good, so are you. What am I?

3.

Can you punctuate the following so that you can read it with meaning?

That that is is that that is not is not that that is is not that that is not that that is not is not that that is is that not not it it is

4.

What makes more noise when they're dead than when they're alive?

5.

You are planning a 12,000 mile trip. Your mechanic tells you that your new tires will only go 8,000 miles and not one mile more. You know that you need to buy spares but aren't sure how many. How many will you need?

6.

What is it that you sit on, sleep in and brush your teeth with?

7.

What is neither inside
a house nor outside a
house, but is still part
of a house?

8.

How many of the following words
are mispelled?

Ukulele   **Sacrilegious**

Obbligato   **Fuschia**

Ecstasy   Graffito

Supersede   *INOCULATE*

9.

Jim and John are on the deck of a ship. The ship is going north. Jim is facing west and John is facing east. Suddenly, without turning around, Jim says to John, "You have a nose bleed." How could he possibly know this without turning around?

10.

One speaker said to the other speaker, "My mother is your mother's mother-in-law." What relationship did the speakers have to one another?"

11.

Can you name at least
two things that fall
but never break?

Can you name at least
one thing that breaks
but never falls?

12.

I purchase one
for 30 cents;
fourteen for 60 cents;
and one hundred
forty four
for 90 cents.
What am I buying?

13.

How many things can you name that have to be broken before they are used?

14.

What eats but never swallows?

15.

There are five
words in the
English language
that end in "cion."
Can you think of
one of them?

16.

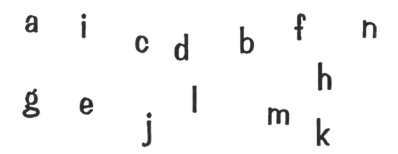

What is the four letter word which
can have three letters removed,
leave five and not change the
meaning of the word at all?

17.

What is it that you throw out when you need it and take in when you don't?

18.

What can you put inside a barrel to make it lighter?

19.

How many things can
you name that are
filled when they are
in use, but empty
when not in use?

20.

What is it that a
rich man doesn't
have, a poor man
has plenty of and
when you die you
take it?

21.

Ten parts of the human body can be spelled with only three letters. Can you name them?

22.

? What has ? eight wheels but is designed to carry one ? passenger? ?

23.

What is it that
was given to you,
still belongs to you,
that you've never
lent to anyone,
but is used by
everyone you know?

23. What Do You See? Answer Key

1. Your reflection.

2. Your shadow.

3. That that is is. That that is not is not. That that is is not that that is not. That that is not is not that that is. Is that not not it? It is.

4. Leaves.

5. Most will say four, but actually only two are needed, since you can take the front two off after four thousand miles and put the spares on. Then you can, after four thousand miles, take the back tires off and put the former front two tires back on. That's the minimal need, which is the goal in cost control.

6. A chair, a bed, and a toothbrush.

7. Windows and doors.

8. From the list, only "fuschia" is misspelled…it should read "fuchsia." And the word "mispelled" is also misspelled.

9. Jim and John were facing each other right from the start.

10. Father and child or paternal uncle/aunt and nephew/niece.

11. Night falls, leaves fall, day breaks.

12. House address numbers.

13. An egg, walnut, a horse, etc.

14. Acid/rust.

15. Suspicion, Coercion, Epinicion, Scion, Internection.

16. Five. Cross out the F, I, E and leave the Roman numeral V.

17. An anchor.

18. Holes.

19. Shoes, pitcher, frame, canteen, salt and pepper shaker, etc.

20. Nothing.

21. Arm, toe, eye, jaw, gum, hip, leg, lip, ear, and rib.

22. A pair of roller-skates.

23. Your name.

From Mundane to Ah Ha!
Using Training Objects

Activity Summary

An activity that encourages trainers to generate creative uses of common objects to facilitate the transfer of training.

Goals

- To develop a list of potential training uses for a group of common objects as a creative exercise.

- To explore training topics and develop a list of potential common objects that can be utilized.

Group Size

From 8 to 20 trainers, preferably 10 to 12.

Time Required

Approximately 2 hours.

Materials

- At least one object for each participant. Objects could include, but are not limited to, a boomerang, chalk, darts, Sharpies®, a magnifying glass, work gloves, puzzles, magic cards, a first aid kit, detergent, candy bars, pizza cutters, jump ropes, glitter, heart-shaped lights or Post-it™ Notes, mothballs, lint brush, Tootsie Roll® bank, or smiley bookmarks.

- One large gift bag for each group. The bag needs to be large enough to hold all the objects for one group.

- One From Mundane to Ah-Ha! Pre-Activity Lecturette for the facilitator.

- A copy of the From Mundane to Ah-Ha! Worksheet 1 for each participant.

- One From Mundane to Ah-Ha! Post-Activity Lecturette for the facilitator.

- A copy of the From Mundane to Ah-Ha! Worksheet 2 for each participant (for the Variation).

- A pencil for each participant.

- A flip chart and felt-tipped markers for each group.

- Masking tape.

- One rubber band.

- One small bag of M&Ms® for demonstration purposes.

Physical Setting

Participants can work at tables or seated in a circle or small cluster. The maximum number of participants is determined by the size of the room. The number of groups is dependant on the room setup and number of participants in the training. If space allows, working at tables is best.

Facilitating Risk Rating

Low.

Preparation

Place enough common objects in gift bags, one bag per group, so that each person has one item. Consider having multiple groups use the same objects so there is a maximum of twenty or thirty different objects in the room and thus discussion is limited.

Trainer's Note

Resources may be found in several places:

- Your local Dollar stores may have some interesting items; it's also good to check back frequently, as their inventory changes often.

- Oriental Trading Company: orientaltrading.com or (800) 875-8480.

- Trainer's Warehouse: trainerswarehouse.com or (800) 299-3770.

- *From Mundane to Ah Ha! Effective Training Objects* by Linda Eck Mills includes a CD containing ninety-six colored pictures of the objects in the book. www.theconsultantsforum.com/eckmills.htm.

Process

1. Using the Pre-Activity Lecturette, introduce the session and explain that the use of an object as an anchor point during training will increase retention of the material.

2. Break participants into table groups with four to five people at each table. Distribute Worksheet 1 and a pencil to each participant. Distribute one bag with objects to each group and tell participants that each individual is to select *one* object from the bag. Tell participants that each of them is to write at least one way to use the object he or she drew in training on Worksheet 1. (10 minutes.)

3. Direct the participants to pass their objects and their corresponding worksheets clockwise within the group and repeat Step 2 until they receive their original objects back. Allow approximately 10 to 15 minutes for the task, giving the participants a 2-minute warning before calling time. (10 minutes.)

4. Ask the small group members to share their ideas with one another and to discuss additional ways to utilize the objects. Give each group a flip chart and markers and tell them to select a scribe to record objects and several of their unique uses on their flip charts. Allow approximately 20 to 30 minutes for the task, giving a 2-minute warning before calling time. (30 minutes.)

5. Ask a representative from each group to present the uses for each object to the total group. Allow about 25 minutes for sharing. (25 minutes.)

6. When all groups have finished reporting, allow approximately 20 to 25 minutes to debrief the activity. Use flip-chart sheets to record answers to the following questions:

   - Which object we discussed would you be most likely to use in your training programs? Why?

   - Did all members of your group have the same ideas for each object? What were some differences?

- Was it difficult to incorporate a specific object into topics that you train? Which object was that? Why would it be difficult to incorporate?

- How would the use of objects help to make your training points more memorable?

(25 minutes.)

7. Summarize the session by referring to the posted flip-chart sheets and give the Post-Activity Lecturette. Be sure to tell the participants that there are a variety of factors that influence the use of a specific object. Make the point that no one object fits every occasion.
(10 minutes.)

Variation

Use Worksheet 2, and have the participants list the topics for which they conduct training. Then have the groups brainstorm what objects could be used to get points across. This could be done after the use of Worksheet 1, instead of after Step 5, or as a separate activity. Have each group use the same bag of objects as they used for Worksheet 1, allowing 10 to 30 minutes.

References

Eck Mills, L.S. (2005). *From mundane to ah ha! Effective training objects.* Bernville, PA: Dynamic Communication Services.

———

Submitted by Linda S. Eck Mills.

Linda S. Eck Mills, MBA, *owner of Dynamic Communication Services, is a professional speaker and educator. Her passion and expertise in active training and presentations, communication skills, and time management results in high-energy workshops that guarantee audience involvement, provide a unique presentation approach, and create a memorable and powerful learning opportunity full of tips and techniques. Linda is the author of numerous articles and books, including* From Mundane to Ah Ha! Effective Training Objects.

From Mundane to Ah Ha! Pre-Activity Lecturette

We've all heard the saying, "A picture is worth a thousand words." Today you will discover that objects are worth a whole lot more and can make learning an "Ah Ha!" event!

How many of you have ever tried to get your point across and your audience just didn't get it?

[Ask for a show of hands.]

Would an object or picture make the point memorable? Many times we forget that everyone doesn't think the same way we do or grasp a new concept on the first try. Using a common object helps tremendously.

Let's boost your creativity by looking at two objects together before you begin this exercise.

[Hold up the package of M&M candy.]

What can these M&Ms represent or symbolize in training?

[Answers could include: (a) diversity in the workplace; (b) customer service (not all customers are alike); (c) employee supervision (not all employees can or need to be supervised the same way); d) we are more alike than different; (e) something sweet can brighten your day; or (f)inside we are all the same.]

[Hold up a rubber band.]

What can this rubber band refer to?

[Answers could include the following: (a) holding things together; (b) stretching your ability; (c) being stretched too much results in increased stress; (d) a broken rubber band could represent the result of being unproductive; (e) time stretched to the limit; (f) the staff is stretched to the limit; or (g) if you delegate you won't be so stretched.]

[Proceed with the activity process.]

From Mundane to Ah Ha! Worksheet 1

Object	Potential Uses

From Mundane to Ah Ha! Post-Activity Lecturette

As we have discovered, there is more than one use for an object. This session is only the tip of the iceberg. I hope that this experience has started the wheels turning for you to do something memorable in your training. Start collecting common objects you want to regularly use to build your own training toolbox.

A key point to remember is that any object you use has to serve a purpose. Make sure you tell your audience what the purpose is so that everyone understands why you are going by using the object. The goal is to take training "From Mundane to Ah Ha!"

From Mundane to Ah-Ha! Worksheet 2

Subject/Content Area	Potential Objects

The Real Focus
Strategizing Leadership Behavior

Activity Summary

A process for leaders to consider as they meet the requirements of their work-places.

Goals

- To discuss the concept of leadership.

- To compare perceptions of leadership through the experiences of practic-ing leaders.

- To strategize a leadership action plan in line with requirements of the workplace.

Group Size

Up to 15 participants in leadership positions.

Time Required

Approximately 2 hours.

Materials

- One brief leader profile for each participant.

- One copy of The Real Focus Lecturette for the facilitator.

- One copy of The Real Focus Questionnaire for each participant.

- Whiteboard or flip chart.

- Markers.

- Paper and pens or pencils for participants.

The 2009 Pfeiffer Annual: Training.
Copyright © 2009 by John Wiley & Sons, Inc. Reprinted by permission of Pfeiffer, an Imprint of Wiley. www.pfeiffer.com

Physical Setting

A large room with tables for groups of three to work together.

Facilitating Risk Rating

Moderate.

Preparation

1. Gather profiles and achievements of leaders. Cover leaders across a spectrum of industries, other organizations, and working groups. Prepare brief profiles of the leaders that may include some of the following:

    - Brief bios that identify the organizations they have worked with.

    - Particular assignments demonstrating leadership excellence.

    - Particular strategies adopted.

    - That leader's thoughts on success factors of excellent leaders.

2. Prepare to give The Real Focus Lecturette.

3. Make copies of The Real Focus Questionnaire for participants.

Process

1. Explain that the purpose of the activity will be to focus on leadership qualities. Give the lecturette and stress the need for leaders to shape their leadership behavior to the expectations of their followers.

2. Divide the group into triads. Provide each participant with a profile of a leader, blank paper, and a pen or pencil.

3. Have participants read through the profiles they have received and then take turns within their small groups presenting their leaders and discussing their profiles.
    (10 minutes.)

4. Now tell participants to work together in their groups to prepare lists of leadership traits and behaviors for presentation to the large group.
    (15 minutes.)

5. After time is up, ask one participant from each group to present his or her small group's observations to the large group. Allow for discussion. Record the information on the flip chart/whiteboard.
    (25 minutes.)

6. Provide copies of The Real Focus Questionnaire to participants. Ask them to answer Questions 1 through 4 and then to discuss their answers within their small groups.
   (10 minutes.)

7. Lead a large group discussion of what they have learned and list their ideas on the flip chart.
   (10 minutes.)

8. Ask participants to answer the fifth question and again discuss their responses with the other group members when they are ready.
   (15 minutes.)

9. Call time and bring closure through a formal discussion and a reinforcement of the message that the individual, as a leader, must always deliver on the expectations of this or her followers to be truly effective in the leadership role.
   (5 minutes.)

10. Debrief with the following questions:

    • What have you learned from the leader profiles and your discussion here that you can apply when you are interacting with your own followers?

    • How can you be sure that what you have learned is not lost as you return to the workplace?
    (15 minutes.)

11. Ask participants to make arrangements among themselves to check each other's progress via email at stated times in the future, such as thirty days or three months. Give them time to exchange email addresses or make other plans. Ask them to share some of their ideas with the group and then close the session.
    (10 minutes.)

Variations

• If the group is small, participants could share their responses within the large group rather than breaking into subgroups.

• Instead of preparing the profiles yourself, have each participant select a leader (or you assign one) before the session and bring information about that person to share within the small groups.

Submitted by Mohandas Nair.

Mohandas Nair *is a management educator, a teacher, trainer, writer, and a facilitator of learning. He earned a B.Tech (Mech.) from IIT Kharagpur, India, has a diploma in training and development, and has thirty years of experience in industry and consultancy in the fields of industrial engineering and human resources development. He has published two books, written numerous articles, and facilitated many management development programs.*

The Real Focus Lecturette

Over the centuries, leadership has been defined and explained as the responsibility of one person—the leader. Leaders rallied followers to achieve goals the leaders established. The followers seldom had a say in the matter. They followed orders and generally could not choose whom to follow. That concept of leadership invariably had the followers subjugate their own interests to those of the leader.

Unfortunately, this concept is not in line with the newer idea of an individual's pride in self, in one's ability to and interest in taking charge of one's own life, using one's own knowledge and experience to initiate work processes and initiate change.

In the historical definition of leadership, only the leader suggested ideas and ways to move the system forward. The wealth of knowledge and creative instincts of the mass of followers remained largely untapped. Followers had to "buy into," or at least understand, their leaders' ideas before moving forward. Progress, thus, was often very slow, and some followers "tuned out" entirely.

By not tapping into the immense potential available within every follower, earlier leaders did not allow for much creativity and often hindered progress by insisting that there was only one best way to do a task. There was no room for variance.

When leaders stifle individuality and stunt potential, they can stifle the workers' spirit. People who feel like cogs in the wheel come to act like mere machines, but are not as consistent as machines and lack the capacity to continue without tiring. But if we as the new generation of leaders can unleash the spirit of our followers, we can enable big things to happen.

Today, that earlier concept of leadership has been turned on its head. Leaders can be seen as providing services to followers, supporting them in their work, making resources available, and creating an environment that allows followers to deliver excellence.

For this to happen, followers have to feel empowered and enabled. In the present workplace, younger followers especially want to be in charge of their own work and, if a leader is not up to their expectations, they will not perform to their potential.

Because the "modern" leader plays only a facilitative role, he or she must take followers' expectations into account, rather than choose a directive path. Thus, it can be said that true leadership is about followership.

The Real Focus Questionnaire

1. What have you learned about leadership by participating in this activity?

2. Briefly describe the environment you would like to create in which to lead your followers. What are their expectations from you?

3. What traits and behaviors from other leaders would you like to model in your own work situation?

4. What new traits and behaviors would you like to incorporate to strengthen your leadership style?

5. Identify some things that you need to do when you return to your job to incorporate what you have learned about leadership today.

Signs of Change
Identifying and Overcoming Roadblocks

Activity Summary

Using street signs as metaphors for helping participants predict potential roadblocks that may surface during organizational change.

Goals

- To anticipate potential roadblocks that may surface during organizational change.

- To identify effective strategies for overcoming these roadblocks.

Group Size

A small-to-moderate sized group (4 to 28 people). An even number is necessary to allow participants to work in pairs.

Time Required

90 minutes.

Materials

- One copy of the Signs of Change Worksheet for each participant.

- One pen or pencil for each participant.

Physical Setting

Arrange chairs and tables around the room so that participants can easily work in pairs.

Facilitating Risk Rating

Moderate.

Process

1. Introduce the topic. Say: "Organizational change rarely, if ever, unfolds as planned. The inevitable turbulence is underscored by the old adage, 'The best laid plans often go awry.' For this reason, anticipating potential roadblocks seems like a wise endeavor. This proactive strategy can dramatically increase the chances that change will be successfully implemented on the front lines—and sustained for the long haul."

2. Explain that the goal of this activity is to help them anticipate potential roadblocks that might interfere with a change that they have been asked to help implement. Also point out that this activity will help them identify ways to overcome obstacles to making the change.
   (5 minutes.)

3. Distribute copies of the Signs of Change Worksheet to all participants and give everyone a pen or pencil. Tell them to complete Part 1 of the worksheet and then wait for further instructions. In Part 1, they are to describe an upcoming change that will require them to motivate others (up, down, and/or sideways) to implement it. Allow approximately 3 minutes for this task, giving the participants a 1-minute warning before calling time.
   (5 minutes.)

4. Have participants work with partners to discuss the upcoming changes that they recorded in Part 1 of their worksheets. Allow approximately 10 minutes for this task, giving the participants a 2-minute warning before calling time.
   (10 minutes.)

5. Direct participants' attention to Part 2 of the worksheet. Discuss the five broad categories of potential roadblocks listed there:

   - Resistance from employees

   - Low/no support from leadership

   - Lack of resources

   - Poor planning and organization

   - Unclear/inconsistent communication about change

6. Write these on the flip chart and tell a story about when you personally *failed to anticipate and resolve one of these roadblocks* while trying to implement organizational change.

7. Have the participants work on their own to complete Part 3 of the worksheet, where they will identify the biggest obstacle that they might face while implementing the change that they described in Part 1. Stress that participants should be as specific as possible. Allow approximately 10 minutes for this task, giving participants a 1-minute warning before calling time. (10 minutes.)

8. Have the participants work on their own to complete Part 4 of the worksheet, choosing street signs that symbolize the biggest roadblocks they anticipate facing. Tell them to be sure to articulate how the sign they choose symbolizes their roadblock. Allow approximately 5 minutes for this task, giving participants a 1-minute warning before calling time. (5 minutes.)

9. Have participants discuss with their partners their anticipated roadblocks (Part 3) and the signs they chose to symbolize them (Part 4). Allow approximately 10 minutes for this task, giving the participants a 2-minute warning before calling time. (10 minutes.)

10. Have participants work on their own to complete Part 5 of the worksheet, where they will articulate why it's important to overcome their predicted roadblocks and the potential consequences if they don't. Allow approximately 5 minutes for this task. (5 minutes.)

11. Have participants discuss with their partners their responses to Part 5. Allow approximately 15 minutes for this task, giving a 2-minute warning. (15 minutes.)

12. Say: "At this point, you've realized that it's critically important to overcome your anticipated roadblocks, but how much control do you REALLY have over these predicted problems? While driving, we usually take detours to avoid roadblocks and other obstacles that impede our progress. Even though we might take unexpected routes, we still arrive at our intended destinations. This can be a useful metaphor when talking about the roadblocks that we inevitably face while trying to implement organizational changes. It's important for us to realize that we have the power to navigate around roadblocks

that threaten to impede our progress. We just have to be open to taking a different path. At some time or other, we have all been guilty of saying, 'I can't.' Today, let's challenge ourselves to stop making excuses. Instead, let's ask ourselves: 'What CAN we do to make our change a success?'"

13. Direct the participants' attention to Part 6 of the worksheet. Say: "Part 6 contrasts 'Red Light Statements' and 'Green Light Statements.' Red Light Statements are excuses for why your change effort will probably fail. For example: 'I can't motivate others to change.' 'I can't make the leadership of the company care.' 'I can't get the resources I need.' 'I can't improve how this change is planned and organized.' 'I can't improve how change is explained and communicated.' Conversely, Green Light questions are questions that you can ask yourself to ensure that your change will be successful. These questions demonstrate accountability and ownership. For example: 'How can I use my interpersonal influence to motivate others to change?' 'How can I leverage my current resources to create change?' 'How can I influence leadership to care about the change?' 'How can I improve how this change is planned and organized?' 'How can I improve how change is explained and communicated?'"

14. Have the participants ask themselves the "green light questions" and then respond to the questions in Part 6 of the worksheet. Explain that they should plan detours or ways to overcome their predicted roadblocks. Allow approximately 10 minutes for this task.
(10 minutes.)

15. Instruct participants to discuss the plans they created in Part 6 with their partners. Allow approximately 20 minutes for this task, giving participants a 2-minute warning before calling time.
(20 minutes.)

16. Summarize the lesson by saying: "During this activity we identified potential roadblocks that can disrupt organizational change. We also identified effective strategies for overcoming these obstacles." Ask, "Based on what you learned during this activity, what can you do differently to ensure your change is successfully implemented?" Listen to participants' ideas. Challenge them to share their ideas with at least one colleague who can help them champion the implementation of their change in their workplace. Express encouragement and confidence in the participants' abilities to lead and influence successful change implementation efforts.
(15 minutes.)

Variation

Have a single team that is responsible for the change implementation process complete this activity together. This activity can foster an open dialogue about each team member's concerns and predictions of possible roadblocks as well as strategies for overcoming them.

Submitted by Travis L. Russ.

Travis L. Russ, Ph.D., *is an assistant professor of communication at Fordham University in the School of Business Administration. As a professional consultant, he designs and facilitates learning solutions for clients in the corporate, educational, and non-profit sectors. His expertise includes organizational change, workplace communication, leadership, and diversity. He has published numerous development programs and academic articles.*

Signs of Change Worksheet

Part 1

Describe an upcoming change that requires you to motivate others (up, down, and/or sideways) to implement it.

Part 2

Below are five general categories of roadblocks that can interfere with successful change implementation.

- Resistance from employees

- Low/no support from leadership

- Lack of resources

- Poor planning and organization

- Unclear/inconsistent communication about change

Part 3

Describe the BIGGEST roadblock you anticipate facing while trying to implement the change you described above. Be very specific.

Part 4

Circle ONE of the following signs that symbolizes the roadblock you described above.

How and why does the sign you circled above symbolize your predicted roadblock?

Part 5

Why is it important to overcome your predicted roadblock?

What might happen if you don't overcome this roadblock?

Part 6

Today, challenge yourself to stop making excuses for why your change won't work. The following listing contrasts "Red Light" statements and "Green Light" questions. What **can** you do to make your change a success? What **do** you have control over?

Red Light Statements	Green Light Questions
Excuses for why your change will fail.	Accountability questions for ensuring the success of your change.
I CAN'T...	HOW CAN I ...
• Motivate others to change.	• Use my interpersonal influence to motivate others to change?
• Make leadership care.	• Leverage my current resources to create change?
• Acquire the resources I need.	• Influence leadership to care about the change?
• Improve how the change is planned/ organized.	• Improve how this change is planned/organized?
• Improve how the change is explained/ communicated.	• Improve how change is explained/ communicated?

After asking yourself the green light questions above, what steps can you take to overcome your roadblock?

What will successful change look like?

Introduction
to the Editor's Choice Section

Unfortunately, in the past we have had to reject exceptional ideas that did not meet the criteria of one of the sections or did not fit into one of our categories. So we recently created an Editor's Choice Section that allows us to publish unique items that are useful to the profession rather than turn them down. This collection of contributions simply does not fit in one of the other three sections: Experiential Learning Activities; Inventories, Questionnaires, and Surveys; or Articles and Discussion Resources.

Based on the reason for creating this section, it is difficult to predict what you may find. You may anticipate a potpourri of topics, a variety of formats, and an assortment of categories. Some may be directly related to the training and consulting fields, and others may be related tangentially. Some may be obvious additions, and others may not. What you are sure to find is something you may not have expected but that will contribute to your growth and stretch your thinking. Suffice it to say that this section will provide you with a variety of useful ideas, practical strategies, and creative ways to look at the world. The material will add innovation to your training and consulting knowledge and skills. The contributions will challenge you to think differently, consider a new perspective, and add information you may not have considered before. The section will stretch your view of training and consulting topics.

The 2009 Pfeiffer Annual: Training includes two editor's choice selections. Keep in mind the purpose for this section—good ideas that don't fit in the other sections. The submission by Mark Allen and Nanette Miner are perfect examples of items that are valuable to the readers of the *Training Annual*, but simply do not fit in any of the other categories.

Articles

The Corporate University Phenomenon: A Look Ahead, by Mark Allen

Twenty-One Questions to Ask Before Designing Any Training Program: The Sixty-Minute Needs Analysis, by Nanette Miner

The Corporate University Phenomenon
A Look Ahead
Mark Allen

Summary

Corporate universities have truly become a global phenomenon. Given the thousands in existence in North America and the incredible growth in the numbers of corporate universities in Europe and Asia, it is safe to say that corporate universities can be considered to be a vital part of the success of many organizations and not in danger of disappearing as another ephemeral fad.

This article examines the trends in the corporate university movement and discusses what these trends portend for the future. After starting with a definition of corporate university, the author explores these trends, including the growth in strategic importance, globalization, appropriate uses of technology, evaluation, and finally the shift from knowledge to wisdom.

Corporate Universities Defined

In *The Corporate University Handbook* I offered the following definition:

> "A corporate university is an educational entity that is a strategic tool designed to assist its parent organization in achieving its mission by conducting activities that cultivate individual and organizational learning, knowledge, and wisdom." (Allen, 2002, p. 9)

Some parts of this definition are worthy of discussion. A bit later in this article, I will discuss the final words in the section on learning, knowledge, and wisdom. For now, I want to point out that the phrase "conducting activities" was deliberately vague. Many corporate universities grew out of traditional training departments. However, the most sophisticated corporate universities now realize that there are many ways to develop people in addition to training. These corporate universities integrate numerous functions that are designed to develop people and expand organizational capabilities.

If there is one word that is most important in this definition, it is definitely "strategic." What most distinguishes a corporate university from a traditional training department is its strategic nature. While training departments are important, their importance is often tactical. A corporate university's contribution is strategic. This brings us to the first trend shaping the future of corporate universities, an increasing trend for organizations to use their corporate universities as strategic business partners.

The Strategic Role of Corporate Universities

When corporate universities first became popular in the United States, many organizations wanted to become part of the fad. So they quickly renamed their training departments as corporate universities. There were two problems with this approach. First, the corporate university movement was not a fad—it was (and is) a strategic tool to help organizations develop people and expand capabilities. More importantly, merely changing the name of something does not make it more important or more strategic. These were still training departments handling the important function of training (with the same level of quality as before the name change), but were no more or no less strategic than they were before.

This approach had another problem. Once people realized that the name change was really a meaningless gimmick, it doomed subsequent attempts to develop a true corporate university. People remembered the initial effort and were not willing to buy into the next attempt.

The important truth is that it does not matter what you call it—an "institute" can do a great job of strategically growing human capital, whereas a corporate university that is ill-conceived and poorly executed will not help an organization. As a matter of fact, in Europe, the word "university" is rarely used—institutes and academies are much more prevalent (Renaud-Coulon, 2002).

The key to success is for the corporate university to make strategic contributions to achieving the organization's goals. One method for checking on this is to examine whether the head of the corporate university (again, it does not matter whether he or she is called a "dean," a "director," or anything else) has a "seat at the table." If the corporate university chief has the ear of the senior executives, is invited to key strategic planning sessions, and can give input to senior executives, then the corporate university is likely a strategic contributor. If the corporate university is buried somewhere deep in the organization chart and reports to someone who reports to someone who is not in a particularly strategic role, then success is unlikely. In truth, the number one variable in determining the likely success of a corporate university is support from senior executives, especially the CEO.

Globalization of Corporate Universities

I started this article by asserting that corporate universities have become a global phenomenon. I mean two things by this. First, the corporate university, while tracing its roots to the United States (as far back at least as the 1940s with the establishment of Northrop University), now exists on every continent. There are thousands in North America. Growth in Europe has been explosive over the past decade. Asia, particularly China, has shown tremendous growth in the numbers (and sophistication) of corporate universities over the past few years. Australia has long had successful corporate universities (Dickson, 2002). Numerous corporate universities are beginning to emerge in South America and Africa.

But globalization also refers to the reach of corporate universities in companies that do business internationally. As in any other organization, a multinational corporation can benefit greatly from a well-executed corporate university, which can assist in developing the skills needed to manage a multinational corporation, while also assisting in creating consistency in organizational culture, focus, strategy, and even a common vocabulary (Shaw, 2005).

However, numerous challenges are inherent in implementing a global corporate university (Cohen, 2007). Among these are differences in cultures, languages, behavioral norms, and even time zones. Technology can help bridge some of these gaps, but as we will discuss in the next section, technology is not always a panacea.

Appropriate Uses of Technology

Seven years ago, I attended a conference called "Virtual Corporate University Week." The theme of the conference was that corporate universities were eliminating their brick-and-mortar classrooms and converting all instruction to so-called "e-learning." Hundreds of people who were either planning to implement or had implemented a virtual corporate university attended this conference. Now, six years later, I no longer hear of plans to convert corporate universities to a 100 percent virtual format, and I know of none that currently operate in that fashion.

So how is it that the use of technology in learning has seemingly moved backward, even as the technology itself has greatly improved? There were several problems with e-learning, the largest of which was that the focus was usually on the "e" and not on the learning. Many people viewed e-learning as a cost-effective method to widely distribute instruction. The problem was that the goal of a corporate university is not to distribute instruction—it is to help people learn. If people are not engaged by an online course or if they are not completing it, they are not learning. So this cost-effective solution was not a solution at all, therefore it was not effective, therefore the cost, while possibly less than classroom instruction, was not worth the investment. Too much of the focus was on the technology itself, instead of concentrating on learning. And it turns out that some people just do not like to learn using technology.

One problem with the notion of the virtual corporate university is the mistaken assumption that there can be a single method for distributing learning throughout an organization. The simple truth is that people have different learning styles and preferences. No solution can work for everyone, so the best corporate universities use many different methods.

Does this mean that I am advocating the abandonment of technology? Not at all. When used properly, technology can assist learning. Usually, it is best utilized to enhance classroom learning, not replace it. But as Roger Schank (2007) argues, the focus needs to be on the learning, not the medium of delivery. Figure out what people need to know and then discuss the best organization of that curriculum, design the learning, figure out who is best to deliver it, and then determine the best medium. It is not that technology cannot be of great use to corporate universities; it is just that, in many cases, the potential has not yet been realized.

I think the future trend will be to use technology more wisely. Instead of viewing it as a solution to all problems, it will be used when it can have the most impact in assisting learning. Of course, knowing what kind of impact it is having requires the ability to measure success, and that brings us to the topic of evaluation.

Evaluating Corporate Universities and Their Programs

One of the most enduring problems in the corporate university world is the question of evaluation. Corporate university leaders are plagued with the question of what to measure. Should they select one or more of Kirkpatrick's levels (Kirkpatrick, 1994), should they utilize Jack Phillips' ROI Methodology (Phillips, 1997), or some of the newer concepts on the market (Kiely, 2002; Kirkpatrick & Kirkpatrick, 2005; Phillips & Phillips, 2005)? There is no universal answer to that question. In fact, the only good answer is, "It depends." In this section, I will reveal what it depends on.

Kirkpatrick's four-level model posits a hierarchy ranging from reaction to learning to behavior change to results. While most corporate university directors profess a desire to know about behavior change and results, the truth is that the vast majority of programs are measured at Levels 1 and 2, not 3 and 4. The reason for this, of course, is that Levels 1 and 2 are easy and inexpensive to measure, while Level 4, in particular, is perceived as being complicated and costly.

But a corporate university does not exist merely to make people happy, or even just to enhance learning. It exists to deliver results (in terms of individual or organizational performance). So while it would be nice to know that people like your offerings and are learning from them, that is not enough to justify the investment in your corporate university. In order to see a return on that investment, there has to be some benefit to the organization.

Now the question becomes, "What results should we be looking for?" And the answer to that question becomes apparent when you ask yourself the single most crucial question in the corporate university world: "What are the results we are trying to achieve?" While it may seem obvious that this question should be asked, you would be amazed at how many corporate universities are started without a clear picture of the goals they are trying to achieve. Sometimes, organizations start a corporate university because they believe it would be beneficial, but they have not thought it through deeply enough to figure out how it can strategically assist the organization in meeting its goals. Other times, the stated goals are too nebulous, for example, "to create a world-class workforce." This does not clearly state what the desired goals and outcomes are. These are the types of organizations that struggle with the measurement question.

On the other hand, some organizations have clearly articulated goals for their corporate universities. For example, "to give our people the skills they need to increase sales" or "to improve the quality of our products or services" or "to increase employee retention." These companies have no problem in figuring out what to measure: They measure, in order, sales, quality, or retention. Note that these are not complicated learning metrics, nor are they very costly to measure. In fact, often the best measures of the success of your corporate university are things that you are already routinely measuring. It just turns out that, when these are goals of the corporate university or its programs, they also turn out to be Kirkpatrick Level 4 measures—they demonstrate the impact of your learning efforts.

So the first step is to impose the discipline to ask yourself what you are really trying to accomplish with your corporate university. The answer needs to be as specific as possible. Chances are, if you can clearly articulate the goals of your corporate university, you will then know what to measure. The key is to have a clearly articulated mission for your corporate university. (And if you can't clearly articulate those goals, then measurement is not your greatest problem).

All of this adds up to a process called "Mission-Based Metrics" (Allen & McGee, 2005). The trend is for more corporate universities to measure what is really important, rather than either measuring what is cheap and easy or going to the other extreme and measuring everything. By focusing on the corporate university mission and the organizational goals, the question of what to measure (and even how to measure) often becomes very simple to answer. And by focusing on what you are trying to accomplish, you not only are in a better position to measure it, but you are more likely to achieve it. And this brings us to our last trend, a focus on ensuring that people use the knowledge we give them—a process I call "wisdom management."

Wisdom Management: Moving from Knowledge to Wisdom

Since their inception, the goal of corporate universities has been to impart knowledge to members of an organization. While this is an admirable goal, it is often not enough. Knowledge that is in someone's head but never used does not benefit the organization. Only the application of knowledge truly pays off.

Thus, we need to expand our focus from knowledge to wisdom, with wisdom being defined as "the creative use of knowledge" (Harvard Business School Publishing, 1999). Many organizations have recently embraced the notion of "knowledge management." Their focus is to acquire, organize, share, store, and distribute knowledge throughout the organization. While these efforts are greatly beneficial, we need to go beyond knowledge and start implementing "Wisdom Management."

In *The Next Generation of Corporate Universities*, I provide this definition: "Wisdom management is a planned and systematic process by which an organization manages how its employees use and apply their knowledge and skills in ways that benefit the organization" (Allen, 2007, p. 391).

This shifts the focus away from the acquisition of knowledge and toward the use of it. And it is not just use that matters—the key words in the definition are "in ways that benefit the organization." Remember, knowledge that is not applied does not benefit the organization.

You will notice that this discussion parallels the discussion above about evaluation. Merely acquiring knowledge (learning), is not the goal; therefore it is not the only thing to measure. The use of knowledge in ways that benefit the organization is the goal, so results (in Kirkpatrick's language, Level 4) are what matter.

The concept of wisdom management also is congruent with the strategic role of corporate universities. Learning for the sake of learning is valued by many individuals and in many societies; however, that is not a strategic initiative for most organizations. Learning that manifests itself in ways that benefit the organization is strategic.

How wisdom management is put into place in an organization will depend on the organization's goals and its corporate university mission. The application of wisdom management will flow directly from the strategic objectives of the corporate university.

For example, Enclos Corp., a U.S.-based specialty subcontractor in the construction industry, created Enclos University in part to develop people to become senior project managers, a process that would normally take twelve to fifteen years. Through a wisdom management initiative that was focused on accelerating the process, Enclos is employing a combination of classroom training, on-the-job learning, and job rotations to shorten the process to eight years. The key is focusing on what has to be learned and how it is to be used to ensure that senior project managers not only have acquired the appropriate knowledge, but have already demonstrated the use of the requisite skills.

In conclusion, the corporate university of the future (and by this I mean the near future) will be a strategic tool of its parent organization. It will be a global entity that uses technology appropriately, that measures based on its goals (and more importantly has a clearly articulated set of goals), and employs wisdom management to ensure that the knowledge and skills it teaches are used and applied in ways that benefit the organization. Corporate universities that fit this model will be valuable contributors to their organizations' success.

References

Allen, M. (2002). *The corporate university handbook*. New York: AMACOM.

Allen, M. (2007). *The next generation of corporate universities*. San Francisco, CA: Pfeiffer.

Allen, M., & McGee, P. (2005). Measurement and evaluation in corporate universities. In J.E. Lane & M.C. Brown (Eds.), *Examining unique campus settings: Insights for research and assessment* ("New Directions in Institutional Research," Number 124). San Francisco, CA: Jossey-Bass.

Cohen, E. (2007). Global considerations for corporate universities. In M. Allen (Ed.), *The next generation of corporate universities*. San Francisco, CA: Pfeiffer.

Dickson, I. (2002). Corporate universities in Australia and Southeast Asia. In M. Allen (Ed.), *The corporate university handbook*. New York: AMACOM.

Harvard Business School Publishing. (1999). *Buckman laboratories* (Video 800-502). Boston, MA: Author.

Kiely, L. (2002). Measurement in corporate university learning environments: Is it gonna show? Do we wanna know? In M. Allen (Ed.), *The corporate university handbook*. New York: AMACOM.

Kirkpatrick, D.L. (1994). *Evaluating training programs*. San Francisco, CA: Berrett-Koehler.

Kirkpatrick, D.L., & Kirkpatrick, J.D. (2005). *Transferring learning to behavior: Using the four levels to improve performance*. San Francisco, CA: Berrett-Koehler.

Phillips, J.J. (1997). *Return on investment in training and performance improvement programs*. Boston, MA: Butterworth-Heinemann.

Phillips, J.J., & Phillips, P.P. (2005). *ROI at work*. Alexandria, VA: ASTD Press.

Renaud-Coulon, A. (2002). Corporate universities in Europe. In M. Allen (Ed.), *The corporate university handbook*. New York: AMACOM.

Schank, R.C. (2007). Splendid learning: Why technology doesn't matter. In M. Allen (Ed.), *The next generation of corporate universities*. San Francisco, CA: Pfeiffer.

Shaw, S. (2005). The corporate university: Global or local phenomenon. *Journal of European industrial training, 29*(1), 21–39.

Mark Allen, Ph.D., *is a faculty member in organizations and management at Pepperdine University's Graziadio School of Business and Management. He has published two books on corporate universities (*The Next Generation of Corporate Universities *in 2007 and* The Corporate University Handbook *in 2002). He serves as a consultant to corporate universities and has spoken to audiences all over the world about the topic. He serves on the boards of The Global Consortium of Corporate Universities and of The University of Farmers. He may be reached at mallen@pepperdine.edu.*

Twenty-One Questions to Ask Before Designing Any Training Program
The Sixty-Minute Needs Analysis
Nanette Miner

Summary

In your work as a trainer, you'll often be faced with a request for training from someone who assumes he or she knows what the problem is and that training can solve it. Before you begin to plan a session though, it's worthwhile to spend an hour discussing with the requestor the 21 questions posed in this article to ensure that the problem has been correctly identified and to determine whether or not training is the appropriate solution.

Performance problems can be caused by a myriad of things; perhaps your organization has undergone a downsizing, or perhaps a department is understaffed or its equipment is unreliable. Unfortunately, many managers and organizations assume that poor performance is directly linked to a lack of skill or knowledge that can be solved by training. In my more than twenty years of consulting experience, I've found that what is initially presented as a training problem is often something else entirely.

Before embarking on any training program, it is imperative that a needs analysis be conducted in order to pinpoint the exact cause of poor performance and to ascertain if the poor performance can be solved by applying training. Unfortunately, most organizations skip the needs analysis, assuming that they already know the cause.

The following twenty-one questions will help you to pinpoint the true cause of a performance problem and also help with the design process by ascertaining what training truly needs to be created. Ask these questions of the individual in the organization who is requesting that you design and develop a training program to address an assumed training issue.

1. What Is the Problem You Are Experiencing?

Often you'll hear a request along the lines of, "My sales team needs training on teamwork." Well, that's putting the cart before the horse, isn't it? Ask the requestor to give you a big-picture view of the factors he or she thinks are contributing to the poor performance. Do not accept the definition of the performance problem (in this case, lack of teamwork) until you hear more about the work environment, the intended audience, their job-related duties, and so forth.

2. What Symptoms Led You to Believe This Was a Problem?

Notice the key word "symptoms." Very often what presents as a performance problem is truly a symptom of a deeper or related organizational problem. For instance, a large publishing company believed it needed customer service training because it came in dead last (in the customer service category) in a survey published by its industry magazine. When more investigation was done, it was determined that the organization was suffering from an inadequate technology system that led to the *symptom* of poor customer service.

3. Who Is Your Audience (Age, Tenure, Education, and So Forth)?

Having an understanding of who the potential audience is often provides clues to their on-the-job performance capabilities. Perhaps the staff were all hired within the last year and lack an historical perspective of how their job is done. Perhaps the staff is near retirement age and is starting to "coast" in the job. I often work with organizations that find lack of performance is caused by staff that utilizes English as a second language and a simple translation of work procedures could solve the performance problem, rather than more training conducted in their non-native language.

4. What Are Their Typical Workday/Overall Job Responsibilities?

This question can help you to spot *process* breakdowns that can *appear* to be performance breakdowns. For example, a manufacturing firm intended to conduct cross-training because its machinery broke down so often that many of its personnel simply had nothing to do until their machines were fixed. It was discovered that the machinists were not doing preventative maintenance. Once a stricter protocol was put in place regarding preventative maintenance, the need for cross-training was moot.

5. What's Their Work Environment Like?

The work environment can have a large impact on performance ability. Perhaps tools aren't where they are supposed to be. Perhaps processes that are interrelated are hundreds of yards apart. Perhaps the work environment is so noisy that communication frequently breaks down. Until you understand the environment in which your potential trainees work, you will not understand what factors may be contributing to their lack of performance.

6. Why Do *You* Think This Is a Training Need?

Remember, the person requesting that you design and deliver training has his or her own perspective on the situation. When this question was posed to a retail executive, his response was that a particular department's reports were consistently wrong and therefore they must not know how to use the reporting software. The executive made a huge leap from the evidence of erroneous reports to employees' lack of skill or knowledge. The intended trainees will also have their own perspectives, so it's a good idea to ask them, at some point, whether they feel a need for training based on the evidence at hand. When further investigation was done with the intended trainee group from the retail organization mentioned above, it was discovered that the employees knew how to use the software quite well but lacked basic math skills.

7. Have They Been Able to Do _____ in the Past?

Fill in blank with the assumed lack of knowledge or skill. If the answer to this question is *no*, then you may in fact have a training need. But if the answer to the question is yes, then there's typically something else at play. If the workers could do the task at some point in the past, but now they cannot, investigate what has changed in their environment.

8. What Organizational Factors Might Be Playing a Role?

When organizations are in flux, a sense of ennui trickles down to every individual's performance. If the organization has been talking about an acquisition or merger, it can cause people to change their work habits. If a downsizing has occurred and more work needs to be accomplished with fewer people, it's logical that poor performance will follow. Perhaps the department has had three different managers in the last eighteen months, and every manager has had a different perspective on how the work should be done; eventually, people start to second-guess their abilities and perform at a minimal level in order to "play it safe."

9. What Training Already Exists?

Often you'll find that a "training problem" is a frequent issue within the organization, and it has been addressed in the past. Determining what training already exists is helpful in two ways: (1) it helps you to determine what training people have had in the past and alerts you to look for reasons why that training did not "stick" and (2) it should minimize your need to reinvent the wheel because it's probable that you can repurpose the existing training content.

10. Have You Looked For Off-the-Shelf Training Solutions?

Before determining that a custom training solution is necessary, ask the requester of the training whether he or she has spent any time looking for generic, off-the-shelf, training solutions. Why reinvent the wheel? Very often, topics such as customer service, financial acumen, software, and soft skills training are already in existence and can be a low-cost, highly effective training solution. It's also possible to find a product that "almost fits" and to request that the vendor modify it or repurpose it for your organization's needs. Either way, you will save time and money.

11. What Training Has the Audience Had?

Similar to Question 9, the answer helps you to ascertain what knowledge or skill your expected training audience has already acquired. It's not necessary for this training to have occurred through your organization. For example, perhaps some workers have had college-related experiences that make them more capable than others. Or perhaps a few workers at your organization were previously employed by one of your vendors or competitors. Very often you'll find a range of tenure; the "older" workers will have had training that was delivered a few years ago, while the "newer" workers are at a loss. Again, if you discover that they have had *no* training, you may indeed have a training problem on your hands. But if training has been delivered to the audience, and they *still* are not doing the job as expected, other factors are at play, and it is your job to discover what those factors are.

12. Does the Audience Think They Need Training?

This is a *great* question because whether or not your audience *needs* training is only half the equation—the other half is whether the audience is *willing to accept* training. One manufacturing organization that was trying to cross-train its workforce had a problem with trainees simply not showing up to the classes! No matter what they did to entice or cajole the workforce, the workers simply would not leave their stations to go to the training because they did not feel it was of benefit to them.

13. What If We Don't Train Them? What's the Worst That Will Happen?

Sometimes, an intervention is more expensive than the problem being experienced. A retail organization that had a 112 percent turnover at the hourly level was contemplating providing management training with the expectation that better managers would equate to happier staffers and therefore increase tenure. With just a bit of research, it was determined that training really would not be worthwhile for two reasons: (1) in the retail industry, 112 percent turnover is not that bad and (2) the company really had a hiring issue—choosing to employ teenagers without a strong work ethic and being in an urban location without a nearby bus route, which often impacted their employees' ability to arrive at work.

14. How Will This Training Tie to Business Goals?

If there is no expected business outcome from the training, it will be hard to enlist the support of the organization; it's possible that your project will be canceled if it seems to be a "nice to know" topic. Your time and effort are valuable commodities, so you want to ensure that there is a true business goal such as increased sales, decreased accidents, reduction in personnel, or the like.

15. What's Most Important to You in Solving This Problem: Quality, Speed, or Cost?

Three factors are always in play in project management: quality, speed, and cost. You cannot have all three. The same is true in training. If a training program is to be created and delivered within a short time frame (speed is most important), it will require a good deal of money to make it happen and it's possible that quality will suffer. By the same token, a quality job will require time and money. By asking the project requestor which is most important, you will have a good understanding of where to apply your efforts.

16. What Resources Can You Give Me?

This question tests the commitment of the project requester. Too often you'll find that the requester is trying to make his or her training problem your problem. There's only so much that you can do in your role as a trainer; by asking what resources the project requester is willing to commit, you gain an understanding of how much that individual is willing to invest in the success of the training. It's possible that you may need an office in their facility, or access to an internal database, or access to subject-matter experts. Think about what resources you would need to be successful and ask for them early in the process.

17. Who Will Sign Off on the Final Design?

Every once in a while you will discover that the person who is requesting the training is not the ultimate decision-maker. It's important to discover early who has final authority. I once worked with the director of operations to develop new hire training for a fifteen-store retail organization. We spent over forty hours each creating content and materials, only to be told, when we presented them to the vice president of operations, that we had taken them entirely in the wrong direction. Who would have thought that the director of operations didn't know what the organization was trying to achieve? Now I always ask, "Who will ultimately approve this training?"

18. Do You Know of Other Industries or Companies Experiencing the Same Problem? How Are They Addressing It?

I find it hard to believe that most organizational needs are so unique that no one else has dealt with them. Try to avoid reinventing the wheel. Check with your industry association and/or your competitors to see whether they are also experiencing the same need. In a best-case scenario, you may be able to purchase or license something they have already created. As an example, the National Lumber and Building Material Dealers Association created a stellar forklift-safety video-training program and sold it from their association website for a mere $99.

19. What Is the Life Expectancy of This Course?

Will the course be a one-time offering? Will it be quarterly? Will it be delivered on a weekly basis? Maintaining the program requires extra effort on your part. Are parts of the course subject to government regulations and therefore will need to be checked and updated periodically? Are there forms that may become obsolete? Will trainers change? If so, the leader materials must be exceptionally detailed. Knowing the shelf life of the training program will influence your design approach.

20. How Will the New Knowledge/Skills Be Reinforced After the Training?

Remember, you can only do so much as the trainer; eventually the trainees must go back to the job and start using their new knowledge and skills. People never leave a training program having mastered everything they were taught, so some time must be spent back on the job reinforcing what was learned. One organization attempted to change the way that their salespeople answered the phone. Unfortunately, the managers didn't go to the training and didn't really see a need for changing the way the phone was answered. Within a week the salespeople were back to answering the phone the "old way" and the training program and the trainer were implicated in this failure.

21. How Will We Know the Problem Has Gone Away? What Will Be Different?

Beware of requestors who say (or imply), "I don't know what I want, but I know it's not this." If *they* don't know what improved performance looks like, you certainly will not be able to envision it. Without a clear definition of performance turnaround, how will you know when you've achieved it? Don't accept a training assignment from someone who's essentially telling you, "I'll know it when I see it."

One of the issues that we as trainers have faced for decades is our inability to truly identify the value we return to the organization. By finding out the answers to these twenty-one questions, which take about an hour, you will be in a much better position to create and offer training initiatives that will clearly return business results to your organization.

Nanette Miner, Ed.D., *is the founder and managing consultant for The Training Doctor, LLC, an instructional design firm with offices in Connecticut and South Carolina. Now in its seventeenth year, The Training Doctor specializes in creating customized training curriculums for workforce personnel. Dr. Miner is also the founder of The Accidental Trainer, a non-profit organization dedicated to giving subject-matter experts basic instructional design skills.*

Introduction

to the Inventories, Questionnaires, and Surveys Section

Inventories, questionnaires, and surveys are valuable tools for the HRD professional. These feedback tools help respondents take an objective look at themselves and at their organizations. These tools also help to explain how a particular theory applies to them or to their situations.

Inventories, questionnaires, and surveys are useful in a number of training and consulting situations: privately for self-diagnosis; one-on-one to plan individual development; in a small group to open discussion; in a work team to help the team to focus on its highest priorities; or in an organization to gather data to achieve progress. You will find that the use of inventories, questionnaires, and surveys enriches, personalizes, and deepens training, development, and intervention designs. Many can be combined with other experiential learning activities or articles in this or other *Annuals* to design an exciting, involving, practical, and well-rounded intervention. Each instrument includes the background necessary for understanding, presenting, and using it. Interpretive information, scales, and scoring sheets are also provided. In addition, we include the reliability and validity data contributed by the authors. If you wish additional information on any of these instruments, contact the authors directly. You will find their addresses and telephone numbers in the "Contributors" listing near the end of this volume.

The 2009 Pfeiffer Annual: Training includes three assessment tools in the following categories:

Individual Development

Vulnerability to Fraud Survey, by H.B. Karp and Jonathan D. Taylor

Consulting, Training, and Facilitating

Change Readiness Checklist, by Sherene Zolno

Organizations

New Organizational Role Stress (NORS) Scale, by Avinash Kumar Srivastav

Vulnerability to Fraud Survey

H. B. Karp and Jonathan D. Taylor

Summary

As the population ages, the occurrence of investment fraud is on the upswing. People must be more aware of their own susceptibilities to being exploited. The Vulnerability to Fraud Survey was created based on the extensive work of The Consumer Fraud Research Group. This instrument identifies three basic categories of scams, those that center on the need for Conformity, those that focus on having good Character, and those that play to the need for Control.

The survey is presented in the context of ten situations. In each situation there are three options, one from each of the three categories. The respondent is asked to respond to what extent he or she would be influenced by each option in each of the ten situations. The survey is self-scored, yielding one score for each of the categories. The three scores are then plotted on a model that points the respondent to the category that is most like to influence his or her choices. The impact of the other two categories is displayed as well. Options are discussed.

Background

In 2004, the NASD Investor Education Foundation awarded a research grant to WISE Senior Services in Los Angeles to investigate the problem of consumer fraud that targets older Americans. This resulted in the publication, The NASD Foundation Fraud Study Final Report. While this research looked at two types of fraud, lottery fraud and financial investment fraud, this survey is focused solely on the latter. Several major and important findings have come from this extensive research.

1. Investment fraud victims (IFVs) score higher on financial literacy tests than non-victims. Their status as victims may be due to the fact that, because they are more literate and better educated, they think that they are above being fooled and are therefore more ego-involved. This may make them less aware of external cues and more susceptible to a con.

2. Most fraud pitches are tailored to match the psychological needs of the victims.

3. The same tactics used in fraud pitches by con artists are also used in legitimate sales pitches by sales reps.

4. Greed is as much a contributing factor in a scam as it is in a legitimate business or sales transaction.

5. In comparing the profile of the investment fraud victim (IFV) to that of a non-victim, the IFVs significantly/are more likely to be:
    a. Male
    b. Living with someone else
    c. Have more education
    d. Be married
    e. Enjoy higher incomes
    f. Be more optimistic
    g. Be more likely to listen to a sales pitch
    h. Experience more difficulties from negative life events
    i. Under-report fraud victimization

Types of Scams

The NASD Final Report identified thirteen specific types of scams that were used in collecting the data. These scams are listed below:

	Scam	Description
1.	Phantom Fixation	Dangling the prospect of wealth
2.	Scarcity	Making a product seem rare to increase its value
3.	Source Credibility	Claiming to be from a legitimate business
4.	Comparison	Showing a more expensive price with the offered price
5.	Friendship	Playing the victim's friend

6.	Commitment	Making the victim commit early, then using it against him of her later on
7.	Social Consensus	Making it seem as if everyone is buying this particular product or service
8.	Reciprocity	Doing a small favor for the victim to obligate him or her
9.	Landscaping	Structuring the situation so that all roads lead to a sale
10.	Profiling	Identifying the victim's "hot buttons" through extensive questioning
11.	Authority	Con artist plays authority figure, making the victim an "agent"
12.	Fear	Intimidating the victim
13.	Dependent	Con artist plays young, helpless individual, putting victim in a parental role

Themes: The Thirteen Scams

There are many ways in which con artists dupe investors. Upon close inspection, the thirteen scams listed above can be broken down into three distinct categories: conformity, character, and control. *Conformity* focuses on the victim wanting to be seen as being "in" by acting as though only the very few shrewd investors will have access to the best investment opportunities. The *character* category is used to prey on the victim's need to see him- or herself as having a high ethical, moral, and/ or intellectual character. The third category, *control*, involves cons that prey on the victim's susceptibility to the authority and power of other people or institutions or the need for power and control for him- or herself.

The thirteen scams can be sorted by category as follows:

1. Conformity (the need to be seen as a savvy investor)
   a. Phantom fixation
   b. Scarcity
   c. Comparison
   d. Social consensus

2. Character (the need to be seen as having high character)
   a. Friendship
   b. Commitment
   c. Reciprocity
   d. Landscaping
   e. Dependent
   f. Profiling

3. Control (the need to respond to authority or power)
   a. Authority
   b. Fear
   c. Source credibility

See Figure 1 for how the categories fit together.

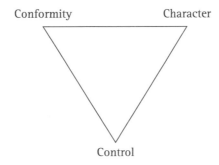

Figure 1. Fraud Vulnerability Response

The assumption the researchers made was that everyone, no matter how savvy, has some proclivity to being conned by someone at some point. Thus, it is helpful to have a feel for what your own tendencies and vulnerabilities are so that you are at least more aware of them.

Using the Vulnerability to Fraud Survey in Training

As the incidence of fraud increases, particularly those scams that are directed to the senior members of our society, more and more public and private training has arisen to educate people about the problem. The Vulnerability to Fraud Survey was created:

- To provide a relevant activity to offset the passive participant role that most straight presentations in this area produce.

- To provide a means for participants to identify with the problem on a personal, subjective level, as well as on an intellectual, objective one. Recognizing one's own potential vulnerability to being duped can go a long way in preventing people from becoming victims of fraud.

It takes thirty-five to forty minutes to fill out and discuss the survey in a group. While this survey can be used with any size group, it is particularly applicable for large groups in which the opportunity for interpersonal interaction is limited.

Reliability and Validity

No reliability or validity data are available. The purpose of the survey is to provide a means for increasing personal involvement and for launching discussion.

Administering the Survey

If using the survey in training, start by having the respondents take the survey before presenting any content. Simply distribute the survey, go over the instructions, and answer any questions respondents may have about the survey itself.

You may choose not to hand out the Scoring Sheet until the respondents have all completed their surveys. In this case, present the NASD findings and discuss them after everyone has completed his or her survey; then have respondents score their own surveys and discuss their results in subgroups. You may choose to share the data from the Rationale Sheet or use it to promote discussion.

H. B. Karp, Ph.D., *is an associate professor of management at Hampton University in Hampton, Virginia. He is also the owner of Personal Growth Systems, a management consulting firm in Chesapeake, Virginia. Dr. Karp received his Ph. D. in industrial/organizational psychology from Case Western Reserve. He has consulted with a variety of Fortune 500 and government organizations in the areas of leadership development, team building, conflict management, and executive coaching. He specializes in applying Gestalt theory to issues of individual growth and organizational effectiveness. He has authored over ninety publications and has written several books, including* Personal Power: An Unorthodox Guide to Success *and* The Change Leader: Using a Gestalt Approach with Work Groups. *Most recently, he was lead author on* Bridging the Boomer-Xer Gap: Creating Authentic Teams for High Performance at Work, *which was* ForeWord *magazine's 2002 Gold Winner for Best Book in Business & Economics.*

Jonathan D. Taylor, Ph.D., *is an associate professor of finance at Hampton University in Hampton, Virginia. In 2000, he received a Ph.D. in decision sciences from the Massachusetts Institute of Technology and began teaching finance at Washington University's Olin School of Business. He has published several articles on conflicts of interest between investment managers and their clients.*

Vulnerability to Fraud Survey

Hank B. Karp and Jonathan Taylor

Instructions: The ten statements below describe *different* situations. Assume that the three options given are the *only ones available* to you in each case. Distribute 10 points across each question in terms of how you would tend to respond. Remember that 0 is a score, so you are free to use it like any other number. Be sure that your total response to each question adds up to 10. Here are a few examples:

1. My preference in ice cream flavors is:
   - 3   A. Chocolate
   - 0   B. Vanilla
   - 7   C. Strawberry
   - Total = 10

2. In terms of vacations, I would prefer going to:
   - 5   A. The mountains
   - 3   B. The beach
   - 2   C. A big city
   - Total = 10

Make the following assumptions for each of the situations presented below:

1. You are interested in the product or service being offered and are contemplating purchasing it.

2. There is nothing suspicious or unreasonable about the person making the presentation.

3. The presentation itself seems reasonable and worthy of consideration.

Spread 10 points across the three options in each case, remembering that you are to assume there are *no other options available*.

1. A sales rep is working with you on buying a car. You are leaning toward purchasing the new car because:
   - A.___The price appears to be considerably lower compared to what other dealerships have asked.
   - B.___The sales rep made a clear extra effort to give you a good price.
   - C.___This agency reputedly sells twice the number of cars as any other in the region.

2. You started with a new stock brokerage firm several months ago. Your broker has suggested that you purchase a small block of a new IPO that is about to come out. You are really considering this because:
   A.___You are one of very few people who know about this upcoming offering.
   B.___If you passed on this, your broker would think that you were really a beginner.
   C.___Your broker has been Broker of the Month for the last six consecutive months.

3. A young, attractive college student is selling magazine subscriptions door-to-door. You are thinking about buying a few because:
   A.___The price is 70 percent off the newsstand price.
   B.___The student needs the commission to help pay next semester's tuition.
   C.___All the magazines are first-rate publications.

4. You have just relocated to a new city. Your realtor has been showing you homes in the price range you specified. The last home you saw really caught your interest and you are considering making an offer because:
   A.___The realtor has just persuaded the owner to come down 15 percent on the price.
   B.___The realtor really seems to know what's important to you and has pointed these aspects out to you.
   C.___There are very few homes this good in the area and if you pass on this it could be months before you find another in this range.

5. You are thinking of buying a condominium for investment purposes in a new development. You might buy the one you saw last week because:
   A.___The choice units are already almost gone.
   B.___The developer sent a car around to take you to and from the building.
   C.___The developer promised that if you could bring in two other people to hear the offer, he could give you an additional discount.

6. A casual acquaintance, whom you have known for several years, recently came to you with a good tip. She said there is an estate sale coming up soon that will have several very undervalued paintings for sale. You may go and purchase some of these because:

   A.___It's a rare chance to make a killing.
   B.___You owe her a favor and she has made the gesture.
   C.___She has a master's in fine arts degree and is known to be somewhat of an art expert.

7. You clearly need a new vacuum cleaner. The Best Deal Shopping Channel is offering one that would meet your needs. You are considering buying this because:

    A.___The deal will only last another three minutes.

    B.___The sales presentation seemed to answer every question you might have had.

    C.___The inventor of this cleaner was featured in the most recent issue of *Newsweek*.

8. You have very little life insurance and have accepted an invitation to a seminar to hear about buying more. Friends have told you that, because you are a senior citizen, you really don't need any more. You don't think this is necessarily so, and are leaning toward buying a policy because the presenter has assured you that:

    A.___The premium seems quite small next to the payout.

    B.___If you don't buy, those you leave behind will be strapped with a financial burden.

    C.___Because of your age, there is little likelihood that another company will insure you.

9. You are at home watching TV when there is a knock at your door. The person there introduces himself and tells you that he and his workers have just finished resurfacing a neighbor's driveway. He noticed that your driveway could use resurfacing and it seems that he accidentally brought more resurfacing material than he needed. He offers to resurface your driveway. You consider this because:

    A.___Eight people in the surrounding neighborhood have used his service and are extremely happy with the results.

    B.___He is very personable and reminds you of your favorite nephew.

    C.___He points out that if you wait another three months, you may have to dig up and replace your entire driveway.

10. You have just received a letter from Estonia explaining that a minor royal has been arrested and needs to get his money out of the country. If you agree to help, you stand to get a percentage of the amount taken out. You are aware of the obvious scam letters flooding the American populace coming from poorer countries, but this one sounds legit, as the writer says he was referred to you by an old friend of yours and gives the friend's name. You are going to check this out and might go along with it because:

    A.___The percentage could make you independently wealthy.

    B.___You seem to be the only one who can really help this person.

    C.___The letter is on the stationery of the Financial Minister of Estonia.

Vulnerability to Fraud Survey Scoring Sheet

Instructions:

1. Add the numbers you gave for each of the three categories A, B, and C:

   A _____ + B _____ + C _____ = 100

   Conformity   Character   Control

2. Now place a mark for each score on the appropriate vector on the diagram below.

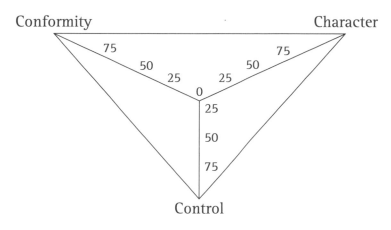

Scoring Vector

3. Connecting the three marks will point you to the category of "con" to which you are most vulnerable. It will also show the extent to which you are likely to be influenced by the other two categories as well.

Vulnerability to Fraud Survey Rationale Sheet

Item		Tactic
1.	A	Comparison
	B	Friendship
	C	Source credibility
2.	A	Phantom fixation
	B	Landscaping
	C	Source credibility
3.	A	Comparison
	B	Dependent
	C	Source credibility
4.	A	Phantom fixation
	B	Profiling
	C	Fear
5.	A	Scarcity
	B	Reciprocity
	C	Authority
6.	A	Phantom fixation
	B	Friendship/Reciprocity
	C	Source credibility
7.	A	Scarcity
	B	Landscaping
	C	Source credibility
8.	A	Comparison
	B	Commitment
	C	Fear
9.	A	Social consensus
	B	Friendship
	C	Fear
10.	A	Phantom fixation
	B	Dependent
	C	Source credibility

Change Readiness Checklist

Sherene Zolno

Summary

The Field Assessment™ model (Zolno, 2008) (see Figure 1), introduced the author's idea that a whole system change intervention, one that creates sustainable change in a complex organization, must be designed to intervene in the three key aspects of a system: its style, strategy, and structure (the "whole field"). Such an integrated approach increases the organization's potential for achieving its goals by generating a critical mass for change. Ensuring that the organization's employees are ready for change is critical. The checklist provided here can be used to gauge the readiness of employees for change.

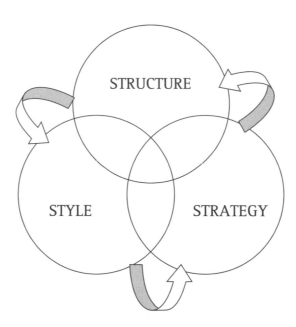

Figure 1. The Field Assessment Model

Consulting to or leading an organization that is going through major change requires bringing a *whole system perspective*, coupled with an *appreciative eye*, to the design of the intervention. You must create an integrated intervention plan that can foster change in multiple parts of the organization at the same time. Such a comprehensive intervention can bring about a profound shift in the organization's identity and its view of its future and way of doing business. This type of whole system approach to a change intervention is more likely to support the organization in reaching its "tipping point"—the point of critical mass—that moves the organization forward.

The success of any major change effort is dependent to a large extent on the readiness level of the organization's employees. "Readiness" is here defined as the degree to which employees are predisposed to support change, as opposed to ignoring or resisting it.

Recent research, particularly in the arena of social construction and system change, suggests that organizational change occurs as part of intentional collective action (Fuller, Griffin, & Ludema, 2000; Gergen, 1994; Weisbord, 1987). The authors report that complex change in an organization is most likely to be successful when people within that system are fully engaged in a cooperative process of creating it.

Support for change comes about "by connecting people to the organization's strategy, capturing their imaginations, respecting their contributions, and energizing the change process" (Zolno, 2002). Recognizing and supporting the key role employees play in effecting complex change increases employee readiness to support that change.

I've found it to be especially powerful when employees are clear about their strengths and positively acknowledged for their successes in the past. The sense of capability that results leads to their confidence in their ability to make a change. After all, employees are repeating successes of the past, but within a new context. Thus, a link between past, present, *and* future capacities is forged . . . and this brings readiness for change.

The Change Readiness Checklist can help you to determine employee "readiness" for change, as well as identify strategies required to help employees get ready to participate in and support a change initiative. You can fill out the checklist based on your own observations, or use the eleven questions to gather data on the organization from others. In order to facilitate use as a handout to others, the explanations of the importance of each rating are given on the Interpretation Sheet.

References

Fuller, C.S., Griffin, T.J., & Ludema, J.D. (2000). Appreciative future search: Involving the whole system in positive organization change. *Organization Development Journal, 18*(2), 42–53.

Gergen, K.J. (1994). *Realities and relationships: Soundings in social construction.* Cambridge, MA: Harvard University Press.

Weisbord, M.R. (1987). *Productive workplaces: Organizing and managing for dignity, meaning, and community.* San Francisco, CA: Jossey-Bass.

Zolno, S. (2002). Appreciative inquiry: New thinking at work. In E. Biech (Ed.), *The 2002 annual, volume 2: Consulting.* San Francisco, CA: Pfeiffer.

Zolno, S. (2008). Getting smart about system change. In E. Biech (Ed.), *The 2008 Pfeiffer annual: Training.* San Francisco, CA: Pfeiffer.

Sherene Zolno, RODC, *executive director of The Leading Clinic, is a researcher, educator, and consultant whose expertise includes working with leadership teams and assisting organizations in identifying strategic intention, improving operations, and transforming culture. Her research-based New Century Leadership™ program and Timeline for Tomorrow process are the foundation for whole system change in several major organizations. Zolno served on ASTD's OD Professional Practice Area Board. Her writing has been published in ASTD's* Research Monograph, *in OD Network's* OD Practitioner *and* VisionAction *journals, in* Consulting Today, *and in the 2000, 2002, and 2008* Annuals.

Change Readiness Checklist

Sherene Zolno

1. Employees feel valued and hopeful about the future of the organization.

0	1	2	3	4	5

   Don't feel valued;   Feel; valued
   feel hopeless   feel hopeful

2. Employees are involved in planning for the change.

0	1	2	3	4	5

   Employees   Employees
   are not involved   are involved

3. The purpose of the change is clear to employees.

0	1	2	3	4	5

   Purpose   Purpose
   is unclear   is clear

4. Employees believe there is a *need* for the upcoming change.

0	1	2	3	4	5

   No need   Need for
   for change   change

5. There is good communication regarding the change.

0	1	2	3	4	5

   Communication   Communication
   is not good   is good

6. The "cost" of making the change is not high, and the potential rewards seem greater than the potential losses.

0	1	2	3	4	5

   Cost too   Cost is
   high;   appropriate;
   rewards   rewards
   too low   outweigh losses

7. The compatibility of the change with the present system is perceived to be high.

0	1	2	3	4	5
Low compatibility					High compatibility

8. Credible people in the organization are advocating the change and genuinely support it, and there is respect for and trust in the change sponsor or change agent.

0	1	2	3	4	5
Credible people do not support; no trust					Credible people support; high trust

9. Employees believe there will be adequate organizational support for the change.

0	1	2	3	4	5
Resources not available					Resources available

10. Key job characteristics that are being changed will have a positive impact on the employees.

0	1	2	3	4	5
Negative impact on job characteristics					Positive impact on job characteristics

11. Employees have been through well-executed changes in the past and are confident in and in touch with their capacity to implement the present suggested change.

0	1	2	3	4	5
Not confident					Confident

Change Readiness Checklist Interpretation Sheet

1. **Employees feel valued and hopeful about the future of the organization.** It is important to honor the contributions of employees to past successes, building a platform for the future based on strengths.

2. **Employees are involved in planning for the change.** It is human nature for people to support what they helped create, so employees need to have a key role in co-creating any major organizational change.

3. **The purpose of the change is clear to employees.** Employees need a good understanding of why the sponsors are implementing the change. Otherwise they may be anxious and suspicious in the absence of information.

4. **Employees believe there is a *need* for the upcoming change.** Even if employees fully understand the *rationale* for the change, they may not agree that a change is needed.

5. **There is good communication regarding the change.** Even if the change affects only a few people, communication can be easily distorted.

6. **The "cost" of making the change is not high, and the potential rewards seem greater than the potential losses.** For employees to be motivated to make a change, a reward for accomplishment must be provided in the form of something they truly value, and it must compensate for any physical, intellectual, or emotional price they perceive they will pay.

7. **The compatibility of the change with the present system is perceived to be high.** Compatibility relates to how closely employees view the change aligning with existing organizational values or with their own personal beliefs and values, especially any that employees hold as fundamental or "sacred."

8. **Credible people in the organization are advocating the change and genuinely support it, and there is respect for and trust in the change sponsor or change agent.** Employees must see that others whom they value support a change initiative.

9. **Employees believe there will be adequate organizational support for the change.** If the change requires scarce organizational resources (money, time commitments by certain managers, new equipment/facilities, specialized training, etc.), employees may not see the value of changing. Also, operating budgets can be overburdened with the cost of planning, purchasing, and implementing the organizational change.

10. **Key job characteristics that are being changed will have a positive impact on the employees.** Employees will be more accepting of a change if they perceive that it will increase their autonomy and the value the organization places on them or their jobs. Resistance is increased if employees believe a change will block or significantly restrict the achievement of their own personal ambitions, negatively impact their social relations, or involve a significant challenge that is likely to go un-rewarded.

11. **Employees have been through well-executed changes in the past and are confident in and in touch with their capacity to implement the present suggested change.** Change involves learning, and learning usually involves mistakes. When people are not given the freedom to make mistakes while learning, they become afraid and easily discouraged. Employees must perceive that they already possess the skills and knowledge required for implementing the change, or that the necessary training will be provided by the organization.

New Organizational Role Stress (NORS) Scale

Avinash Kumar Srivastav

Summary

Revalidation of the ORS Scale identified the existence of a new type of stress we called Role Underload. The New Organizational Role Stress (NORS) Scale represents an enhanced framework for measuring role stress comprising eleven types. The NORS Scale uses seventy-one items to measures Inter-Role Distance, Role Stagnation, Role Expectation Conflict, Role Erosion, Role Underload, Role Overload, Role Isolation, Personal Inadequacy, Self-Role Distance, Role Ambiguity, and Resource Inadequacy. Reliability of the new scale was tested on a sample collected from 319 respondents. High value of Cronbach's alpha coefficient (0.863) obtained for the NORS sample has established the internal consistency reliability of the NORS Scale. The article describes the development of the NORS, along with its administration and scoring.

Background

Role stress is experienced due to problems encountered in role performance. High role stress reflects poor quality of role design; it jeopardizes the role occupant's well-being and his or her role performance. Assessing the level of role stress and containing it within a reasonable limit are therefore important for all types of organizations (Srivastav, 2006). The first framework of role stress was developed by Kahn, Wolfe, Quinn, Snock, and Rosenthal (1964). It comprised three types of role stress (*Role Conflict, Role Ambiguity,* and *Role Overload*). Scales for measuring role conflict and role ambiguity were developed by Rizzo, House, and Lirtzman (1970). A scale for measuring role overload was developed by Beehr, Walsh, and Taber (1976). Pareek (1982) expanded the framework of role stress, developing a scale to measure eight types of role stress (*Inter-Role Distance, Role Stagnation, Role Ambiguity, Role Erosion, Role Overload, Role Isolation, Role Inadequacy,* and *Self-Role Distance*). The extended framework represented the real problems in organizational roles that remained unexplained by the earlier framework. Role stress framework was further improved by Pareek (1983), who developed a fifty-item *Organizational Role Stress* (ORS) scale to measure ten types of role stress: *Inter-Role Distance* (IRD), *Role Stagnation* (RS), *Role Expectation Conflict* (REC), *Role Erosion* (RE), *Role Overload* (RO), *Role Isolation* (RI), *Personal Inadequacy* (PI), *Self-Role Distance* (SRD), *Role Ambiguity* (RA), and *Resource Inadequacy* (RIn).

Revalidation of the ORS Framework

Revalidation of ORS framework was done by Srivastav and Pareek (2008) through confirmatory factor analysis of fifty items of the ORS scale measured on 453 respondents. The study uncovered the need for enhancing the framework of role stress to include a new type of role stress called *Role Underload* (RU), clearly distinguishing it from RE. It also pointed out (1) low validity of subscale for SRD, (2) mixing up of RE and RS items, and (3) unacceptable validity of thirteen.

Development of the Instrument

Development of the NORS (New ORS) Scale was guided by the scope for improvement identified for the ORS framework, subscales, and the scale as a whole.

1. Scope for improvement was identified as follows:

    a. Making use of the results of revalidation of the ORS framework reported above.

    b. Analyzing each item of the ORS scale for possible improvement according to the following guidelines for item design (Srivastav & Pareek, 2008).

        •   Multiple-choice options or seeking multiple responses through any single item should be avoided; conjunctions like "and/or," should not be used as far as possible.

        •   Negative statements may lead to confusion and attract defensive behavior; their use within a subscale should be limited; when feasible and relevant, positive statements should be substituted.

- Stress items make the respondents uncomfortable and may lead to defensive behavior; their use within a subscale should be limited; when feasible and relevant, comfort items should be substituted.

- Complex sentences (which are confusing or difficult to understand) should be replaced with simple sentences (which are clear and easy to understand).

   c. Obtaining feedback on ORS subscales and items from experts, ORS scale users, and previous respondents.

2. ORS items were redesigned in line with the above-mentioned item design guidelines to enhance their validity.

3. A new subscale was designed for measurement of RU, making use of RE items indicating desire to do more, adding newly designed items representing intention to harness unutilized capacity and potential.

4. New subscales were finalized, using modified ORS items, including newly designed items, or deleting redundant ORS items, as necessary for enhancing subscale validity, distinguishing RS from RE and RU from RE. It was not considered necessary to maintain an equal number of items in each subscale.

5. The NORS Scale was finalized by mixing the items of eleven constituent subscales at random. A regular pattern of ordering the subscale items was consciously avoided to discourage possible manipulation of response by the respondents.

Rationale

The NORS framework represents an enhanced framework comprising eleven types of role stress: IRD, RS, REC, RE, RU, RO, RI, PI, SRD, RA, and RIn. RU is not a part of the ORS; it is newly included in NORS framework. Concept of RO and RA are similar in both ORS and NORS frameworks. Design rationale for the NORS framework is explained below.

1. IRD represents difficulty in balancing between organizational and non-organizational roles. Just as organizational responsibilities can have a disturbing influence on non-organizational responsibilities, non-organizational responsibilities can also have a disturbing influence on organizational responsibilities. An IRD subscale in ORS framework does not capture the disturbing influence of non-organizational responsibilities on organizational

responsibilities. An additional item for the purpose has been included in an IRD subscale under the NORS framework.

2. RS is not only due to lack of personal growth, but it can also be due to lack of career growth. Besides stagnating in the current role, RS can also manifest in stagnating in the previous role. Lack of career growth and stagnating in the previous role are not captured in the RS subscale under ORS framework. Two additional items for the purpose have been included in the RS subscale under the NORS framework.

3. REC can arise from conflict between different expectations from the same party or from conflict between expectations from different parties. The REC subscale in ORS does not specifically capture conflicts that may arise (a) between colleagues and seniors and (b) between colleagues and juniors. Two additional items for the purpose have been included in the REC subscale under the NORS framework.

4. The RE subscale in the ORS has a clear division; two items represent deprivation or erosion, but three items represent desire to do more. Non-deprivation items have been excluded from the RE subscale under the NORS framework. RE can manifest in the role not making an impact in the organization. It may also arise when reward for some of the tasks performed by the role occupant is given to others. The RE subscale in the ORS framework does not consider these two aspects. Two additional items for the purpose have been included in the RE subscale under the NORS framework.

5. The RU subscale under the NORS framework is based on three items in the RE subscale in ORS that indicate desire to do more. It includes two additional items related to desire to harness one's unutilized capacity and potential.

6. The RI manifests in lack of teamwork with connected people. This has not been considered under the ORS framework. An additional item for the purpose has been included in the RI subscale under NORS.

7. PI can result from lack of experience. This has not been considered in the ORS framework. An additional item for the purpose has been included in the PI subscale under the NORS.

8. SRD can arise from conflict between self and role in terms of needs and beliefs. These have not been considered in the ORS framework. Two additional items for the purpose have been included in the SRD subscale under the NORS.

9. RIn can arise in spite of all resources, including the required number of people being available, if they do not have adequate competence for their respective roles. RIn can also manifest when the required equipment for role performance is not available. These were not covered explicitly under the ORS framework. Two additional items for the purpose have been included in the RIn sub-scale under the NORS.

NORS Items

The NORS Scale makes use of forty-nine out of fifty items of the ORS-scale. One item of the ORS scale has not been used. Only one item of the ORS scale has been used in its original form. Forty-eight items of the ORS scale have been modified. The NORS Scale includes twenty-two new items. The nature of NORS Scale items is shown in Table 1.

Table 1. Nature of NORS Items

NORS Scale Item Numbers	Remarks
13, 14, 21, 25, 33, 36, 38, 48, 50, 55, 56, 61, 64, 65, 66	Fifteen new items included for enhancement of role stress framework.
34, 41, 62	Three new items included for avoiding multiple-choice options in ORS scale items 9, 13, 36.
63, 16, 43, 69	Four new items included to enhance clarity in ORS scale items 6, 23, 26, 46.
1-12, 15, 17–20, 22–24, 26–32, 35, 37, 39, 40, 42, 44–47, 49, 51–54, 57–60, 67, 68, 71	Forty-eight items are based on revision of ORS scale items 1–44, 46, 48–50.
70	This item is the same as ORS scale number 45.
2, 6-10, 12, 14, 16, 18, 20, 22-24, 26, 28, 31, 32, 34, 35, 39, 43–45, 47, 49–51, 55, 56, 58, 60, 62, 64, 66, 67, 69, 71	Thirty-eight inverted items; their scores need to be inverted before processing for interpretation. Actual score of 1, 2, 3, 4, 5 would become 5, 4, 3, 2, 1, respectively.

Description of the Instrument

The New Organizational Role Stress (NORS) Scale is a generic instrument for the measurement of stress experienced in organizational roles. Comprising seventy-one items, it measures eleven dimensions or types of role stress, catering to all types of roles and all types of organizations. Knowledge of one's role stress profile is useful for individuals and organizations to enhance their well-being and effectiveness (Srivastav, 2006).

Dimensions of the Instrument

There are eleven dimensions or types of role stress, as explained below:

1. *Inter-Role Distance (IRD):* Arises due to difficulties in balancing between organizational and non-organizational roles.

2. *Role Stagnation (RS):* Arises due to lack of development or growth; one may keep on stagnating in the older role instead of taking up the newer role.

3. *Role Expectation Conflict (REC):* Arises due to conflict among role expectations from significant people.

4. *Role Erosion (RE):* Arises when some functions of one's role are performed by others or when reward for one's performance is given to others.

5. *Role Underload (RU):* Arises when role occupant desires to utilize his or her underutilized potential or capacity to make higher contributions to the organization.

6. *Role Overload (RO):* Arises when there are too high or too many expectations from one's role.

7. *Role Isolation (RI):* Arises due to lack of interactions with those connected with role performance.

8. *Personal Inadequacy (PI):* Arises due lack of competence for role performance.

9. *Self-Role Distance (SRD):* Arises when there is a conflict between the self and the role in terms of image, needs, or values.

10. *Role Ambiguity (RA):* Arises due to lack of clarity in role expectations.

11. *Role Inadequacy (RIn):* Arises due to lack of external resources for role performance.

Scoring the Instrument

Eleven types of role stress, as explained above, are measured through the direct or inverted scores of designated items as follows. Inverted items are marked with an asterisk (*). Inverted score is obtained by subtracting the direct score from 6. As a result of inversion, scores of 1, 2, 3, 4, 5 would become 5, 4, 3, 2, 1, respectively.

Average of the designated direct or inverted items for a role stressor scores the role stressor in the range of 1 to 5. To translate the score in the range of 0 to 10,

1 is subtracted from the average item score corresponding to the role stressor and the remainder is multiplied by 10 and divided by 4. The scoring framework is shown below.

(1) IRD = [{(6* + 12* + 27 + 37 + 38 + 52)/6} − 1] × 10/4

(2) RS = [{(3 + 13 + 20* + 28* + 39* + 58* + 66*)/7} − 1] × 10/4

(3) REC = [{(29 + 40 + 41 + 53 + 59 + 61 + 63 + 65 + 68)/9} − 1] × 10 /4

(4) RE = [{(4 + 7* + 14* + 21)/4} − 1] × 10/4

(5) RU = [{(1 + 11 + 19 + 25 + 36)/5} − 1] × 10/4

(6) RO = [{(15 + 30 + 42 + 54 + 70)/5} − 1] ×10/4

(7) RI = [{(8* + 16* + 22* + 31* + 43* + 44* + 62* + 64* + 67* + 69*)/10} − 1] × 10/4

(8) PI = [{(32* + 45* + 56* + 60* + 71*)/5} − 1] × 10/4

(9) SRD = [{(5 + 9* + 17 + 23* + 33 + 46 + 48)/7} − 1] × 10/4

(10) RA = [{(2* + 18* + 26* + 34* + 49* + 57)/6} − 1] × 10/4

(11) RIn = [{(10* + 24* + 35* + 47* + 50* + 51* + 55*)/7} − 1] × 10/4

Score for Total Role Stress (TRS) is obtained by adding individual scores for the eleven types of role stress. TRS is scored in the range from 0 to 110.

Norms

Eleven types of role stress were measured on 258 respondents from public- and private-sector banks, and using the NORS Scale yielded the very first norms for the new scale. These are shown in Table 2, listing the mean and standard deviation for the twelve role stress variables (eleven types of role stress and total role stress). A role stressor can be seen as "high" when its score exceeds its mean plus half its standard deviation; it can be taken as "low" when its score falls below its mean minus half the standard deviation; it can be taken as "medium" when it falls in between low and high limits above.

Administration

First, respondents are introduced to what role stress is and its implications at the individual and organizational levels and learn about the utility of role stress

Table 2. Norms for NORS

Stress Variable	Mean	Standard Deviation
IRD	4.62	1.54
RS	4.49	1.30
REC	3.57	1.68
RE	4.68	1.50
RU	6.06	1.88
RO	4.63	1.76
RI	5.21	1.29
PI	5.15	1.67
SRD	4.22	1.29
RA	4.63	1.45
RIn	5.11	1.37
TRS	44.04	4.32

(N = 258: Public and Private Sector Bank Executives)

profiles at the individual and organizational levels. Then a brief explanation is given of the eleven types of role stress under the NORS framework.

Guidelines for scoring are explained, followed by distribution of the NORS Scale and pens or pencils.

After the administration, scoring time of about thirty minutes is given to the respondents. It may be noted that allowing them a longer time could pave the way for data errors due to possible manipulation of their natural responses to the items.

The NORS Scoring Matrix is distributed to the respondents after they complete scoring all seventy-one items. Respondents are advised to (a) enter their item scores in the pre-assigned boxes on the Scoring Matrix, taking care to invert the scores in respect of items marked with an asterisk (*); (b) compute the averages of direct/inverted item scores in each row; (c) subtract 1 from the row average, multiply the remainder by 10, divide the product by 4, and enter the result in the designated box for the final score for the related role stressor/type of role stress; (d) add the scores for all the role stressors to compute their total role stress score; and (e) enter their total role stress on the Scoring Matrix.

Using the NORS for Organization Development

The process of identifying prominent role stressor(s) can be used to find both problems and opportunities for improvement at the individual and organizational level (Srivastav, 2006). The following approach is suggested:

1. Obtain group scores for each role stressor by averaging the scores for the relevant role stressor for all the respondents.

2. Obtain the group score for total role stress by adding together the group scores for all role stressors.

3. Identify maximum and minimum scores for each role stressor at the individual and group levels. Communicate these to the group and ask those having the maximum score for each role stressor for some thoughts about why their scores are so high, facilitating the group discussion.

4. Similarly, obtain feedback from those having minimum scores for each role stressor and facilitate a group discussion about how to increase or decrease the various role stressors.

5. Identify role stressor(s) at the organizational level and communicate these to the respondents, facilitating a discussion of action plans for dealing with them (Srivastav, 2006).

6. Identify and privately communicate prominent role stressor(s) at the individual level to any respondents who are interested, helping people to formulate strategies and action plans for dealing with them (Srivastav, 2006).

Reliability

The NORS Scale was administered to 319 role occupants from a state police organization, three public-sector banks, two private-sector banks, and a private-sector business school. NORS data was used (after inverting the scores for the inverted items) for assessing the internal consistency reliability of the new scale using the SPSS package. Cronbach's alpha coefficient for the seventy-one-item NORS Scale was found to be 0.863. Sensitivity of Cronbach's alpha coefficient to exclusion of each one of the items was also tested. By excluding any one item at a time, the Cronbach's alpha coefficient changed in a very narrow range from 0.859 to 0.868. Because each value of alpha is higher than 0.8 and the range of its variation is only 0.009, a high degree of internal consistency among the items of the new scale was confirmed. It can therefore be concluded that the NORS Scale has an acceptable reliability.

Recommendation

Further research is recommended for determining the validity of the NORS Scale and finding the correlates and norms for the eleven role stressors measured in different organizations for a variety of roles.

Acknowledgments

Valuable guidance received from Dr. Udai Pareek is gratefully acknowledged. Dr. K.S. Gupta reviewed the previous version of the manuscript and made useful suggestions. He also used the NORS Scale and collected data from a state police organization in Bangalore. Mr. Christo F.V. Fernandes used the NORS Scale and collected data from bank personnel in Goa.

References

Beehr, T.A., Walsh, J.T., & Taber, T.D. (1976). Relationship of stress to individually and organizationally valued states: Higher order needs as a moderator. *Journal of Applied Psychology, 61,* 41–47.

Kahn, R.L, Wolfe, D.M., Quinn, R.P., Snoek, J.D., & Rosenthal, R.A. (1964). *Organizational stress: Studies in role conflict and ambiguity.* New York: John Wiley & Sons.

Pareek, U. (1982). *Organizational role stress scales.* Ahmedabad, India: Navin Publications.

Pareek, U. (1983). Organizational role stress. In L.D. Goodstein & J.W. Pfeiffer (Eds.), *The 1983 annual.* San Francisco: CA: Pfeiffer.

Rizzo, J.R., House, R.J., & Lirtzman, S.I. (1970). Role conflict and ambiguity in complex organizations. *Administrative Science Quarterly, 15,* 150–163.

Srivastav, A.K. (2006, October/December). Role stress audit for organizational development. *Indian Journal of Training and Development,* XXXVI(4), 81–97.

Srivastav, A.K., & Pareek, U. (2008). Measurement of stress in organizational roles: Revalidating the framework. In E. Biech (Ed.), *The 2008 Pfeiffer Annual: Training.* San Francisco, CA: Pfeiffer.

Avinash Kumar Srivastav, Ph.D., *holds an MS in electronics and communication engineering and a Ph.D. in management in the organizational behavior area. He is the dean (research) at Icfai Business School, Bangalore, India. He has served as external consultant to International Labor Organization; executive director, ITI Ltd., Bangalore; and OD advisor, change management advisor and corporate HR director in Jakarta. Dr. Srivastav has authored fifty national and international publications on different aspects of organizational behavior and development, including those in international conference proceedings and refereed journals. He was the editor of* R & D Management, *published by Tata McGraw-Hill, New Delhi. Dr. Srivastav is the consulting editor for ICFAI's* Journal of Organizational Behavior.

New Organizational Role Stress (NORCS) Scale

Avinash Kumar Srivastav

Instructions:

1. Read the statements one by one, in a sequence from 1 to 71; read only when you are ready to score the item.

2. Score a statement before reading the next statement.

3. Score on the basis of your first natural reaction to each statement, without trying to determine the ideal response. It should not take more than 30 minutes to complete the seventy-one statements.

4. Record your score for each statement in the space provided, as 1, 2, 3, 4, or 5.

   Score 1 for never or rarely, 2 for occasionally, 3 for sometimes, 4 for frequently, 5 for always or very frequently feeling the same way as the statement.

5. It is necessary to record your score for each statement.

Item Number	Statement	Score
1	I would like to accept higher responsibilities than what I have been doing.	
2	My role has been properly defined.	
3	I am stagnating in my current role.	
4	Certain functions belonging to my role are being performed by others.	
5	My role demands that I do what is against my judgment.	
6	My role in the organization allows me time to pursue my interests outside.	
7	My role is important for the organization.	
8	I am able to receive the required attention of those connected with my role.	
9	My role provides me opportunities to use my expertise.	
10	Information required for performing in my role is available to me.	
11	I would like to contribute much more than what I have been doing.	
12	My role in the organization allows me to give time to my family as needed.	
13	Even after moving to a new role, I continue doing tasks belonging to my old role.	
14	My role is making an impact in the organization.	
15	Workload in my role is very heavy.	

(Continued)

Score 1 for never or rarely, 2 for occasionally, 3 for sometimes, 4 for frequently, 5 for always or very frequently feeling the same way as the statement.

Item Number	Statement	Score
16	I am able to obtain the required time from those connected with my role.	
17	I would like to do things for the organization that are quite different from what I am doing in my role.	
18	The scope of my job is clear to me.	
19	I would like to do more challenging tasks than what I have been given.	
20	I am learning in my role for taking on higher responsibilities.	
21	Rewards for certain tasks performed in my role are given to others.	
22	There is sufficient interaction between my role and other connected roles.	
23	Work in my role is related to my interests.	
24	Resources of different kinds are adequately provided for performing in my role.	
25	I would like to use my unutilized potential in my role.	
26	Priorities in my role are clear to me.	
27	My role in the organization interferes with my family life.	
28	I am able to prepare for taking on higher responsibilities.	
29	My seniors have conflicting demands from my role.	
30	Quality of work is compromised because of excessive workload in my role.	
31	I can easily consult with people connected with my role.	
32	I have the required knowledge to take up the responsibilities in my role.	
33	Work in my role is conflicting with my values.	
34	Responsibilities of my role are clear to me.	
35	The required number of people are available for effective performance in my role.	
36	I would like to use my unutilized capacity in my role.	
37	My responsibilities inside the organization interfere with my responsibilities outside the organization.	
38	My responsibilities outside the organization interfere with my responsibilities inside the organization.	
39	I am able to prepare for challenges of my role.	
40	My colleagues have conflicting demands from my role.	
41	My juniors have conflicting demands from my role.	
42	I have too many responsibilities in my role.	
43	People connected with my role can easily consult with me.	
44	I am involved in joint problem solving with people connected with my role.	
45	I have the required skills to take on the responsibilities in my role.	

Item Number	Statement	Score
46	Work in my role is conflicting with my needs.	
47	Financial resources required for effective performance in my role are available.	
48	Work in my role is conflicting with my beliefs.	
49	Expectations of people connected with my role are clear to me.	
50	My subordinates have the required competence to perform effectively in their roles.	
51	Facilities required for effective performance in my role are available.	
52	My friends demand much more time from me than what is permitted by my role in the organization.	
53	My clients have conflicting demands from my role.	
54	Some of the demands on my role need to be reduced.	
55	Equipment required for effective performance in my role has been provided.	
56	I have the required experience for my role.	
57	Certain aspects of my role are vague.	
58	My role offers opportunities for personal growth.	
59	The expectations of my seniors are conflicting with the expectations of my juniors.	
60	I am well prepared for my role.	
61	The expectations of my colleagues are conflicting with the expectations of my seniors.	
62	I am involved in collaborative planning with people connected with my role.	
63	The demands of my clients are conflicting with the demands of organizational members.	
64	I am involved in teamwork with people connected with my role.	
65	The expectations of my colleagues are conflicting with the expectations of my juniors.	
66	My role offers opportunities for career growth.	
67	I can discuss important matters related to my role with the connected people.	
68	I have conflicting expectations in my role.	
69	I am able to obtain the required help from those connected with my role.	
70	I feel overburdened in my role.	
71	I have the required training to complete the responsibilities in my role.	

New Organizational Role Stress (NORS)
Scale Scoring Matrix

Name of Respondent:

Note: Items marked with and asterisk (*) are inverted items; their scores are derived by inverting the original score; after inversion, a score of 1, 2, 3, 4, or 5 becomes 5, 4, 3, 2, or 1, respectively.

6*	12*	27	37	38	5	Row Average (A)		IRD $(A-1) \times 10/4$

3	13	20*	28*	39*	58*	66*	Row Average (A)	RS $(A-1) \times 10/4$

29	40	41	53	59	61	63	65	68	Row Average (A)	REC $(A-1) \times 10/4$

4	7*	14*	21	Row Average (A)	RE $(A-1) \times 10/4$

1	11	19	25	36	Row Average (A)	RU $(A-1) \times 10/4$

15	30	42	54	70	Row Average (A)	RO $(A-1) \times 10/4$

8*	16*	22*	31*	43*	44*	62*	64*	67*	69*	Row Average (A)	RI $(A-1) \times 10/4$

32*	45*	56*	60*	71*	Row Average (A)	PI $(A-1) \times 10/4$

5	9*	17	23*	33	46	48	Row Average (A)	SRD $(A-1) \times 10/4$

2*	18*	26*	34*	49*	57	Row Average (A)	RA $(A-1) \times 10/4$

10*	24*	35*	47*	50*	51*	55*	Row Average (A)	RIn $(A-1) \times 10/4$

Total ORS = IRD + RS + REC + RE + RU + RO + RI + PI + SRD + RA + RIn =

Introduction

to the Articles and Discussion Resources Section

The Articles and Discussion Resources Section is a collection of materials useful to every facilitator. The theories, background information, models, and methods will challenge facilitators' thinking, enrich their professional development, and assist their internal and external clients with productive change. These articles may be used as a basis for lecturettes, as handouts in training sessions, or as background reading material. This section will provide you with a variety of useful ideas, theoretical opinions, teachable models, practical strategies, and proven intervention methods. The articles will add richness and depth to your training and consulting knowledge and skills. They will challenge you to think differently, explore new concepts, and experiment with new interventions. The articles will continue to add a fresh perspective to your work.

The 2009 Pfeiffer Annual: Training includes thirteen articles, in the following categories:

Communication: Feedback

Try Feedforward Instead of Feedback, by Marshall Goldsmith

Communication: Technology

Sink or Swim: Surviving the Leadership and Organizational Challenges Caused by the Rapid Advances in Information Technology, by William J. Shirey

Groups and Teams: Group Development

**Cognitive Task Analysis and Its Applications in Talent Management, by Yusra Visser and Ryan Watkins

---

**Talent Management Topics

Groups and Teams: Techniques to Use with Groups

Simulation Stimulation: The Rise of Rank-Ordered, Consensus-Building Simulations, by Lorraine L. Ukens and Alan Richter

Consulting/Training: OD Theory and Practice

The ADDIE Training Intervention Model and the Organization's Major Functions: An Experiential Learning Strategy, by Christopher A. Chaves

Consulting/Training: Strategies and Techniques

Best If Used by . . . or a Systematic Approach to Maintaining Training Materials, by Marilyn Martin

Consulting/Training: Interface with Clients

**Where Does Training Report in the Organization? by Jean Barbazette

Facilitating: Theories and Models

Does Informal Learning Make Business Sense? by Jay Cross

Facilitating: Techniques and Strategies

Making the Training Content Come Alive: Ten Types of Training Activities, by Sivasailam "Thiagi" Thiagarajan

Facilitating: Evaluation

**Linking Learning Strategy to the Balanced Scorecard, by Ajay M. Pangarkar and Teresa Kirkwood

Leadership: Strategies and Techniques

**How Leaders Think: Developing Effective Leadership, by Homer H. Johnson

Leadership Development: The Value of Face-to-Face Training, by Barbara Pate Glacel

Leadership: Top-Management Issues and Concerns

**The Importance of Organizational Culture in a World of Change: Building Your Leadership Team of the Future, by Richard T. Rees, Allen C. Minor, and Paul S. Gionfriddo

---

**Talent Management Topics

As with previous *Annuals*, this volume covers a wide variety of topics. The range of articles presented encourages thought-provoking discussion about the present and future of HRD. We have done our best to categorize the articles for easy reference; however, many of the articles encompass a range of topics, disciplines, and applications. If you do not find what you are looking for under one category, check a related category. In some cases we may place an article in the "Training" *Annual* that also has implications for "Consulting" and vice versa. As the field of HRD continues to grow and develop, there is more and more crossover between training and consulting. Explore all the contents of both volumes of the *Annual* in order to realize the full potential for learning and development that each offers.

Try Feedforward Instead of Feedback*

Marshall Goldsmith

Summary

The ability to provide feedback is frequently deemed a necessary skill for both leaders and employees. Yet, many people—especially leaders—may be reluctant to hear or act on feedback. In this article, the author presents a different concept—feedforward—that is based on looking to the future rather than critiquing the past. He describes a simple exercise that can be used to help people practice feedforward and then presents reasons why feedforward can be more productive than feedback.

Providing feedback has long been considered an essential skill for leaders. As they strive to achieve the goals of the organization, employees need to know how they are doing. They need to know whether their performance is in line with what their leaders expect. They need to learn what they have done well and what they need to change. Traditionally, this information has been communicated in the form of "downward feedback" from leaders to their employees. Just as employees need feedback from leaders, leaders can benefit from feedback from their employees. Employees can provide useful input on the effectiveness of procedures and processes and as well as input to managers on their leadership effectiveness. This "upward feedback" has become increasingly common with the advent of 360-degree multi-rater assessments.

But there is a fundamental problem with all types of feedback: It focuses on a past, on what has already occurred—not on the infinite variety of opportunities that can happen in the future. As such, feedback can be limited and static, as opposed to expansive and dynamic.

---

*Adapted from *Leader to Leader,* Summer 2002

A Feedforward** Exercise

Over the past several years, I have observed more than ten thousand leaders as they participated in a fascinating experiential exercise. In the exercise, participants are each asked to play two roles. In one role, they are asked provide feedforward—that is, to give someone else suggestions for the future and help as much as they can. In the second role, they are asked to accept feedforward—that is, to listen to the suggestions for the future and learn as much as they can. The exercise typically lasts for ten or fifteen minutes, and the average participant has six or seven dialogue sessions. In the exercise participants are asked to:

- Pick one behavior that they would like to change. Change in this behavior should make a significant, positive difference in their lives.

- Describe this behavior to a randomly selected fellow participant. This is done in one-on-one dialogues. It can be done quite simply, such as, "I want to be a better listener."

- Ask for feedforward—for two suggestions for the future that might help them achieve a positive change in their selected behavior. If participants have worked together in the past, they are not allowed to give *any* feedback about the past. They are only allowed to give ideas for the future.

- Listen attentively to the suggestions and take notes. Participants are not allowed to comment on the suggestions in any way. They are not allowed to critique the suggestions or even to make positive judgmental statements, such as, "That's a good idea."

- Thank the other participant for his or her suggestions.

- Ask the other person what he or she would like to change.

- Provide feedforward—two suggestions aimed at helping the other person change.

- Say, "You are welcome" when thanked for the suggestions. The entire process of both giving and receiving feedforward usually takes about two minutes.

- Find another participant and keep repeating the process until the exercise is stopped.

**The term "feedforward" was coined in a discussion that I had with Jon Katzenbach, author of *The Wisdom of Teams, Real Change Leaders,* and *Peak Performance.*

When the exercise is finished, I ask participants to provide one word that best describes their reaction to this experience. I ask them to complete the sentence, "This exercise was. . . ." The words provided are almost always extremely positive, such as "great," "energizing," "useful," or "helpful." The most common word mentioned is "fun!"

What is the last word that most of us think about when we receive feedback, coaching, and developmental ideas? Fun!

Reasons to Try Feedforward

Participants are then asked why this exercise is seen as fun and helpful as opposed to painful, embarrassing, or uncomfortable. Their answers provide a great explanation of why feedforward can often be more useful than feedback as a developmental tool.

1. We can change the future. We can't change the past. Feedforward helps people envision and focus on a positive future, not a failed past. Athletes are often trained using feedforward. Racecar drivers are taught to "Look at the road ahead, not at the wall." Basketball players are taught to envision the ball going into the hoop and to imagine the perfect shot. By giving people ideas on how they can be even more successful, we can increase their chances of achieving this success in the future.

2. It can be more productive to help people be "right" than to prove they were "wrong." Negative feedback often becomes an exercise in "Let me prove you were wrong." This tends to produce defensiveness on the part of the receiver and discomfort on the part of the sender. Even constructively delivered feedback is often seen as negative, as it necessarily involves a discussion of mistakes, shortfalls, and problems. Feedforward, on the other hand, is almost always seen as positive because it focuses on solutions—not problems.

3. Feedforward is especially suited to successful people. Successful people like receiving ideas that are aimed at helping them achieve their goals. They tend to resist negative judgment. We all tend to accept feedback that is consistent with the way we see ourselves. We also tend to reject or deny feedback that is inconsistent with the way we see ourselves. Successful people tend to have a very positive self-image. I have observed many successful executives respond to (and even enjoy) feedforward. I am not sure that these same people would have had such a positive reaction to feedback.

4. Feedforward can come from anyone who knows about the task. It does not require personal experience with the individual. One very common positive reaction to the previously described exercise is that participants are amazed by how much they can learn from people they don't know! For example, if you want to be a better listener, almost any fellow leader can give you ideas on how you can improve. He doesn't have to know you. Feedback requires knowing about the person. Feedforward just requires having good ideas for accomplishing the task.

5. People do not take feedforward as personally as feedback. In theory, constructive feedback is supposed to "focus on the performance, not the person." In practice, almost all feedback is taken personally (no matter how it is delivered). Successful people's sense of identity is highly connected with their work. The more successful people are, the more this tends to be true. It is hard to give a dedicated professional feedback that is not taken personally. Feedforward cannot involve a personal critique, because it is discussing something that has not yet happened! Positive suggestions tend to be seen as objective advice; personal critiques are often viewed as personal attacks.

6. Feedback can reinforce personal stereotyping and negative self-fulfilling prophecies. Feedforward can reinforce the possibility of change. Feedback can reinforce the feeling of failure. How many of us have been "helped" by a spouse, significant other, or friend, who seems to have a near-photographic memory of our previous "sins" that are shared with us in order to point out the history of our shortcomings? Negative feedback can be used to reinforce the message, "This is just the way you are." Feedforward is based on the assumption that the receiver of suggestions can make positive changes in the future.

7. Most of us hate receiving negative feedback, and we don't like to give it. I have reviewed summary 360-degree feedback reports for over fifty companies. The items "provides developmental feedback in a timely manner" and "encourages and accepts constructive criticism" almost always score near the bottom on co-worker satisfaction with leaders. Traditional training does not seem to make a great deal of difference. If leaders became better at providing feedback every time the performance appraisal forms were "improved," most should be perfect by now! Leaders are not very good at giving or receiving negative feedback. It is unlikely that this will change in the near future.

8. Feedforward can cover almost all of the same "material" as feedback. Imagine that you have just made a terrible presentation in front of the executive committee. Your manager is in the room. Rather than make you "relive" this humiliating experience, your manager might help you prepare for future presentations by giving you suggestions for the future. These suggestions can be very specific and still delivered in a positive way. In this way, your manager can cover the same points without feeling embarrassed and without making you feel even more humiliated.

9. Feedforward tends to be much faster and more efficient than feedback. An excellent technique for giving ideas to successful people is to say, "Here are four ideas for the future. Please accept these in the positive spirit that they are given. If you can only use two of the ideas, you are still two ahead. Just ignore what doesn't make sense for you." With this approach, almost no time is wasted on judging the quality of the ideas or "proving that the ideas are wrong." This "debate" time is usually negative; it can take up a lot of time, and it is often not very productive. By eliminating judgment of the ideas, the process becomes much more positive for the sender, as well as the receiver. Successful people tend to have a high need for self-determination and will tend to accept ideas that they "buy," while rejecting ideas that feel "forced" upon them.

10. Feedforward can be a useful tool to apply with managers, peers, and team members. Rightly or wrongly, feedback is associated with judgment. This can lead to very negative—or even career-limiting—unintended consequences when applied to managers or peers. Feedforward does not imply superiority of judgment. It is more focused on being a helpful "fellow traveler" than on being an "expert." As such, it can be easier to hear from a person who is not in a position of power or authority. An excellent team-building exercise is to have each team member ask, "How can I better help our team in the future?" and listen to feedforward from fellow team members (in one-on-one dialogues).

11. People tend to listen more attentively to feedforward than feedback. One participant in the feedforward exercise noted, "I think that I listened more effectively in this exercise than I ever do at work!" When asked why, he responded, "Normally, when others are speaking, I am so busy composing a reply that will make sure that I sound smart that I am not fully listening to what the other person is saying. In feedforward the only reply that I am allowed to make is 'Thank you.' Since I don't have to worry about composing a clever reply, I can focus all of my energy on listening to the other person!"

In summary, the intent of this article is not to imply that leaders should never give feedback or that performance appraisals should be abandoned. The intent is to show how feedforward can often be preferable to feedback in day-to-day interactions. Aside from its effectiveness and efficiency, feedforward can make life a lot more enjoyable. When managers are asked, "How did you feel the last time you received feedback?" their most common responses are very negative. When managers are asked how they felt after receiving feedforward, they reply that feedforward was not only useful, but it was also fun!

Quality communication—between and among people at all levels and every department and division—is the glue that holds organizations together. By using feedforward—and by encouraging others to use it—leaders can dramatically improve the quality of communication in their organizations, ensuring that the right message is conveyed, and that those who receive it are receptive to its content. The result is a much more dynamic, much more open organization—one whose employees focus on the promise of the future rather than dwelling on the mistakes of the past.

Marshall Goldsmith, Ph.D., *has recently been named by the American Management Association as one of the fifty great thinkers and leaders who have impacted the field of management over the past eighty years. Dr. Goldsmith has a Ph.D. from UCLA. He has been asked to teach in the executive education programs at Dartmouth, Michigan, MIT, Wharton, Oxford, and Cambridge Universities. He is the co-author or editor of nineteen books, including* The Leader of the Future *(a BusinessWeek best-seller),* Global Leadership: The Next Generation, *and* The Art and Practice of Leadership Coaching.

Sink or Swim
Surviving the Leadership and Organizational Challenges Caused by the Rapid Advances in Information Technology

William J. Shirey

Summary

The rapid advances in information technology have resulted in significant leadership and organizational challenges. The wide-spread use of computers, email, cell phones, voice mail, and other high-tech devices often leaves workers with an inability to accurately capture useful and relevant information in a timely manner. The exponential increase in information available exacerbates this problem. "Information overload" is a significant issue for many organizations. Leaders will require unique skill sets to take advantage of new information technology without falling victim to it. Organizations will need to adapt as well. Burton and Obel's (1998) Multi-Contingency Model of Organizational Theory offers a useful methodology to help answer the question, "What different information technologies are required for different organizational designs?" However, the literature is lacking in addressing the training required to take advantage of new information technology.

Over a quarter of a century ago, Naisbett (1982), in his book *Megatrends*, recognized many of the challenges in moving from an industrial society to an information society. He suggested then: "We are drowning in information but starved for knowledge" (p. 24). Today, the challenge remains and organizations continue to struggle with how best to utilize information technology (IT) as it continues to progress at an exponential rate. This article focuses on three areas: (1) information technology and the associated influence it is having on organizations due to rapid advances in the field, (2) leadership challenges in light of the enormous amounts of data now available, and (3) organizational implications in this environment many describe as the "information age."

Rapid Advances in Information Technology

Former U.S. Secretary of Defense Donald Rumsfeld (2003), in an article on military transformation and the war on terrorism, describes moving out of the industrial age and into the information age by saying that, "Instead of opposing armies, we face terrorists who move information at the speed of an email, money at the speed of a wire transfer, and people at the speed of a commercial jetliner" (p. 1). Just as the Department of Defense is attempting to transform in this information age, so too will other organizations outside of government and outside of America. For example, a Reuters (1998) report entitled, "Out of the Abyss: Surviving the Information Age," highlights 1,070 business managers, at various levels, from eleven different countries, who were surveyed in an effort to try to understand the issues related to the rapid advances in information technology. It is a global issue that must be clearly defined and understood if organizations are to avoid being smothered by information.

Information Technology Defined

The term "information technology" conjures varying thoughts from computers to cell phones. There is no doubt that workers are bombarded by more information today than ever before. Computer technology is advancing so rapidly that a computer purchased in one year is outdated by the next. Computer processing speed has doubled every two years for the last thirty years (Shenk, 1997). Information flows into the average home via television with more channels and diverse programming than ever. Telephones and cell phones with voice mail are becoming smaller and more capable.

While these advances are apparent in the home as well as the office, for the purposes of this paper, the focus will be on information technology as it relates to business. In that context, a definition suggested by Burton and Obel (1998) fits best for this study: "Information technology includes computers, email, voice mail, video-conferencing, databases, expert systems, and other electronic means to store, analyze, move, or communicate information in an organization. Information technology is then a means for an organization to process information" (p. 230). In light of this definition, one might consider what benefits have been reaped due to the rapid improvements in information technology.

Progress or Problem?

A theme stressed in current literature is the paradoxical situation of having a huge amount of useful and relevant information at our fingertips that is often difficult to obtain in a timely manner (Edmunds & Morris, 2000). "The problem is that in the workplace when one has a pile of paper to read, in addition to an escalating amount of emails to scroll through; when faxes frequently arrive and the telephone is constantly ringing; the perception of being overloaded with information is very difficult to avoid" (Edmunds & Morris, 2000, p. 19). The sheer volume of information available can be overwhelming.

Information Volume

Shenk (1997) reported that paper consumption in the United States tripled between 1980 and 1990; 60 percent of the average office worker's time was spent processing paper documents; and the typical business manager read one million words per week, or the equivalent of one and a half full-length novels per day. Over nine thousand periodicals are published in the United States each year and almost one thousand books throughout the world are published daily. More new information has been produced within the last three decades than in the last five millennia (Nelson, 2001). "A single edition of *The New York Times* contains more information than a 17th-Century Britisher would encounter in a lifetime" (Swenson, 1992, p. 85).

Swenson (1999) describes the exponential increase in the volume of information individuals now receive. In a chart showing total mail messages passed yearly (email and surface mail) from 1900 to 2000, the number of messages is relatively constant until 1985. However, between 1985 and 1995 total mail messages increase exponentially by a factor of 15 to 20.

Most of us are aware of the amount of junk mail that arrives in our mailboxes. While laws are being passed to reduce junk mail, junk email or "spam" is increasing at an alarming rate. It is estimated that the amount of spam email has tripled since 2005 (Email Spam, 2007). It appears that spam will require more time to manage and be an increased burden for businesses in the future (Roberts, 2003). It is difficult to capture the total amount of data coming into our offices and homes; however, there is little doubt that we are in the midst of what many have termed an information explosion. With so much written about the enormous amount of information volume, it is worth clarifying the term "information."

Data Versus Information

It is important to differentiate between data and information. Often the term "information" is used when "data" may be more appropriate. For this paper, data is defined as "the raw material on which the human mind works to make information"

(Edmunds & Morris, 2000, p. 19). Data becomes information when it is processed and put into some useful context. It is most helpful when it can be integrated with other knowledge.

Integration: A Step Toward Progress

Technology will continue to advance, and more data will be available than one can hope to process. In that light, integration will be fundamentally critical. Nicholas Donofrio (2003), a senior vice president for IBM, describes the importance of integrating work flow, data flow, and application flow. He says, "People who figure out how to use the information technology capability and their system-level thinking to create ways of making this integration happen [will be] the winners in the future" (p. 5). The tendency in dealing with huge leaps in technology and large amounts of information is to compartmentalize it into small chunks we are comfortable with. While this is helpful to a point, Swenson (1992) suggests that information overload has caused integration to be absent from the contemporary American landscape and further suggests that it needs to be emphasized to encourage transformation.

Kimble, Grimshaw, and Hildreth (1998) did an empirical study of information overload with data collected from the United Kingdom and Europe. Although the degree of information overload varies globally, it is still helpful to review results drawn from the empirical data of a relatively large sample size (1,500). Kimble, Grimshaw, and Hildreth found that for electronic communication to be effective, there is a need to establish a context in which the message can be interpreted. They state that "for human to human communication to be successful there is a need to supply a context to transform the data into information" (p. 2). Although this happens naturally in face-to-face communication, in electronic communication, many contextual clues are missing. Without the ability to see one's expression or to question specific information, it is possible for a message to come through garbled. Van Winkle (n.d.) suggests that information technology often diminishes workplace efficiency. Whether via efforts to improve integration or context, something is required to make sense of all the data and information being thrown at the average worker in the 21st Century (Saffo, 1997).

Penalty for Underestimating the Rapid Advances in Information Technology

There are two key areas in which failing to recognize the importance of information technology issues can be costly to the organization. First, large amounts of data or information in the work environment can cause health and motivational problems. Van Winkle (n.d.) states: "The barrage of data to which we are constantly exposed carries a cost, both physically and mentally." He also cites Shenk (1997) in describing the effects of information overload, which include cardiovascular stress, weakened vision, confusion and frustration, impaired judgment, and decreased benevolence to others. A worker with any of these symptoms will not be properly motivated and the organization will suffer.

Second, advances in information technology can be a magnet and take away from our time to critically think and analyze. Anyone who has "surfed" the Internet or "channel surfed" on the TV can identify with the temptation to let your mind wander and lose focus on the task at hand. Similarly, researchers who greedily download and save files without sorting, sifting, reading, and discriminating confuse volume of information with successful integration of information. McKenzie (1997) suggests, "Perhaps we need to replace that old message ['How long does it have to be?'] with 'less is more.' Wisdom has more to do with distillation and reduction than volume. While we may want to search widely, we must harvest sparingly and wisely" (p. 4).

One area of interest to organizations is training. Understanding the impact of changes in information technology should allow one to prepare for those changes. Van Winkle (n.d.) cites several indicators of problems that can be related to training, including how we inefficiently use phones, conduct meetings, and organize our work. For example, if employees are routinely using email to communicate with someone only fifty feet away, there is probably a problem. Employees will need to have different skill sets to negotiate the new information landscape of the 21st Century. Leaders will need to be prepared to train workers to integrate large volumes of data, put it into context, and then have time to think critically about this information before applying it.

Leadership Challenges

With more information available, one of the most significant challenges for the 21st Century leader is understanding where and how to devote one's efforts to best accomplish organizational goals. Comparing and contrasting two different views of leadership can help understand the challenge.

The Totally Connected Leader

First, consider the leader who fully embraces information technology to the point of being controlled by it. In a *New York Times* article, Matt Richtel (2003) accurately captures the picture.

> Mr. Lax, a 44-year-old venture capitalist, is sitting in a conference for telecommunications executives at a hotel near Los Angeles, but he is not all here. Out of one ear, he listens to a live presentation about cable television technology; simultaneously, he surfs the Net on a laptop with a wireless connection, while occasionally checking his mobile device—part phone, part pager and part Internet gadget—for email. Mr. Lax flew from Boston and paid $2,000 to attend the conference, called Vortex. But he cannot unwire himself long enough to give the presenters his complete focus. If he did, he would face a fate worse than lack of productivity: he would become bored. "It's hard to concentrate on one thing," he said, adding, "I think I have a condition." The ubiquity of technology in the lives of executives, other businesspeople and consumers has created a subculture of the Always On—and a brewing tension between productivity and freneticism. For all the efficiency gains that it seemingly provides, the constant stream of data can interrupt not just dinner and family time, but also meetings and creative time, and it can prove very tough to turn off. (p. 4)

This description provides a succinct and accurate picture showing one end of the spectrum regarding the application of information technology. The scene highlights the potential for information technology to cause individuals and organizations to become dysfunctional.

The Collaborative Leader

In contrast, Roepke, Agarwal, and Ferratt (2000) describe a leadership approach at 3M to transform information technology from a back-office support role to one that characterizes IT as a strategic partner or enabler. This concept moves the senior information technology executive from a director title reporting under the Finance Department to a chief information officer title and member of the executive management team. Instead of IT professionals and management being tied through a "job" contract, this approach emphasizes the development of relationships in which workers are committed to the relationship and the organization. The weakness of this approach is the extensive time required to develop this capability and the complexity of the social processes required to develop it. However, the movement from a hierarchical command-and-control philosophy to one that is more collaborative is significant. The leadership model suggests eight model behaviors: initiative, emotional self-management, cooperation, customer service orientation, self-confidence, achievement orientation, flexibility, and interpersonal understanding. While costly in terms of time and effort, this collaborative example demonstrates a transformational approach to leadership and information technology. The findings indicate that an investment in leadership capability can help align IT with the business vision. This alignment encourages efficiency and prioritization.

The Pareto Principle

The ability of a leader to prioritize is emphasized by Maxwell (2002) through the Pareto Principle (also commonly called the 20/80 principle). He elaborates on the concept that prioritization is tied to efficiency and success. The Pareto Principle states that 20 percent of your priorities will give you 80 percent of your production. In other words, if an individual or organization spends their time, energy, money, and personnel on the top 20 percent of their priorities, the result is a four-fold return in productivity. This can be significant when applied to information technology. For example, with regard to reading, 20 percent of the document (email, report, book, study, briefing, etc.) generally contains 80 percent of the content. Unfortunately, there is no empirical evidence to support this theory. Therefore, it is probably unrealistic to put too much weight on this principle. However, it is useful to consider that by properly prioritizing the use of information technology in the spirit of the 3M initiative above, one can avoid the dysfunctional habits of Mr. Lax. Imagine the benefit. If 20 percent, or a small amount of one's time, could produce 80 percent or most of the results, much more time could be spent contemplating how to work smarter, rather than harder.

Leaders Need Time to Think

All leaders need time to take a step back and think; time to try to see the forest, as well as the trees. The importance of this practice is discussed by Birkerts (1994) in *The Gutenberg Elegies,* in which he discusses the concept of deep reading and deep thinking. Birkerts maintains that it is contemplative, probing, and reflective reading that lies at the heart of the search for truth. He relates wisdom not to the knowing of facts, but to the understanding of human nature and the processes of life. Birkerts mentions that the historical roots of deep reading and deep thinking were in early times when few people owned books. Therefore one book in the home, like the Bible, was read over and over in search of understanding (McKenzie, 1997).

This illustration highlights the importance of meditation and reflection in leadership. It is during such times of contemplation that one considers how best to lead. Because leadership involves influencing people, time is required to build relationships. Although information technology is a great aid to maintaining connectivity with workers, it can also be a stumbling block to building relationships.

Air Force General Hal Hornburg (2002) saw this threat from his position as the leader of Air Combat Command. He warned,

> I see squadron commanders who are in a three-point stance with their ears
> laid back at their computer terminal, ready to pounce on that email that
> hasn't yet arrived. What we need to do is make technology our friend, not
> our enemy. Holding direct conversations with our people is what we need to
> do. When you need service, you [need to] talk to a human being instead of
> to a recording. We need to get away from these form letters. We have to put a
> personal touch on being a leader and a subordinate and get back to dealing
> with people as individuals rather than just processing them through and con-
> sidering them a capability.

One can sense the frustration this general has with letting information technology drive our leadership instead of vice versa. Maxwell (2002) reminds us, "People
don't care how much you know until they know how much you care" (p. 76).

New Skill Sets Required for Successful Leaders

There is significant evidence to indicate that new skill sets will be required to deal
with the avalanche of information coming into organizations today. In an environment in which there is more data and information available than anyone can possibly digest, leaders will need to learn how to deal with the complexities associated
with processing and distributing IT products. Krill (2003) points out that some
leaders will feel as though they have missed something unless they review all available data. Leaders who tend to be micromanagers will have to learn to make decisions without personally reviewing every piece of information available. Leaders
must also consider how much information is enough to make an appropriate decision for a given issue. Establishing boundaries and deadlines will be important to
enable leaders to take control of the information coming their way. For example, in
some circumstances, an 85 percent solution may be satisfactory when compared to
the 100 percent solution that will require much more data and time.

McKenzie (1997), although somewhat dated in his observations compared to
Krill, sees the need for multi-tasking and the support of "intelligent agents" such
as search engines to filter the continuing barrage of important new information
skimmed sizzling off the networks as fast as it hits the wires. In addition, leaders will need to possess the ability to review large amounts of information and
sort them for accuracy and usability. Nelson (2001) describes this as the ability
to determine quickly whether the data or information retrieved meets the search
criteria—and is also valid and useable. In many cases, this means that the data
or information must be timely. Similarly, leaders will have to understand how
to use filters in order to receive accurate information. This will require an understanding of how to filter out that which is irrelevant, while not excluding relevant
documents.

Unfortunately, the training required to develop the skill sets above is rarely addressed. While there is significant agreement on what skills are required, there is little discussion on how to achieve them. The rapid advances in information technology will require more than just knowledge-level skills to operate a particular software program. More importantly, integration and processing skills will need to be part of IT training programs for the future. The emphasis will need to be on how to apply the skills described above and how to adapt as technology continues to advance. Those organizations that are proactive in this regard stand to reap significant benefits. As the information environment transforms, so too must the leadership.

Transformational Leadership

The leadership challenges associated with the rapid advances in information technology seem to call for a transformational style of leadership. Transformation has been described as new technology, combined with new concepts of operations, and new organizational structures (Major General David Deptula, personal communication, October 2002). This definition seems to be useful in the context of embracing the rapid advances in information technology. As new IT systems are implemented, leaders must develop new concepts of operations and consider organizational changes.

The transformational leadership model described by Bass and Avolio (1994) is comprised of four factors: (1) idealized influence, (2) inspirational motivation, (3) intellectual stimulation, and (4) individualized consideration. These factors can be helpful in analyzing the issues a leader should consider when implementing new information technology. For example, under individualized consideration, a leader should consider the individual differences in workers' ability to embrace new IT solutions. A two-way (verbal) exchange of information to assess progress can be useful if "management by walking around" is practiced. Under intellectual stimulation, leaders can encourage followers to be innovative and creative by questioning assumptions, reframing problems, and approaching old situations in new ways. Under inspirational motivation, the leader, in the context of IT, can motivate followers by making them more aware of potential outcomes and inducing them to transcend their own self-interest for the sake of the organization (Yukl, 2002).

Leadership style is one of the most important factors in encouraging innovation. Jung, Chow, and Wu (2003) found in their empirical study that there is a direct positive link between transformational leadership and organizational innovation. Although the study involved a small sample size (thirty-two), in one country (Taiwan), and from one industry (electronics), it provides a basis for further research. Organizational innovation will be critical in the 21st Century information technology environment.

Organizational Implications

Information Processing as an Organizational Metaphor

Several authors have contributed ideas to stimulate thought on how to design organizations to account for advances in information technology. Morgan (1997) uses the metaphor of an information processing brain to describe organizations. Every aspect of an organization is involved in information processing. He describes organizations as institutionalized brains that process information and then fragment, routinize, and bound the decision-making process to make it manageable. Morgan admits to some limitations in this metaphor. First, it emphasizes a centralized view of the organization. Second, too much emphasis is placed on relating the individual information processing capabilities of an individual to organizations. However, Morgan's metaphor is still helpful.

Galbraith, in a much earlier but seminal work, observed that uncertainty appeared to make a difference in organizational structure. His studies confirmed that "the greater the task uncertainty, the greater the amount of information that must be processed among decision-makers during task execution in order to achieve a given level of performance" (Galbraith, 1974, p. 28). Galbraith argued that organizations will choose a strategy that will result in either a reduction in the need for information processing or an increase in the capacity to process information. Although Galbraith's work is now over thirty years old, it still provides a useful basis for understanding the relationship between information processing and organizations.

Lee and Whitley (2002) suggest that information technology, specifically the Internet, is transforming the way time is perceived, used, managed, and disciplined. They recognize the complexities in the relationship between time and information technology. Lee and Whitley point out that IT is able to speed up business processes and thereby save time. However, this may not be true in all organizations. In more complex organizations where information processing is not routine, this may not be the case. As mentioned previously, new information technology can slow down information processing and cause dysfunction in an organization if not integrated properly.

Organizational Structure

Robbins (1997) recognizes that as times change so does the organizational structure. He suggests that computer technology and the trend toward empowering employees has made the more traditional concepts of chain of command, authority, and unity of command less relevant today. All employees can now access, in seconds, information that twenty years ago was available only to top management. Similarly, anyone at any level can communicate with anyone else without going through formal channels. In some ways, information technology can flatten the traditional hierarchal organizational structure.

These thoughts are consistent with Hunter's (1999) findings regarding the influence of information technology on organizational structure. He recognized that information technology is no longer viewed merely as a means to automate routine processes,-but is increasingly seen as an enabler of multiple functions within the organization. In measuring centralization within organizations, Hunter found that, generally, routine tasks were associated with centralized structures and non-routine tasks were associated with decentralized structures. He found that increased IT use was always associated with decentralization.

Burton and Obel (1998) integrated both the work of Hunter and Galbraith in their Multi-Contingency Model of Organizational Theory. The basis for their thinking about organizations is also based on an information processing view. They attempted to explain the interplay between information technology and organizations without resorting to an independent variable, dependent variable approach. Their focus was on what information technology should be adopted by the organization to be compatible with the organizational configuration and the organizational properties. They suggested different organizational design configurations to describe how information technology should fit into different types of organizations. For example:

1. If the organization is highly formal, then IT should incorporate rules and routines.

2. If formalization is low, then IT should augment available information with email, voice mail, and shared databases.

3. If the organizational configuration is a matrix, then IT should use email, voice mail, video-conferencing, and shared databases.

4. If the organizational complexity is low, and particularly the vertical differentiation is low, then the IT should facilitate quick hierarchical flow and the aggregation of information (p. 232).

Although the empirical evidence is lacking in their study, their model is useful and offers an approach that can easily be applied.

Technology and Organizational Culture

Determining what specific type of information technology best fits in an organization is not an easy task. However, Collins (2001) offers the following key points to consider from his research involving organizations that have moved from good to great:

- Good-to-great companies *think* differently about the role of technology.

- Great companies respond to technological change with thoughtfulness and creativity, driven by a compulsion to turn unrealized potential into results; mediocre companies react and lurch about, motivated by fear of being left behind.

- Great companies never use technology as the primary means of igniting a transformation.

- Eighty percent of good-to-great executives did not even mention technology as one of the top five factors in their transformation.

- Great companies avoid fads and are pioneers in the application of *carefully selected* technologies.

- Technology by itself is never a primary root cause of either greatness or decline.

These very practical findings provide useful general guidelines from research that is reasonably current, relevant, and objective.

Potential Help with Solutions

Collins, and especially Burton and Obel, offer the most in-depth and scholarly approach with regard to a methodology for integrating technology into organizations. Scherkenbach (1992), in compiling the lessons from Total Quality Management and Dr. Deming, highlights the importance of leadership. He emphasizes that leadership is ultimately responsible for helping people, machines, and gadgets to do a better job.

Leaders are expected to identify the requirement for training in an organization, and then ensure that the requirement is met. There is little written to emphasize the importance of preparing training programs to integrate new information technology. Edmunds and Morris (2000) emphasize the importance of technology being a tool and not the driver in an organization and also offer several solutions to information overload that could be part of organizational IT training. They suggest adopting a personal information management strategy, integrating software solutions such as push technology and intelligent agents, providing value-added information (filtered by software or information specialists), and increasing information literacy. Several of the solutions suggested by Edmunds and Morris are aimed at reducing the volume of data and information coming into the organization.

Although Saffo's (1997) work is somewhat dated, he understood clearly that IT tools are needed to improve information processing. He suggested that "information overload" is not a consequence of too much information confronting us, but a problem with the effectiveness of "sense-making" tools. Although, Saffo did not name specific tools, he agreed that one should be careful to avoid chasing such tools as they become more sophisticated and substituting them for human judgment. Interestingly, he also suggested that the machine-wise leader of the future will not only know when and how to use information technology tools, but will also know when to switch off the computer completely; a subtle suggestion regarding the importance of not becoming addicted to IT devices.

Kirsh (2000) provides another perspective that suggests that workers should expect to be overwhelmed as information technology increases. He defines this condition as "cognitive overload" and predicts that it is here to stay as a brute fact of modern life. However, Kirsh does offer some potential solutions. First, he suggests changing the physical layout of work spaces to gain efficiencies. Second, he recommends changing business practices to allow workers to solve problems faster and more accurately. Last, he advocates developing better techniques for conducting meetings, for personal time management, for recording results, for accessing corporate memory, for dealing with interruptions, and for coordinating activity at both an individual and group level. Kirsh's study highlights that the problem of dealing with large volumes of information to the point of "overload" is here to stay. This forecast provides a challenge for both leaders and organizations of the future.

Conclusion

Information technology is becoming more important than ever in organizations today. More data is at our fingertips than we can process, and the volume of data is increasing exponentially. For this data to become useful information, it must be put into context and integrated. While this offers much promise for the future, the consensus in the literature is that there is an inability to accurately capture useful and relevant information in a timely manner. In some cases, this can result in information overload. This dysfunctional situation can be a de-motivator, causing both mental and physical heath problems.

Innovative leadership is required to reap the full benefit of information technology advances. Email, voice mail, cell phones, and other high-tech tools can be magnets and detract from leadership. Leaders can become so connected with IT devices that they leave little time to build essential relationships with their followers. Leaders of the future will need skill sets that allow them to embrace information technology and not fall victim to it. The transformational style of leadership seems to fit best in this environment.

Organizations will also have to adapt to the rapid advances in information technology. Several researchers have used the information processing metaphor to describe organizations. Those studies are helpful for understanding how organizational structure must change to reap the benefits of new technology. Burton and Obel's (1998) Multi-contingency Model of Organizational Theory offers the most in-depth and useful methodology to answer the question, "What different information technologies are required for different organizational designs?" There are several solutions with the potential to ease the growing pains associated with integrating new information technology into an organization. These include adopting a personal information management strategy, integrating software solutions such as intelligent agents or filters, and increasing information literacy through training.

The advances in information technology continue to be mind-boggling. Compared with just ten years ago, information processing is significantly different. The literature indicates that this rapid growth will continue. As more data becomes available, we must consider more efficient ways to turn the data into useful information that will lead to understanding, wisdom, and insight.

References

Bass, B.M., & Avolio B.J. (1994). Improving organizational effectiveness through transformational leadership. In G.R. Hickman (Ed.), *Leading organizations: Perspectives for a new era*. Thousand Oaks, CA: Sage.

Birkerts, S. (1994). *The Gutenberg elegies: The fate of reading in an electronic age*. Boston, MA: Faber and Faber.

Burton, R.M., & Obel, B. (1998). *Strategic organizational diagnosis and design* (2nd ed.). Boston, MA: Kluwer Academic Publishers.

Collins, J.C. (2001). *Good to great*. New York: HarperCollins.

Donofrio, N.M. (2003). Innovation for the new era. *Vital Speeches of the Day, 69*(23), 721.

Edmunds, A., & Morris, A. (2000). The problem of information overload in business organizations: A review of the literature. *International Journal of Information Management, 20*, 17–28.

Email Spam. Retrieved November 10, 2007, from http://en.wikipedia.org/wiki/E-mail_spam

Galbraith, J. (1973). *Designing complex organizations*. Reading, MA: Addison-Wesley.

Galbraith, J. (1974). Organizational design: An information processing View. *Interfaces, 4*(3), 28–36.

Hornburg, H.M. (2002, March 13). Speech presented at the meeting of the Air Armament Summit. Eglin Air Force Base, Florida.

Hunter, S. (1999). Information technology and organization structure (doctoral dissertation, Duke University). *Dissertation Abstracts International, 60,* 803.

Jung, D.I., Chow, C., & Wu, A. (2003). The role of transformational leadership in enhancing organizational innovation: Hypotheses and some preliminary findings. *The Leadership Quarterly, 14*(4/5), 525–544.

Kimble, C., Grimshaw, D.J., & Hildreth, P.M. (1998). The role of contextual clues in the creation of information overload. In *Matching technology with organisational needs: Proceedings of 3rd UKAIS Conference* (pp. 405–412). New York: McGraw-Hill.

Kirsh, D. (2000). *A few thoughts on cognitive overload.* Retrieved November 10, 2007, from http://interactivity.ucsd.edu/articles/Overload/published.html

Krill, P. (2003, January 7). *Overcoming information overload.* Retrieved November 10, 2007, from InfoWorld website: http://archive.infoworld.com/articles/ca/xml/00/01/10/000110caoverload.xml

Lee, H., & Whitley, E.A. (2002). Time and information technology: Temporal impacts on individuals, organizations, and society. *The Information Society, 18*(4), 235–240.

Maxwell, J.C. (2002). *Leadership 101.* Nashville, TN: Thomas Nelson, Inc.

McKenzie, J. (1997, March). *Deep thinking and deep reading in an age of info-glut, info-garbage, info-glitz and info-glimmer.* Retrieved November 10, 2007, from www.fno.org/mar97/deep.html

Morgan, G. (1997). *Images of organization.* Thousand Oaks, CA: Sage.

Naisbitt, J. (1982). *Megatrends: Ten new directions transforming our lives.* New York: Warner Books.

Nelson, M.R. (2001, January). *We have the information you want, but getting it will cost you being held hostage by information overload.* Retrieved November 11, 2007, from www.acm.org/crossroads/xrds1-1/mnelson.html

Reuters. (1998). Out of the abyss: Surviving the information age. London: Author.

Richtel, M. (2003, July 6). *The lure of data is addictive.* Retrieved November 11, 2007, from http://query.nytimes.com/gst/fullpage.html?res=9502E3D81E3AF935A35754C0A9659C8B63

Robbins, S.R. (1997). *Essentials of organizational behavior* (5th ed.). Upper Saddle River, NJ: Prentice Hall.

Roberts, P. (2003, July 1). Report: Spam costs $874 per employee per year. *InfoWorld.* Retrieved November 10, 2007, from www.infoworld.com/article/03/07/01/HNspamcost_1.html

Roepke, R., Agarwal, R., & Ferratt, T.W. (2000). Aligning the IT human resource with business vision: The leadership initiative at 3M. *MIS Quarterly, 24*(2), 327–353.

Rumsfeld, D.H. (2003, November 24). A 21st-century DoD. *Wall Street Journal.* Retrieved November 11, 2007, from www.globalsecurity.org/military/library/news/2003/11/mil-031124-usia02.htm

Saffo, P. (1997). Are you machine wise? *Harvard Business Review, 75*(5), 18–28.

Scherkenbach, W.W. (1992). *The Deming route to quality and productivity.* Rockville, MD: Mercury Publishing Services.

Shenk, D. (1997). *Data smog: Surviving the information glut.* London: Abacus.

Swenson, R.A. (1992). *Margin.* Colorado Springs, CO: NavPress.

Swenson, R.A. (1999). *Hurtling toward oblivion.* Colorado Springs, CO: NavPress.

Van Winkle, W. (n.d.). *Information overload.* Retrieved November 10, 2007, from www .gdrc.org/icts/i-overload/infoload.html

Yukl, G.A. (2002). *Leadership in organizations* (5th ed.). Upper Saddle River, NJ: Prentice-Hall.

William J. (Joe) Shirey, Ph.D., *is president of ISE Consulting, an organization development firm helping organizations to manage change through strategic planning, executive coaching, and improved leader-follower communication. Prior to his work at ISE Consulting, Dr. Shirey was a senior strategic planning analyst with Lockheed Martin and served in the Air Force as a fighter pilot and staff officer. He has a BS in management from the U.S. Air Force Academy and a Ph.D. in organizational leadership from Regent University.*

Cognitive Task Analysis and Its Applications in Talent Management

Yusra Visser and Ryan Watkins

Summary

Cognitive task analysis can be used to determine the thinking processes necessary to perform a given task at an optimal level, information that can be used to effectively recruit and manage personnel. In this article, the authors define cognitive task analysis and its value and describe a detailed process for conducting the analysis.

The purpose of a cognitive task analysis is to systematically define the decision requirements and psychological processes used by expert individuals (i.e., performers) in accomplishing results.

Talent Management Applications

Task analysis is used to identify, analyze, and systematically document the actions taken and the inputs used to accomplish results at this time. Cognitive task analysis is one specific type of task analysis, and it is used to define the mental processes and steps underlying performance in a specific area. In the organizational context, cognitive task analyses are often used to document the cerebral steps that individuals or teams are either using or should be using in order to contribute results. The cognitive task analysis, as opposed to other task analysis processes, focuses on the routinely overlooked thinking processes (rather than observable behaviors) used by performers to make decisions, apply heuristics, adapt logic models, and solve problems.

Within talent management, from recruiting and promoting to mentoring and coaching, the results of a cognitive task analysis can provide you with the necessary insights to align performers with desired performance. Such insights are especially important in today's knowledge-based economies. By identifying and defining the cognitive processes associated with highly proficient performance, the cognitive task analysis findings (especially when combined with the results of other performance analysis processes) can guide your decisions about how to best support the range of talented individuals working for your organization; decisions that would otherwise be have to be made based on assumptions about what it takes to be a high performer within different roles. Some advantages and disadvantages are listed below.

Advantages

- A cognitive task analysis generates detailed, precise information on the nature of expert level performance in a specific task of interest.

- When implemented correctly, cognitive task analysis techniques are a highly valid source of information on expert cognitive processes.

- A cognitive task analysis provides systematic procedures (rather than hit-or-miss steps) for ascertaining the cognitive processes used by experts and high-level performers.

Disadvantages

- Analysis of the data gathered during a cognitive task analysis can be time-intensive.

- Cognitive task analysis does not always capture other non-cognitive attributes necessary for accomplishing results (such as physical capabilities, access to resources, and interpersonal relationships).

- The results of a cognitive task analysis can be misleading when expert performers have performance capacities beyond that of others (for example, a cognitive task analysis can be done with high-performing professional athletes but implementation of cognitive processes alone will not duplicate performance).

Conducting the Analysis

Familiarizing Yourself with the Domain Area

To kick off the cognitive task analysis process, think about how results are accomplished in the positions or roles for which you are interested in applying the cognitive task analysis method. If you are planning to conduct your cognitive task analysis in a performance area for which you have little background knowledge or experience, now might be a good time to take a moment and learn some of the basics about the domain, the domain-specific terminology, and what constitutes high-level performance in the domain area.

There are a variety of different ways in which you could gather both cursory and detailed information on the domain area. Here are a few suggestions:

1. Informally or formally interview professionals in the domain area and ask them to explain in layman's terms the broad brush strokes of performance in the domain area (Clark, Feldon, van Merrienboer, Yates, & Early, 2006). As the professionals provide you this insight, be sure to ask them to define unfamiliar terms and to provide examples for key concepts or approaches. These kinds of interviews help you make the connection to the real-world practices and procedures that are associated with the performance area.

2. Contact recruiters or high-level decision makers who routinely hire performers in the domain area. Ask them what criteria they would use to determine whether someone is highly proficient in the area. Consider asking them how they might assess in a short amount of time whether someone is an expert or a novice in the domain area.

3. Look over job descriptions, training materials, and other written documentation about the performance area (Clark, Feldon, van Merrienboer, Yates, & Early, 2006). By reviewing extant documents, you will be better prepared to conduct interviews with experts, and you will also be able to later identify discrepancies between existing training/performance support materials and expert performance.

4. Determine whether any systematic inquiry has been conducted by researchers on expertise, expert performance, or novice-expert differences in the domain area of interest. In recent years there has been much interest in the study of expertise, and systematic studies on the psychology of expertise have been conducted in a broad variety of domain areas. If such research has been conducted in your area of interest, the findings would likely be of immense value to your task.

Identifying Tasks for Further Exploration

Once you have started to develop some understanding of the domain area, the next order of business is to use the results from your preliminary review to get a better sense about key cognitive tasks that you should consider studying using the cognitive task analysis approach. Your goal is to gather information on (a) tasks that are important, frequent, and highly critical within the performance that you are studying and (b) tasks or problems within the performance area that allow for discrimination between expert and novice performance (these tasks are sometimes referred to as "representative tasks").

Two of the most effective methods that you can use to begin defining tasks of interest for the knowledge elicitation phase of the cognitive task analysis (described below) are *observations* and *interviews*. For both of these methods, you will want to identify some of the domain's high performers to use as a source of information; performers you observe at this stage in the process are not the same performers you intend to use for the actual "knowledge elicitation" process. When doing interviews, you may opt to take a "go with the flow" approach, or you can ask the experts to focus on a specific aspect or task related to the domain area. The key thing you want to walk away with is a better understanding of the knowledge structures associated with the task area, as well as some of the main types of the decision-making, evaluation, and synthesis processes that experts have to work through to perform effectively in the domain (Clark, Feldon, van Merrienboer, Yates, & Early, 2006). Ideally, you will complete some interviews before you conduct observations, because this will ensure that you can focus your observation on those tasks that are really central to the performance area.

It is best to conduct the observations in the "real-world" setting in which the experts normally perform. During the observations, place yourself in an unobtrusive location and watch the experts as they engage in the tasks of interest. Observe and record the performers' actions, making special note of those moments in which it seems that they are actively engaged in problem solving, decision making, or other types of cognitive processes. To make the observations as useful as possible, make sure to (a) avoid interrupting the experts during the observations and (b) avoid communicating either positive or negative judgment regarding their performance (Clark, Feldon, van Merrienboer, Yates, & Early, 2006).

Having completed both interviews and observations, you should now be ready to map out the tasks of interest in more detail. Look over your notes and identify the steps, sub-steps, knowledge, and skills that comprise the tasks that you wish to study further. Strive to use a concept mapping or flowcharting application (such as Microsoft Visio, Inspiration, or CMAP) to create visual representations of the relationship between the tasks, subtasks, and knowledge in the performance area. Ideally, your visual representations will have a hierarchical structure, with the highest-level cognitive processes at the top and underlying knowledge and skills underneath. As you refine your visual representations, consider sharing them with professionals in the performance area. Ask the professionals to identify any errors, omissions, or inconsistencies. Once your visual representation is more-or-less stabilized, use it to identify one or two specific performance tasks that you will use during the knowledge elicitation phase.

Lay the Foundation for Expert Knowledge Elicitation

The demands placed on your organization's experts and highest performers are likely to be considerable. For this reason, it is very important that you ensure that you do advance planning for the knowledge elicitation. Below are some planning tips that will ensure that the data collection and analysis for the cognitive task analysis are as efficient as possible.

1. Determine whether your knowledge elicitation phase will be focused on codifying high-level performance or on identifying those cognitive processes that distinguish novices from highly competent performers.

2. Select the knowledge elicitation method(s) that you would like to use to identify, cluster, link, and prioritize the critical cognitive decisions that are routine in high-level performance in the domain area. All of these knowledge elicitation methods can be used with expert performers. If you intend to also gather information from novices, however, it is recommended that you select either interviews or concurrent verbal protocol analysis as knowledge elicitation methods, since the other techniques assume a high level of domain knowledge.

   a. *Structured and unstructured interviews:* Using a combination of interviews, the expert is asked to list key steps, decision points, procedures, and so on for the performance area of interest.

   b. *Concurrent verbal protocol analysis:* The expert is asked to verbalize all thought sequences while performing a "representative task" in the performance area of interest.

   c. *Applied cognitive tasks analysis:* Several sequential and structured interviews are conducted with each expert, with each interview generating results that are used to define the subsequent interview.

   d. *Critical decision method (also referred to as "Critical Incident Technique"):* The expert is invited to recall a critical or uncommon situation in the performance area of interest, and the analyst works with the expert to systematically identify decisions, cues, and so on in the context of the critical incident.

3. Create a protocol (or guide) that you can use to structure the knowledge elicitation process. Your protocol will differ depending on which

knowledge elicitation method you select. Below are recommendations for the design of the protocols based on the intended knowledge elicitation techniques:

a. *Protocol for structured and unstructured interviews:* Develop instructions and questions for interviews, focusing on key decision points, procedures for choosing between different options at decision points, and domain knowledge.

b. *Protocol for concurrent verbal protocol analysis:* Develop a script that gives participants information on procedures for verbalizing thought sequences, as well as a few simple problem-solving tasks that can be used to practice the verbalization process. The protocol should conclude with the presentation of the main problem (based on the representative task).

c. *Protocol for critical decision method:* Develop instructions and questions, focusing on key decision points, procedures for choosing between different options at decision points, and domain knowledge in use in the critical incident identified by the expert.

4. Carefully select the experts or high performers you would like to use for the knowledge elicitation.

a. Plan on using several experts as sources of data (Clark, Feldon, van Merrienboer, Yates, & Early, 2006). This will ensure that you can look for consistent trends associated with high performance across individuals.

b. Seek to involve experts who have recently been involved in performing the tasks that are the focus of your cognitive task analysis (Clark, Feldon, van Merrienboer, Yates, & Early, 2006).

c. Determine whether you have access to experts who have also had experience training people in the domain area (Clark, Feldon, van Merrienboer, Yates, & Early, 2006). If you do, those are excellent participants for the cognitive task analysis.

d. Avoid using experts whose advice and insight you solicited during the first two phases ("Familiarizing Yourself with the Domain Area" and "Identifying Tasks for Further Exploration").

5. If the cognitive task analysis will be conducted by someone other than you, identify someone to serve as the cognitive task analyst. Note that it is

highly desirable to choose this individual carefully. Ideally, it is someone who can interact comfortably with the subject-matter expert and who can learn domain/task-specific terminology efficiently.

6. Secure an appropriate location for conducting the knowledge elicitation. Generally, a quiet, spacious location is most desirable. Ensure that the location comes equipped with the tools or resources that the expert may need to use during the knowledge elicitation process.

7. Determine how you will capture the data from the knowledge elicitation process. You may want to use a combination of note-taking, audio recording, and/or video recording. If you decide to use audio or video recording techniques, be sure to obtain participants' permission in advance. Test out the equipment to make sure that it functions properly before you begin the focused knowledge elicitation.

Gather Data Through Knowledge Elicitation Technique

You are now ready to implement the procedures you have outlined for eliciting knowledge from the experts. During the "knowledge elicitation" phase, you apply the technique(s) that you selected in the previous phase (e.g., interviews, verbal protocol analysis), with the goal of gathering the amount and type of data that is needed in order for you to develop a clear sense of the nature of the cognitive processes that underlie performance in the domain area of interest.

Because people generally do not feel immediately at ease with being recorded, and since the process to be used may not be familiar to the expert, it is highly recommended that you run the expert through a short sample session of the knowledge elicitation shortly before conducting the actual knowledge elicitation session. This is particularly relevant if you choose to implement a concurrent verbal protocol analysis, an applied cognitive task analysis, or the critical decision method.

Transcribe and Analyze Data

Here are the steps for transcribing and analyzing the data:

1. If you have recorded the knowledge elicitation session(s), transcribe the recorded information into a text-based format.

2. Prepare the transcripts for further categorization and synthesis by coding them (Clark, Feldon, van Merrienboer, Yates, & Early, 2006). Pay special attention to diagnosing and characterizing key decisions points based on the techniques used, cues signaling the decision points, and the inferences made.

3. Provide a copy of the formatted results from the knowledge elicitation to each of the experts from whom you gathered data (Clark et al, 2006). Allow the expert to make any suggestions for changes or clarifications.

4. Integrate edits and adjustments recommended by the expert.

5. Once coding has been completed, organize the data from each of the transcripts into a format that summarizes and categorizes the data.

6. Compile the summarized data from all of the transcripts.

Format Results for Intended Application

Now it's time to format the results.

1. Using the formatted results from the expert knowledge elicitation sessions, create a single model task analysis, representing all the skills, knowledge, and strategies used by the experts when functioning in the task area (Clark, Feldon, van Merrienboer, Yates, & Early, 2006).

2. Write a summary report of the findings from cognitive task analysis. Your report should include descriptive information on the cognitive processes as well as their relationship with behavioral processes in completing the task. Decide what to include in your report by reflecting on who is going to read the report and how that person will use your findings to guide future performance.

3. The task analysis is an essential ingredient to talent management and should be used as a point of comparison with other assessment data (e.g., surveys, interviews, focus groups) in order to inform decisions about how to best support the talent within your organization.

Table 1 provides a worksheet that you can use to track the cognitive analysis process.

Tips for Success

- Strive to be very systematic in your analysis. Take careful notes about what you learn from the cognitive task analysis and systematically compare those findings with information gathered from other processes (Watkins, 2007).

- Expert performers have often internalized or made habitual many of the key decisions that go into performing the related steps within the

Table 1. Cognitive Task Analysis Planning Guide

Cognitive Task Analysis Activity	Date to Be Completed	Person Responsible for Completion
Develop background on the task and context.		
Identify experts to participate in the task analysis.		
Identify associated knowledge structures.		
Create knowledge representations.		
Determine who will conduct the task analysis.		
Select one or more knowledge elicitation methods.		
Develop appropriate protocols for completing the task analysis processes.		
Complete a formative evaluation of the task analysis protocols through practice sessions.		
Collect information from expert performers through the selected procedures.		
Code and synthesize findings from the task analysis.		
Compare and contrast results from the cognitive task analysis with findings from other performance analysis processes.		
Prepare a report on the findings of the task analysis.		

task. This makes completing a cognitive analysis challenging. Aid expert performers in communicating their cognitive processes by using techniques such as card sorting, process tracing, or concept mapping.

- Use the findings from your cognitive task analysis to inform decisions at multiple stages of the talent management process (for instance, recruiting, hiring, training, coaching, or succession planning).

References and Resources

Clark, R., Feldon, D., van Merrienboer, J., Yates, K., & Early, S. (2006, October 14). *Cognitive task analysis.* Retrieved September 17, 2007, from Center for Cognitive Technology, University of Southern California: www.cogtech.usc.edu/publications/clark_etal_cognitive_task_analysis_chapter.pdf

Cognitive Task Analysis (from NATO): http://ftp.rta.nato.int/public//PubFulltext/RTO/TR/RTO-TR-024/TR-024-$$ALL.pdf

Jonassen, D.H., Hannum, W.H., & Tessmer, M. (1989). *Handbook of task analysis procedures.* New York: Praeger.

Protocols for cognitive task analysis. From the Institute for Human and Machine
    Cognition: http://ihmc.us:16080/research/projects/CTAProtocols/ProtocolsForCog
    nitiveTaskAnalysis.pdf

Watkins, R. (2007). *Performance by design: The selection, design, and development of per-
    formance technologies that achieve results.* Amherst, MA: HRD Press.

Yusra Visser, Ph.D., *is a faculty member at Florida Atlantic University, where she teaches in the Instructional Technology program and coordinates the Digital Education Teacher's Academy. She is lead editor of* Trends and Issues in Distance Education: International Perspectives *(Information Age, 2005) and has published and presented extensively on distance education, instructional design, and international development education.*

Ryan Watkins, Ph.D., *is an associate professor of educational technology at George Washington University in Washington, D.C. He is an author of* Performance by Design *(HRD Press, 2007), the* e-Learning Companion *(Houghton Mifflin, 2004, 2007),* 75 e-Learning Activities *(Pfeiffer, 2005), and* Strategic Planning for Success *(Pfeiffer, 2001), as well as more than sixty-five articles on performance improvement, needs assessment, strategic planning, and e-learning. In 2005, Watkins was also a visiting scientist with the National Science Foundation.*

Simulation Stimulation
The Rise of Rank-Ordered,
Consensus-Building Simulations
Lorraine L. Ukens and Alan Richter

Summary

Simulation activities are an important mainstay in the realm of instructional methods. This article examines two types of simulations (process and content) that can be used to examine behavioral outcomes and their relationships to real-world situations. The relevance of the debriefing session is explored in supporting the simulation as a learning event.

What are simulations, and what makes them valuable as a learning tool? Our early experiences as children start us on the road to learning through play. Play is an essential part of our development, and as adults, we incorporate our early learning to create a manageable version of the real world in which we can practice behaviors and learn from our mistakes. A game will be interesting to adults if it provides a challenge and, therefore, an opportunity to overcome an obstacle with real feelings of success and real learning, even if the situation is virtual.

In essence, a simulation is a contrived situation that contains enough reality to induce a real-world response by those participating in the event. This simulated environment requires the participant to "play" a role, which produces certain actions and behaviors that can be compared to real-life situations. There are two types of simulations: those that pertain to the use of a machine or equipment and those that replicate a social or interpersonal interaction. It is the latter type of simulation that we will be examining here. These activities stress the complex, real-life situations and goals that organizations attempt to implement on a daily basis.

The Use of Simulations

Using simulation as a learning tool is not a new concept. The first war game was created in China around 3000 BC. Since then, war games have been used over the centuries to prepare leaders for the rigors of strategic conflict. Even the development of chess, one of the most successful games in history, was an attempt to simulate two warring armies. Most of the nations that participated in World War I used war-game simulations as preparation for the real thing. After World War II, with the development of the computer, more complex war simulations were developed.

As an outgrowth of war games, other types of simulated activities have entered the world of learning because they allow the learner to explore the elements of a system, change variables, and discover consequences without actually suffering real distress. In order to do this, however, it is important for the learner to understand the analogies between what happened in the simulated experience and what happens in the real world.

As early as 1957, the American Management Association (AMA) adopted simulation as a management development tool, with its Top Management Decision Simulation. Since then there has been a blossoming of simulations in business management programs around the world. So simulations have come of age. In this article we want to focus on a particular kind of simulation—the rank-order, team-consensus type of simulation that has an interesting evolution over the past fifty years.

Almost any simulation can be used as an assessment tool in two key ways:

1. Process: by focusing on social or interpersonal skills and group dynamics, such as assessing the relationship skills or communication skills of a person, or

2. Content: by focusing on teaching how to adopt or assimilate content into the behavior or skill that is being assessed, for example, using flight simulators to teach pilots to fly.

This article will explore both the process and content of simulations, although the focus will be limited to learning soft skills through rank-order team-consensus-building simulations.

Process Simulations

The purpose of this type of activity is to examine the flow of behaviors in a group, where the emphasis is as much on *how* things happen as it is on the final outcome of the simulated event. Group *process* is concerned with the dynamics of the group: group norms and roles, leadership, communication, and dimensions of group effectiveness.

Within the larger context of group process, it is important to examine two distinct dimensions: (1) *task-oriented* process that contributes to task accomplishment and includes planning, goal setting, problem solving, decision making, creativity, and risk taking; and (2) *relationship-oriented* process that explores maintaining good working relationships within the group, including group cohesiveness, collaboration, trust, conflict management, and negotiation.

These activities fall within the category of social-system simulations that focus on interactions among people and the ways that one's beliefs, assumptions, goals, and actions may be hindered or assisted in interactions with others. The primary focus of such simulations is for participants to experience some of the dynamic social processes that are part of the fabric of organized social groups. Working through this type of learning activity can provide a group immediate feedback on how well group members perform.

The components of the process-oriented simulation are (1) a precipitating event, (2) complicating factors, (3) participant roles, and (4) context. All of these components interact with one another to set in motion the interactions among participants that are the core of the simulation. Outcomes depend for the most part on the interpersonal dynamics that evolve as the simulation progresses.

Process simulations provide the context of a plausible but imaginary situation in which group members are free to learn real lessons about how their behavior affects others. For example, the simulation *Common Currency: The Cooperative-Competition Game* (Ukens, 1996) presents participants with the scenario of a union of several smaller countries into a large republic that will convert separate currencies into one new shared system. The game exposes the players to the conflicting goals of cooperation and competition, while demonstrating the interdependence of groups within an organization. It is a lesson in both task and relationship processes because it places emphasis on not only the final result, but also on how these outcomes were achieved.

Working together to solve prescribed challenges, participants practice vital group-process skills that are reinforced through focused reflection and discussion. The participants can make generalizations in terms of attitudes, skills, concepts, paradigms, and so forth. Although the simulation might not be designed to provide learning directly, the debriefing segment of the activity allows for learning to take place.

Survival-type simulations constitute one type of process simulation that is often used in team-building situations to explore the concepts of synergy and consensus decision making. Teams experience first-hand the exciting benefits of group thinking and problem solving. The earliest survival simulation was *NASA Moon Survival*

Task, developed by Jay Hall in 1963 as part of his doctoral dissertation, and also published later as *Lost on the Moon*.

In the late 1950s, Hall was a graduate student at the University of Texas and studied with Robert Blake and Jane Mouton, who developed the Managerial Grid. Blake and Mouton used the film *Twelve Angry Men* as a "predictive tool" by stopping the film mid-track, after the first vote by the jury is cast, and asking their students to predict the order of the next eleven votes of the jury. The point was to see how well individuals and teams could second-guess or predict what will happen, based on their reading of the characters so far into the film. Hall became interested in using this "ranking" technique and began to develop it to examine the decision-making process that might occur in a space capsule, the effect of disagreements among the crew, and how the disagreements might be resolved.

Hall first sent his list of fifteen items to be ranked in terms of usefulness to the astronauts at what is now the Johnson Space Center. The astronauts, according to his colleague and fellow graduate student Warner Burke, were far too busy, so the list was passed to the scientists and engineers at NASA, who provided even better logic for the ranking exercise, and so *NASA Moon Survival Task* was launched, so to speak. Ever since then, survival simulations have remained a very popular team-building tool among corporate trainers and school educators.

There are typically two general approaches to creating consensus survival simulations: (1) *priority-setting simulations*, where participants rank order a list of available items necessary for survival in a particular environment, and (2) *decision-making simulations*, in which participants are presented with situational dilemmas that require the selection of the best choice of action from among several options.

An example of a priority-setting simulation is *Adventure in the Amazon* (Ukens, 1998) where fifteen items must be ranked in order of priority for survival after a plane crashes in the jungle. A more humorous example of a priority-setting simulation, provided by Dale Crossman (formerly of NASA), is to photocopy the Whitman chocolate sampler sheet and have participants rank the chocolate samples from most to least chosen, thereby testing the predictive power of individuals and teams in knowing chocolate preferences.

As an example of the decision-making variety of simulation, *Trouble on the Inca Trail* (Ukens, 2005) requires participants to make choices on the best actions to take in twelve survival situations involving the desert, mountain, and jungle regions of Peru.

Christopher Novak, a consultant with The Summit Team in Marcellus, New York, often uses simulations in his training sessions. He explains that this type of activity helps stimulate real-world behaviors around a neutral topic in which everyone can engage. His impression is that participants generally enjoy these activities because they offer a free-flowing learning environment that can draw in the vast majority of people. People seem to like the "brain-work" associated with the simulations—the opportunities to apply logic, knowledge, and even educated guesses to a process of finding a workable solution.

Content Simulations

Many of the practitioners who designed process-oriented simulations, over time, became somewhat disillusioned with the "content free" or "content-lite" aspect of these exercises and have tried to adapt the framework to teach content as well as process. An example of a content-oriented simulation is *Lost in Cyberspace* (Richter & Willett, 2002), which was developed for Wharton's MBA orientation retreat. Wharton had been using *The Desert Survival Situation* (Lafferty, Eady, & Pond, 1970) for a number of years, but grew tired of it and commissioned a new simulation to also address the growing issue and challenge of global virtual teams.

Unlike most of the "lost"-type simulations, which address problem solving in a physical survival setting, *Lost in Cyberspace* was framed in terms of current business survival and set out to teach some content about the "best practices" of global virtual teams. The simulation scenario involves trying to win an e-commerce project and thereby prioritizing a mix of technology, information, and team or human factors. It also employs the method of individual ranking, followed by team ranking (based on group consensus), then followed by revealing the target rankings, which in turn provides the scoring for the individual and team decisions. In the debriefing, the content is reviewed, which addresses the learning of global virtual team best practices, but the process (especially how decisions were made by each group) is also debriefed, making for a more balanced simulation.

Other examples of "soft" content simulations hark back to the use of Hollywood movies to provide the "case" for review. In the 1980s, as part of leadership development programs, Marshall Goldsmith, then with KGB (the now dissolved consulting firm of Keilty, Goldsmith, and Boone), used to screen *The Bridge on the River Kwai* as the basis for studying leadership. Ratings would be made, individually and then in teams, on leadership characteristics as portrayed by the two leaders in the movie. These ratings were then compared against target ratings based on an objective (as much as possible) reading of the movie. QED Consulting developed similar simulations using the movies *Twelve O'Clock High*, *Hoosiers*, and *Gandhi*. In each case the leadership characteristics would be tailored to the wording of the leadership competencies of the organization undertaking the training. In this way it was almost like evaluating how well (or badly) this leader would work out if he were leading your organization. More recently, Hartwick Humanities in Management Institute (at Hartwick College, Oneonta, New York) began including the use of films as an exciting and innovative tool for learning about leadership. The Institute publishes and distributes Hartwick Classic Film Leadership Cases® and related teaching notes for colleges and universities.

Debriefing Sessions

Regardless of the type of simulation used, the debriefing discussion that follows the simulation activity is critical to the learning process because its goal is to reflect on the relevant dimensions in terms of real-world situations. By carefully examining the participants' experiences through guided reflection, the facilitator moves the learning toward practical application.

A multistage approach is recommended, with each stage identified by a specific question. The main component of the debriefing session should examine three key areas:

- What happened?

- Why did it happen?

- How does this apply to the real world?

The facilitator should discuss both the process and the outcome of the simulated event, although the weighting of these two elements will be determined by the simulation design (primarily process-oriented, content-oriented, or balanced). Participants should be encouraged to reflect on how and why the outcomes occurred, examining the roles they played in determining the final results. This process of forced reflection and subsequent internalization of the possible learning points makes this type of experience worth the time, energy, and money expended by both the individual and the organization.

No matter how much time is devoted to the debriefing session, it is the part of the simulation process that is absolutely essential for learning to occur. The more elegant the design of the simulation, the longer the debriefing session will run compared to the actual simulation. It is also important to remember that, although the facilitator may have a specific intention in mind for the activity, participants may get something else out of the experience that goes beyond this initial objective. Therefore, participant feedback helps determine the actual direction and composition of the debriefing period.

The role of the facilitator is to guide the participants to insights by discussing, reflecting, and questioning what was experienced. Rather than telling the learning points of the simulation activity, an effective facilitator will guide the participants into individual awareness. A successful learning event is one in which the participants leave with at least one powerful and useful insight.

References

Hall, J. (1963). *NASA moon survival task.* Waco, TX: Teleometrics International Inc.

Lafferty, J.C., Eady, P., & Pond, A. (1970). *The desert survival situation.* Chicago, IL: Human Synergistics.

Richter, A., & Willett, C. (2002). *Lost in cyberspace.* San Francisco, CA: Pfeiffer.

Ukens, L. (1996). *Common currency: The cooperative-competition game.* King of Prussia, PA: HRDQ.

Ukens, L. (1998). *Adventure in the Amazon.* San Francisco, CA: Pfeiffer.

Ukens, L. (2005). *Trouble on the Inca trail.* San Francisco, CA: Pfeiffer.

Lorraine L. Ukens, *owner of Team-ing With Success (www.team-ing.com), is a performance consultant who specializes in team building and experiential learning. She is the author of sixteen training activity books and games and is a frequent contributor to other publications. Ukens has a bachelor's degree in psychology and a master's degree in human resource development from Towson University in Maryland, where she also taught as an adjunct faculty for eight years prior to her move to the South.*

Alan Richter, Ph.D., *is president of QED Consulting, specializing in consulting, training, and product development in the areas of leadership, values, culture, and change. He is the author of several training games and simulations, as well as self-assessment tools. Dr. Richter has worked around the world with leading organizations in both the private and public arenas.*

The ADDIE Training Intervention Model and the Organization's Major Functions

An Experiential Learning Strategy

Christopher A. Chaves

Summary

In this article, the author makes the argument that the way students and practitioners of HRD are taught instructional systems design can have a significant impact on their success on the job. It's critical that a clear connection be made between the ISD process and the actual functions within an organization. After laying out one ISD process, the author goes on to provide several short examples and a longer case study to illustrate how the ISD process can be linked to an organization's major line functions.

University-level workforce education and development degree and/or train-the-trainer programs, designed to educate and develop aspiring learners or practitioners of human resources development (HRD) in resolving various organizational human performance challenges, invariably include instructional systems design (ISD) training models within the curriculum. While there are a variety of ISD training intervention models (Morrison, Ross, & Kemp, 2004), most workforce development degree program curricula informs the learner and practitioner about how to effectively conduct occupational analyses, design curriculum, develop course materials, implement the training solution (curriculum), and evaluate the training intervention; this ISD intervention model is better known as ADDIE.

However, many workforce education and development degree program curricula fail to incorporate a module that addresses how all of an organization's major line functions may actually relate to and affect the final training solution for the department or work cell experiencing human performance problems. In this article, the author argues that teaching learners and professional trainers about analyzing open systems architecture (i.e., global economy, government regulations, industry competitors) and cross-functional operations, and how they relate to organizational training interventions can create a better training solution than what is generally accomplished, that is, simply isolating the human performance issue to one or a few localized organizational systems or functions. Essentially, a cross-functional approach to training interventions can, in greater measure, benefit the client organization when the curriculum designer incorporates the input from subject-matter experts who operate within the four major organizational line functions (sales and marketing, design and engineering, accounting and finance, and production and operations). Moreover, learners and practitioners must understand that globalization; national economic structures; government regulations; industry competitors; the role of key suppliers, wholesalers, and retail operations; and especially primary customer feedback must also inform the needs analysis process (see Figure 1).

Second, the article will also assert that, for learners and practitioners of HRD to understand and apply a more comprehensive needs analysis tool investigating potential human performance challenges, a workforce education and development degree or certificate program curricula must require occupational-level experiential learning assignment(s) in an effort to achieve a more complete understanding of how the open system architecture and an organization's major line functions inform a training solution. It has been my experience that ultimately utilizing learners' workplace arenas is the most appropriate place to begin applying training intervention academics. Including and applying learners' subject-matter expertise toward new training intervention analyses model(s) creates better connection and learning for them sooner rather than later, and at a deeper level.

But first, in order to understand how to effectively apply experiential learning assignments to classroom academics, understanding the philosophy and theory behind the diverse nature of experience (ontology) and experiential education is crucial for its proper and subsequent application in a real-world occupational setting. Subsequently, after establishing what the nature of experience and experiential learning approaches appropriate to adult learners can look like, we will shift toward an analysis application model that promises to produce a more comprehensive organizational training intervention strategy.

Theoretical Bases: Experience, Experiential Learning, and Adult Learners

Experience and Education

A review of the foundational literature pertaining to the relationship between experience and education reveals the following early theoretical constructs. The

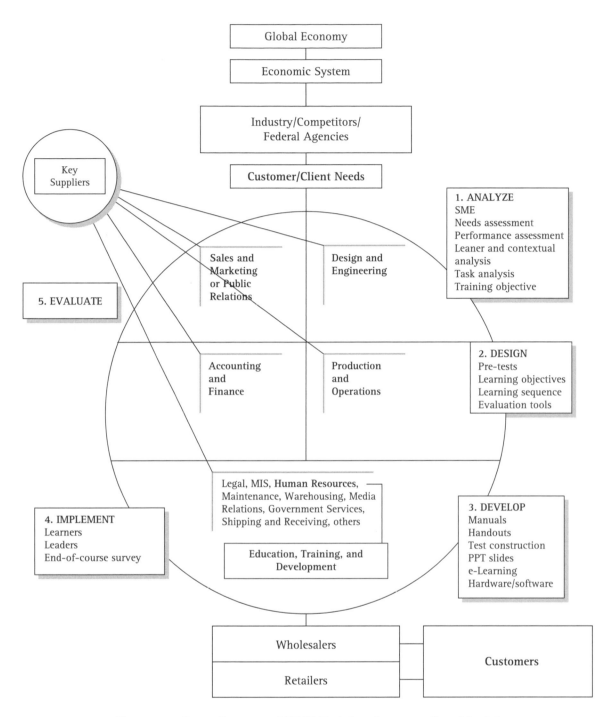

Figure 1. Open Systems ADDIE Training Intervention Model

idea of connecting previous understanding and new experience to current epistemology in efforts to extend human knowledge is certainly not a contemporary one. For instance, Kant (1788) begins his work entitled *Critique of Pure Reason* by asserting that all human knowledge starts with experience. However, according to Kolb (1984) and Jarvis, Holford, and Griffin (1998), the philosophical roots of contemporary experiential education models lie in the writings of Dewey (1938), specifically his work on the relationship between experience and education.

Dewey (1938) in his seminal work, *Experience and Education*, which pertains to how children and people learn generally, argues that "the newer philosophy is found in the idea that there is an intimate and necessary relation between the processes of actual experience and education" (pp. 19–20). He asserts that critical thinking is initiated when an individual perceives a problem and, consequently, attempts to clarify the nature of the problem to arrive at the appropriate solution. As such, "thinking was stimulated by problems that the learner was vitally interested in solving, the learner was both physically and mentally active and alert and engaged" (Dewey, 1938, p. 186). Simply stated, as the individual is compelled by a need to know or personal motivation, he or she can generate solutions to relevant and current problems. However, realizing what can comprise the diversity of human ontology, or the nature of experience, is also important to understanding how and why in-classroom academics (education) can complement and relate closely with new real-world experiences.

Jarvis, Holford, and Griffin (1998) developed six very specific categories of experience nuance that can help us begin to understand more of what can constitute concrete human experiences, especially in regards to experiential learning contexts. The six types of human experience include (1) *primary experience*, which describes a situation in which at least one of the human senses (e.g., hearing, sight, smell, touch, and taste) encounters the social context in which the experience occurs, (2) *secondary experience*, which is a situation in which mediation is provided through a video presentation or via dialectical discussion to describe the experience outside of its social context, (3) *actual experience*, which is understood to be the present real-time activity occurring, (4) *recalled experience*, which can be characterized as a repeated account of an actual experience, (5) *real experience*, which describes an event within its actual context, and (6) *artificial experience*, which is a manufactured experience that uses parts of other actual or real experience to demonstrate a critical point.

Schön (1987) warns, however, that the sole use of primary experience during the initial learning process may not always be appropriate simply because individuals are not omniscient or knowledgeable about events occurring in all places and, therefore, must obviously be informed by secondary sources, as in the case of subject-matter experts. However, adult learners, as compared to younger students, tend to experience educational processes and events much differently due in large part to their level of knowledge, skills, and associated abilities. Knowles's (1984) work on adult learning theory sheds crucial light on the topic.

Knowles and Andragogy

Knowles (1984) introduced us to the concept of andragogy (helping adults learn) and shifted our focus toward how adult learners' psycho-social makeup, prior experiences, and motivations enhance experiential learning strategies; indeed, adult learners comprise the majority of those undertaking formal education programs in workforce training and development. The idea of andragogy suggests that adult students experience learning at different cognitive, psychomotor, and affective levels and, therefore, the teaching paradigm must shift from an instructor-centered to primarily a student-centered transactional experience.

While citing the work of Knowles (1984), Sims and Sims (1995) assert that the learning activity design for adults should be "based on the learners' needs and interests so as to create opportunities for the learners to analyze their experience and its application to their work and life" (p. 3). Andragogy affords the student an opportunity at greater autonomy in coupling learning modes to learning objectives and their intended application.

According to Knowles (1984), the concept of andragogy is based on five critical assumptions about adult learners. These assumptions include:

1. Adults are motivated to learn as they develop needs and interests that learning will satisfy.

2. Adult orientation to learning is life- or work-centered.

3. Experience is the richest resource for adult learning.

4. Adults have a deep need to be self-directing (autonomy).

5. Individual differences among adult learners increase with age and experience" (Sims & Sims, 1995, pp. 3–4).

Of crucial importance to this discussion are andragogy's assumptions that adults are motivated to learn due to personal and professional interests, that they are occupation-centered, that they can use their experience as a reservoir for new knowledge, and that they have an ability and need to be self-directed learners. Next, experiential learning constructs and, in particular, Kolb's (1984) work on experiential learning strategies, can be combined with our understanding of diverse forms of human experience and adult learner characteristics to help us create classroom-level experiential learning approaches for real-world application.

Experiential Learning

Experiential learning programs are known to assist individuals to improve conflict-resolution skills, student development, farming techniques, theoretical modeling, personal growth, and workplace education and training (Saddington, 2001). According to Saddington (2001), Cantor (1997), and Henry (1989), experiential education methods include non-traditional learning objectives, the incorporation of prior learning, social change curricula, work and community placement (internship/ service learning), activity-based laboratory exercises, problem solving, and independent learning. Smith and McCann (2001) argue that experiential education programs can also foster critical thinking and reflection on the part of students by "involving contrasting perspectives from the classroom and from the real-world setting" (p. 205) within learning objectives. Indeed, Itin (1999) and Hutchinson and Bosaki (2000) characterize experiential education as a transactional process, as opposed to uni-directional transmission, whereby an individual experiences changes in feelings, judgments, and knowledge as a result of living through an event or a series of events.

Experiential learning, therefore, is an educational process whereby direct experiences are reflected upon, where previous personal and professional experiences are incorporated, and, as a result, new understanding or changes are produced at the individual and/or group level (Saddington, 2001). The importance of further developing and expanding the use of experiential education curricula is that, according to Haskell (2000), transfer of learning has not been successfully achieved to any significant level through the use of traditional teaching and evaluation methods; achieving transfer of learning is critical, for this, he believes, is ultimately the foundation for thinking, learning, and effective problem solving. Jacobs (1999) argues that experiential education not only assists students in actually engaging the learning process, but helps them to achieve transfer of learning, in particular, outside of the classroom; the workplace is no exception. But what can experiential learning curricula look like for adult learners? Kolb's (1984) work on the experiential learning stages offers a strong model.

Kolb's Experiential Learning Model

According to Jarvis, Holford, and Griffin (1998), Kolb's experiential learning cycle model is essential as a starting point to empirical research on adult learning styles. Additionally, McLaughlin and Thorpe (1993) posit that Kolb's learning cycle model allows for reflection and discovery on the part of adult students, the majority of which are working individuals. Kolb (1984) argues that experiential education programs must be holistic in nature by ultimately linking personal development, education, and work. He posits that, when undertaking an academic exercise, students prefer one or two of the four learning stages he subscribes. The four experiential learning cycle stages include (1) *concrete experiences*, which are those that engage the student with in-class demonstrations, storytelling, films, videos, simulations,

Internet applications, and newspaper article discussion; (2) *reflective observations*, which summon students' perceptions about an issue through brainstorming sessions, open-air discussions, question-and-answer requirements related to HRD course assignments, and journal writing assignments to allow for reflection on learning experiences; (3) *abstract conceptualization*, which creates an opportunity for students to engage in model-building experiences, in writing critiques about the theories and models they investigate; and (4) *active experimentation*, where the students are given the opportunity to soon after apply the material to field work, lab work, case studies, model testing, and individualized activities (Kolb, 1984; Royce, 2001).

Examples of how some of the preceding learning concepts are experienced will be explored within the mini-case study section of this article.

Classroom Academics: The Open System ADDIE Training Intervention Model

Next, we shift the focus to exploring the Open Systems ADDIE Training Intervention Model within the context of learning about how to effectively accomplish occupational analysis and subsequent curriculum design. It is in understanding the universe of the wider organization and associated systems where the learner and practitioner can begin to design better training and development solutions. The learning of this new analysis application model begins with experiential learning academics (curricula), but culminates within the students' workplace setting by utilizing their occupational expertise. First, we begin by exploring the basic Open Systems ADDIE Training Intervention Model (see Figure 1) and its meaning to the needs analysis process.

In general, the Open Systems ADDIE Training Intervention Model prescribes that the learner and practitioner understand that potential training solutions begin with a comprehensive analysis of where the organization's productivity problem might lie (i.e., organizational structures and policies, technology, or operational practices, learners); what required knowledge, skills, and attitudes must inform the final curriculum design (e.g., pre-tests, learning objectives, and evaluation tools); what tangible materials need to be developed to enable the learning objectives to be achieved (e.g., manuals, handouts, checklists, e-learning); when and how to implement the training program (e.g., ASAP or quarterly; in class or online) and for whom (e.g., learners, leaders, and/or key suppliers); employing the right mix of instructional strategies (e.g., lecture, demonstration performance, CBT, or experiential learning); and, last, end with a final comprehensive evaluation of the training program based primarily on the feedback received from the organization's learners upon completion of the course, and indeed, at set subsequent timeframes to measure return on training investment.

Although practitioners use many variations of this model, learners of HRD can benefit most by applying the basic, but effective ADDIE model for most training intervention analyses. However, in an effort to arrive at the genuine root cause(s) of organizational human performance challenges, HRD training professionals should begin with an analysis of potential policies and procedure (non-instructional) problems existing in the organization.

Non-Instructional Considerations

It has sometimes been the case that organizational trainers and/or outside training firms tend to find a training solution for every form of human performance challenge occurring within an organization; training programs do not necessarily solve all organizational performance challenges. Integrity about the final recommendations pertaining to resolving organizational human performance challenges demands analysis also of potential non-skill (policy/procedure) based problem areas. According to Rothwell and Kazanas (1998), organizational analyses must also include investigation about five organizational issues: (1) employee selection practices (e.g., recruitment, job analysis, selection tools and results); (2) employee feedback methods (e.g., coaching, production wall charts, team meetings, 360-degree supervisor reviews, and customer surveys); (3) reward systems (e.g., goal-related, monetary, and non-monetary); (4) job performance aids (e.g., checklists, algorithms, work samples, and procedure manuals); and (5) organizational design (e.g., reporting relationships, information sharing, job responsibilities). It can be the case that some of the above areas may be complicit in the performance problem context to some degree.

The current need for managers and employees to understand and operate within a cross-functional environment necessitates that training solutions affecting production and operations, for instance, be informed by how related functions such as sales and marketing, design and engineering, and accounting and finance actually impact the productivity level of the production or assembly line; this also includes the contribution of key suppliers the producer contracts with regarding its raw material needs. Is within the analysis portion of the training intervention whereby curriculum experts (trainers) can begin to investigate human performance issues using local and extended subject matter experts (SME) found within all major organizational functions.

Analysis and Cross-Functional Collaboration

Critical to the analysis phase of most training interventions is that training professionals assemble key stakeholders within and without the organization experiencing a productivity challenge; the support of high-level leadership to a collaboration process between the organization's major functions is critical. Assembling key stakeholders is essential for gathering the necessary primary and secondary data to inform the final training solution, should one actually be required. Requiring key stakeholders to participate in Delphi method processes regarding analyses results is also crucial and usually carried out by various key cross-functional subject-matter experts (SME) to achieve a comprehensive training solution. This can certainly pose a geographic challenge for firms that operate on a multi-state, national, or global scale. Leveraging technology (i.e., email, video- or web-conferencing tools) when engaging or polling a focus cross-functional analysis team can circumvent most of this challenge.

Four Major Organizational Line Functions

Most organizations, be they organic (i.e., Microsoft) or mechanistic (i.e., military) in nature, are composed of line, and staff functions (i.e., HR, MIS, maintenance, legal, administrative support, and others). In general, within the typical organization (private and public sectors and/or non-profit) operating within a free-market open system economic environment, four major organizational line functions are charged with either marketing, designing, funding, or producing the product or services that the firm is in business to offer the domestic or global economy. For example, the lead function within the private sector firm is the sales and marketing (S&M) department (public relations or office of communications for non-profit and public-sector organizations). This function is responsible for attracting new customers or clients, in addition to maintaining the current customer or client relationship. This is typically accomplished through a marketing mix that includes product, price, place, and promotional strategies. Market research tools are employed to take the best pulse reading of a certain target market consumer. Design and engineering (D&E), the second major function, sometimes known as research and development, is generally informed by S&M with regards to what new and current customers desire in the firm's product or service (e.g., cars, food, or banking services). Designers generate the conceptual plans based largely on customer needs and desires regarding the product or service's features and benefits. The engineering side of this functional area determines whether certain tangible materials (e.g., metals, plastics, fabrics, technologies) can make a certain car model, for example, more fuel efficient; the input of key suppliers becomes critical at this stage.

The third major organizational function(s) includes accounting and finance (A&F). Accounting is generally charged with monitoring organizational flows of funds in and out of the firm; budgetary issues and constraints tend to inform expenditures decisions at all levels, in addition to tax liability issues. Finance, on the other hand, is generally charged with raising funds (e.g., initial public offerings, bank loans), issuing customer credit, and investing company financial resources ultimately for the benefit of the firm's operations, plans, and programs. And fourth, production and operations actually implements D&E specifications concerning products and services to manufacture and utilizes distribution channels to deliver them to various wholesalers or directly to retail stores. The following two organizational examples can serve to illuminate how the four line functions generally operate and interrelate in a company.

XYZ Car Company. The XYZ Car Company's sales and marketing (S&M) function will employ radio, print, television, and Internet media to advertise about this year's new models to current and potential new customers. Much of the new car model features and benefits were based on previous year's customer feedback, which S&M obtained through various market research methods (e.g., surveys, focus groups) or industry regulations. Design and engineering (D&E) had taken this market intelligence data about, for instance, minivan vehicles benefits and features desired by consumers and created the designs, specifications, and engineered for the tangible materials necessary to produce a safe, fuel-efficient, and sporty minivan. Production and operations (POM), in turn, had collaborated with D&E during the design phase providing valuable input about production line technologies, inventory resources, key supplier materials, and human resource requirements, among other things. At time of production, POM simply implemented the designs on the assembly line, which is probably a part of a global supplier and value production chain, often characterized as a vertical disintegration business enterprise model. All the while accounting and finance (A&F) offers customer credit lines, issues equity shares for investors, secures bank loans, and ensures accounts payable and receivables are kept current.

ZYX Restaurant. At ZYX Restaurant, the sales and marketing function may apply promotion strategies that include radio, print (coupon), television, and Internet channels to advertise the restaurant's menu items to the target customer bases. A chef would be responsible for "designing" the menus for the food that the cooks in the kitchen will make (production) and that the serving staff will deliver (operations/distribution). Of course, accounting and finance concerns itself with the restaurant's operating budgets, pay and salaries, accounts payable and receivable, customer credit, overhead, and any expansion plans under consideration. For HRD learners, this process can often be confusing, but can be learned and operationalized within academic contexts designed to teach them about how to conduct effective, cross-functional occupational analysis and the subsequent curriculum design(s). The following case study scenario about an organizational human performance challenge can serve as an example.

Case Study Scenario and Cross-Functional Collaboration

Organization: Orbus Laptop Computer Company (OLCC), operating customer service and call centers in Southern California and Southeast Asia, assembles made-to-order laptops in China and Hungary with a global distribution network.

Human Performance Challenge: Many European, U.S., and Japanese customers are receiving their laptop computers with the incorrect hardware equipment installed (per the earlier description in this article, this is a primary and recalled experience). The experiential learning process begins when HRD learners are assembled into teams of no more than four members; ground rules are established, especially with regard to leadership and followership expectations. Next, after receiving an in-depth briefing about the four major organizational functions, each HRD learner assumes the role of subject-matter expert for one of the four major functions (e.g., sales and marketing, design and engineering, accounting and finance, and production and operations) for OLCC. Each learner is then required to conduct basic research about what his or her role would encompass and require within the assigned major function (artificial experience). The question is: Where does the human productivity challenge lie in OLCC, that of assemblers not correctly installing the requested hardware features (real experience and reflective observations)?

Analysis of Possible Non-Instructional Causes

HRD learners begin the analysis about the problem by exploring the five possible "non-instructional" root causes discussed above (secondary experience and reflective observations). It is assumed that focus groups and survey tools can assist the initial data gathering steps of this part of the analysis. It is important that learners begin the potential non-instructional aspects of the analysis by addressing how the human resources department might conduct employee recruitment/selection practices (reflective observations). In the case of OLCC's order call center employees, what are the necessary prerequisite knowledge, skills, and attitudes (KSAs) pertaining to language skills, customer service skills, cross-cultural literacy, and information technology skills outlined in their job description? In general, similar questions are explored concerning Hungarian and Chinese laptop computer assemblers, in addition to the required tools used for assembling and installing laptop computers and associated components.

This portion of the analysis also requires HRD learners to discuss what employee feedback mechanisms (e.g., wall charts, 360-degree feedback, coaching), or lack thereof, are employed within the organization's world-wide operational environment. Then learners must ask: Does OLCC offer monetary and non-monetary rewards tied to organizational and production goals worldwide? Is the rewards and recognition program managed outside of operations environments so as to undermine favoritism and other "political" issues?

Next, learners consider what type of job performance aids (e.g., checklists, work samples, or manuals) supervisors provide their employees and whether they are attached to actual workplace training programs. And last, given OLCC's global and cross-cultural operations environment, are the reporting relationships characterized as open, effective, and cross-culturally sensitive throughout the organization? Does OLCC employ in-country supervisory and management staff to lead their employees? and Does the leadership understand about connecting customer service and performance goals to overall organizational profitability? This ends a basic analyses process HRD learners can undertake in an effort to eliminate any non-instructional problem areas within the company-wide organization. If the problem does lie within one of the five organizational policy areas, a performance assessment of the laptop computer assembly operations can, nonetheless, be beneficial to spot any minor KSAs-based deficiencies that may be present.

Analyses of OLCC's Four Major Functions

Next, HRD learners are guided to explore where the skills gap may exist at OLCC by also analyzing the four major organizational functions (secondary experience). What will be crucial for this portion of the analyses is that HRD learners are encouraged to use free writing and brainstorming techniques to essentially generate credible hypotheses (abstract conceptualization) concerning what their team believes is the major skills gap causing the human performance challenge.

The team members must unanimously decide what major function holds the major portion of the skills-based problem, present their findings, and receive feedback from their other colleagues in class (artificial experience). Because most human performance problems seem to stem from the POM function, the teams are encouraged to begin the brainstorming process there. Learners are directed to focus on the laptop assembly line operations and to ask what prerequisite and required knowledge, skills, and attitudes an assembly worker requires to effectively accomplish the job; a generic job description for a laptop computer assembler can suffice to initiate the discussion about basic KSAs. It is assumed that if an actual technical training certificate is not required to become a laptop computer assembler at OLCC, the company provides in-house training and development programs to their new assembly-line workers. Does the existing Basic Laptop Computer Assembly Course at OLCC cover adequately the principles, theory, terminology, product nomenclature, operational concepts, and industry jargon base in workers' native language? Is there adequate psychomotor demonstration performance experiences required of students during training, especially with required tools, technologies, and checklists on the assembly line? And third, are assembler trainees also educated about customer service principles such as the lifetime customer value concept, due diligence, and about appreciating due process for internal and external customers? It is safe to assume to some degree that "tailoring" a product to customer specifications and desires may not be a fully accepted ontology among workers operating within a formerly one-size-fits-all centrally planned economic system.

Next, HRD learners can move on to exploring what type of collaboration is required between POM and the other three major functional areas, with D&E in particular (abstract conceptualization and reflective observation). What is the role of key suppliers, if any at this point? Is the problem stemming from Hungarian or Chinese plants, or both, and does the problem seem to happen more consistently during certain worker shifts than on other shifts when perhaps more experienced workers tend to operate? Moreover, has A&F had to reduce or eliminate most funding for assembly-line training? Has OLCC upper management recently decided that S&M will instead receive greater functional funding due to a greater need to increase sales for the near and medium term? Has the S&M budget adequately covered call center and customer service center trainee programs? Might there be a loss in translation between customers' requests, the customer service representative, and the final assemblers overseas? Ultimately, all teams are required to focus on one or two training needs objectives, design the learning objectives and sequence based on the knowledge, skills, and affective requirements of the skills deficient area, and design and develop the assessment tools to measure student learning.

Once this process has been accomplished for the necessary cycles and tested using midterm or final exam tools, HRD learners are then required to apply this same training intervention analysis tool to a real-world workplace human performance issue. It is within the learner's workplace setting where extended experiential learning occurs, wherein classroom academics about real-world case studies are then applied within their own areas of occupational expertise in a self-directed manner (active experimentation).

Implications for Learning and Practice

Human resources development (HRD) academic training programs require both theoretical and experiential learning aspects. The theoretical aspects about the nature of experience, experiential learning methods, and adult learning constructs serve to inform the actual curricular structure and academic exercises in a HRD course. The experiential learning aspects create links between the theoretical bases, learners' experience, knowledge, and motivation within classroom level experiences (i.e., abstract conceptualization) that are based on actual case studies, real-world or otherwise. Ultimately, HRD learners and practitioners can apply foundational theory about human experience, adult learning characteristics, and experiential learning strategies to training intervention analysis tools, one being the Open Systems ADDIE Training Intervention Model.

References

Cantor, J. (1997). *Experiential learning in higher education: Linking classroom and community.* Washington, DC: ERIC Clearinghouse on Higher Education. (ED404948).

Dewey, J. (1938). *Experience and education.* New York: Collier Books.

Haskell, R. (2000). *Transfer of learning: Cognition, instruction and reasoning.* San Diego, CA: Academic Press.

Henry, J. (1989). Meaning and practice in experiential Learning. In W. Weil & I. McGill (1989), *Making sense of experiential learning.* London: SRHE & Open University Press.

Hutchinson, D., & Bosacki, S. (2000, Winter). Over the edge: Can holistic education contribute to experiential education? *The Journal of Experiential Education, 23*(3), 177–182.

Itin, C.M. (1999, Fall). Reasserting the philosophy of experiential education as a vehicle for change in the 21st century. *Journal of Experiential Education, 22*(2), 91–98.

Jacobs, J. (1999). *Experiential education: The main dish, not just a side course.* Washington, DC: ERIC Clearinghouse for Higher Education. (ED438140).

Jarvis, P., Holford, J., & Griffin, C. (1998). *The theory and practice of learning.* London: Stylus Publications.

Kant, E. (1788). *Theoretical philosophy after 1781 (electronic resource).* New York: Cambridge University Press.

Knowles, M. (1980). *The modern practice of adult education: From pedagody to androgogy.* Chicago, IL: Follett.

Knowles, M.A., & Associates (1984). *Andragogy in action.* San Francisco, CA: Jossey-Bass.

Kolb, D. (1984). *Experiential learning: Experience as the source of learning and development.* Englewood Cliffs, NJ: Prentice Hall.

McLaughlin, H., & Thorpe, R. (1993). Action learning: A paradigm in emergence: The problem facing a challenge to traditional management education. *British Journal of Management, 4*(1), 19–27.

Morrison, G.R., Ross, S.M., & Kemp, J.E. (2004). *Designing effective instruction* (4th ed.). Hoboken, NJ: John Wiley & Sons.

Rothwell, W.J., & Kazanas, H.C. (1998). *Mastering the instructional design process: A systemic approach* (2nd ed.). San Francisco, CA: Jossey-Bass.

Royce, D. (2001). *Teaching tips for college and university instructors.* Needham Heights, MA: Allyn & Bacon.

Saddington, T. (2001). *What is "experiential learning?"* Available at www.el.uct.ac.za

Schön, D. (1987). *Educating the reflective practitioner.* San Francisco, CA: Jossey-Bass.

Sims, R.R., & Sims, S.J. (1995). *The importance of learning styles: Understanding the implications for learning, course design, and education.* Westport, CT: Greenwood Press.

Smith, B.L., & McCann, J. (2001). *Reinventing ourselves: Interdisciplinary education, collaborative learning and experimentation in higher education.* Bolton, MA: Anker Publications.

Dr. Christopher A. Chaves *has worked with adult learners for fifteen years in organizational and university-level education, training, and development programs. A former U.S. Air Force member and entrepreneur, he is currently a program coordinator and visiting assistant professor for Southern Illinois University Carbondale (SIUC). Dr. Chaves has previously taught courses in management, marketing, operations management, and business ethics, but currently teaches courses in occupational analysis and curriculum design, teaching methods and materials, and training systems management for SIUC, College of Education, Department of Workforce Education and Development.*

Best If Used by . . . or a Systematic Approach to Maintaining Training Materials

Marilyn Martin

Summary

Reviewing and updating training materials can be a time-consuming task, but it's a necessary one to maintain the usefulness and integrity of training. This article presents a model and questionnaire for assessing your training materials and programs and provides some pointers on how to make sure you keep your training up-to-date and effective.

You've seen the *Best If Used by . . .* date on the side of the milk carton. It keeps us out of trouble, even though we usually also apply the "sniff" test to double-check freshness. Training materials can be a lot like milk—good for us, enjoyable, but to be avoided when it is starting to "turn." So if milk has a date stamp on the carton and you can smell or taste when it has gone bad, how do you know when training materials are "past their peak" of freshness?

For the sake of this article, training materials are any materials created to help people learn: courseware, job aids, troubleshooting guides, e-learning, online performance support, assessments, collateral materials, and so forth.

I've asked a number of my clients and colleagues about their procedures for keeping training materials current and relevant. At best, I found maintenance to be an afterthought, and at worst, non-existent. Looking to the IT industry, I borrowed a best practice for systems maintenance, also known as change control. Using the IT model, here is a framework against which you can assess the relative "freshness" of training content:

- *Adoption*—Are people using the materials?

- *Utility*—How useable are the materials to those people using them?

- *Efficiency*—Is this the most cost-effective way to help people learn today?

- *Business alignment*—How well do the materials meet the needs of the business and how useful are they to learners?

Let's look at each component of the framework individually.

Adoption

Adoption refers to the acceptance of the training materials by people using them. A sign of a high adoption rate is a high level of registrations (or downloads or views, depending on how the material is accessed). For example, if the target audience for a training piece is one hundred people, and only five have downloaded it, you can safely say that the adoption rate is low and begin to look for obstacles that may be preventing higher adoption. Perhaps the piece needs to be better marketed, or it may be ineffective or not relevant. Regardless of the cause, a decision to improve the materials or pull them out of the catalogue should be considered.

Utility

Utility refers to how well the training materials address the learning requirement. Are the training materials well organized? Are good instructional design techniques used? Is there a way for learners to assess their progress? Are other resources and support identified for learners? Unless you can answer yes to all of these questions, it may be time to pull the materials back for an overhaul.

Efficiency

Efficiency is probably one of the most important, yet most overlooked reasons for revamping training materials. With recent technological innovations and on-demand printing options, there are many inexpensive delivery methods available today. Good training managers monitor costs per hour or costs per learner for training programs and are always looking for lower-cost options.

Business Alignment

Business alignment refers to how well business priorities are defined and addressed using the training materials and how satisfied business partners and learners are with them. Training materials that cannot be linked to a positive business result or are not valued by business partners or learners can be seen as a needless expense, something no effective training manager wants in his or her portfolio. Training materials should be monitored on an ongoing basis to ensure that they are in alignment with business needs.

How Good Are Your Training Materials?

So how do you know whether your training materials are baseline, effective, or exemplary? Ah, now we get to the meat of this article. Roll up your sleeves and honestly evaluate your materials using the following questionnaire.

Adoption (Acceptance of the Materials by the Target Audience)

Who is the target audience?

What is the total population?

What is the annual turnover rate in this population?

How many registrations were there last quarter?

How many registrations were there two quarters ago?

How many registrations were there three quarters ago?

What was last quarter's registration rate? (Divide last quarter's registration by total population.)

What was the registration rate two quarters ago? (Divide registration two quarters ago by total population.)

What was the registration rate three quarters ago? (Divide registration three quarters ago by total population.)

Are registration rates trending up, trending down, or stable?   up   down   stable

Is the registration rate acceptable? (You will have to determine an acceptable rate for your organization.)   yes   no

Is the registration rate at least equal to the turnover rate? (Divide turnover rate by 4 to find quarterly turnover.)   yes   no

What are known obstacles preventing the right level of adoption?

Utility (How Well the Training Materials Address the Learning Requirement)

	Baseline	Effective	Exemplary
Organization and Design			
Do the materials provide:			
A syllabus or course outline that explains what is expected of learners?	None or very limited	Some	Extensive
A visual design that communicates information clearly?	None or very limited	Some	Extensive
Alternatives to address accessibility issues?	None or very limited	Some	Extensive
Innovative use of technology to facilitate learning and communication among learners?	None or very limited	Some	Extensive
Instructional Design and Delivery			
Do the materials provide:			
Opportunities for interaction and communication between learners, learners and instructors, learners and subject-matter experts?	None or very limited	Some	Extensive
Visual, textual, kinesthetic, and/or auditory activities to enhance learning?	None or very limited	Some	Extensive
Activities to help learners develop critical thing and/or problem-solving skills?	None or very limited	Some	Extensive
Opportunities for learners to reflect on what they have learned and how they will apply new knowledge or skills?	None or very limited	Some	Extensive
Assessment of Learning			
Do the materials provide:			
Opportunities for learners to determine whether they have met threshold requirements of the course?	None or very limited	Some	Extensive
Alignment of learning objectives and learning assessment activities?	None or very limited	Some	Extensive
Learner self-assessments and/or peer feedback?	None or very limited	Some	Extensive
Learning Support and Resources			
Do the materials provide:			
Name/contact information of instructors, content owners, or subject experts?	None or very limited	Some	Extensive
Information on how to obtain supporting resources, such as articles, books, websites, cassettes, other training programs, etc.?	None or very limited	Some	Extensive

Efficiency (Financial Benchmarks that Help Determine the Cost Effectiveness of the Training Materials)

	Baseline	Effective	Exemplary
Financial Measures			
How does the cost to develop the course compare to other programs?	Higher	Same as	Lower
How do the costs to deliver the program compare with other programs?	Higher	Same as	Lower
Costs per learner?	Higher	Same as	Lower
Costs per hour?	Higher	Same as	Lower

Business Alignment (How Well Business Priorities Are Defined and Addressed)

	Baseline	Effective	Exemplary
Attainment of Business Objectives			
Were business priorities defined?	No or to a very limited degree	Somewhat	Extensively
Were root causes of the problem identified?	No or to a very limited degree	Somewhat	Extensively
Do business partners agree with the priorities, design, and objectives of the training materials?	No or to a very limited degree	Somewhat	Extensively
Do the learning outcomes directly correlate to the root cause of the business problem?	No or to a very limited degree	Somewhat	Extensively
Learner Feedback			
Is there an opportunity for learners to give feedback on course content?	None or very limited	Some	Extensive
Is there an opportunity for learners to give feedback on the use of technology?	None or very limited	Some	Extensive
Learner Satisfaction			
How well did the learners like the content, delivery, experience, and nature of the program?	Not at all or to a very limited degree	Somewhat	Yes

Where Will You Find This Information?

Fortunately, this information is readily available, although it will require a bit of legwork. You can gather information from the following sources:

- Interviews with business partners or sponsors of the training materials

- Review of relevant evaluation data

- Interviews with learners from the target audience—both those who have used the materials and those who have not

- Interviews with subject-matter experts to determine whether the content is correct and/or still relevant

- First-hand review of the materials (use the materials yourself)

- Review of relevant industry benchmark data such as training costs, development and delivery costs, and so forth that is readily available through industry sources

How to Interpret and Act on Your Findings

There may be several reasons for each of your findings and an equal number of courses of action.

Adoption

When looking at adoption rates, think about the number of learners in the pipeline. The more people in the pipeline, the higher your registration rates should be. If registration rates are declining, investigate further to determine the underlying reason(s):

- Audience size is declining or the audience has been saturated, and registration decline is a normal phenomenon.

- Training materials are not meeting the needs of the target audience.

- The training materials are not being marketed properly.

- The materials are no longer relevant or underlying business objectives have shifted or changed.

- Less expensive alternatives have become available as options to the training material.

Utility

When analyzing utility, consider the usefulness of the materials from the learners' perspective. If many of your responses fall within the baseline category, look for ways to improve the materials by tweaking the design and delivery, through improved use of technology, or by providing additional learning resources.

If the size of your target audience is declining rapidly, you may decide to do nothing.

Efficiency

Consider current and ongoing costs for the design (or redesign) and delivery. Look for solutions that lower the overall cost.

Business Alignment

Consider how well the materials meet organizational objectives and how easy it is for learners to achieve performance objectives.

Prioritizing Your Workload

It can be a daunting task to review all training materials and, for that reason, I recommend putting each on a regular schedule—weekly or quarterly—so that you look at all of the courses in your portfolio at least once annually. Review of the materials may be only the first step; it is likely that you will have some materials that will be decommissioned and some that will require additional investigation or rework. By assigning a score to the answers in the questionnaire, you can prioritize which materials require attention first. Baseline courses should take priority over effective courses, and courses with a large target audience, low adoption rate, and crucial business imperative should take the highest priority.

Conclusion

Usually our attention is drawn to improving training materials when there are complaints, known as break-fix in the IT world. Break-fix is the same as fire-fighting and is expensive and disruptive because it is an unplanned activity. Take a tip from our IT colleagues and plan for maintenance by anticipating registration and tracking adoption rates, verifying the usefulness of materials, ensuring the most cost effective methods of design and delivery, and guaranteeing that training materials are aligned with what the business (and learners) want and need.

Marilyn Martin is an independent consultant with over twenty years' experience in performance improvement technologies, including formal and informal workplace learning design, group facilitation, visual language and information display, competency model prototyping and development, and knowledge management. She was a contributing author to The 2007 Pfeiffer Annual: Consulting. *She holds three prestigious industry certifications: Senior Professional HR (SPHR) from SHRM; Certified Performance Technologist (CPT) from the International Society of Performance Improvement; and Certified Knowledge Manager (CKM) from the Knowledge and Innovation Management Professional Society.*

Where Does Training Report in the Organization?*

Jean Barbazette

Summary

In this article, the author briefly describes two types of training structure—centralized and decentralized—discusses the advantages and disadvantages of each type, and provides suggestions for how to overcome the disadvantages for each.

Decentralized and Centralized Training

The two most common places a training function reports to higher management are either as a centralized or decentralized organization. A centralized function has all trainers in an organization working in one group with specific trainers acting as internal consultants to specific business units. The training staff reports to a training manager or chief learning officer who often reports to a vice president of human resources. A corporate university is an example of a centralized training function. A decentralized training function assigns or designates specific trainers acting as internal consultants to work in a business unit and report to an operating manager. Most sales training functions are decentralized with the sales training manager reporting to the vice president of sales. In a decentralized training function, additional training functions would exist in the manufacturing department, corporate offices, etc.

There are advantages and disadvantages to each type of organization, as summarized in Table 1. Whether a training function is centralized or decentralized is not critical to the success of the function. What is critical to success is to capitalize on the advantages and work at overcoming the disadvantages.

---

*From *A Trainer's Journey to Competence* © 2005 Pfeiffer. Used with permission.

Table 1. Advantages and Disadvantages of Where a Training Function Reports

	Centralized Training Function	Decentralized Training Function
Advantages	Trainers physically located together facilitates mentoring new trainers; Cross-training staff is easier to accomplish; It is easier to develop training specialists who have different levels of expertise. Experts can be developed in course development or instruction; A career path in "training" can be developed more easily by performing in a variety of training roles; Training design and delivery are likely to be consistent.	Trainers find it easier to identify skill deficiencies since they "live" in the operation they support. It is easier to develop subject matter expertise with this type of reporting; Trainers more easily develop relationships with the business unit they support because they are present all of the time; The supervisor who sees the results of your work in the business unit is the trainer's manager; The training budget is a line item in the department's budget and not as likely to be cut during tight financial times.
Disadvantages	Trainers need to make a greater effort to develop relationships with the business unit they support since they are sometimes seen as an "outsider"; It may take longer to identify knowledge and skill deficiencies because the trainer must study the business unit from a distance and is not a subject matter expert; The training budget for the entire organization is an easy target during cost-cutting times.	Finding another trainer as a mentor is more difficult when trainers work by themselves; Trainers tend to be generalists who must perform a variety of roles well. This can be difficult for a new trainer whose strength is in subject matter expertise; Finding a replacement or successor can be difficult if trainers are not cross-trained to function in other business units; Training design and delivery varies in quality and consistency; Some organization have "dotted line" reporting to a central training manager, which can be confusing, disruptive, or cause conflict.

Overcoming Disadvantages

Following are suggestions for the centralized function to overcome disadvantages listed in Table 1.

1. Build relationships with the business unit you support. Make scheduled and informal visits to the department in the business unit. Identify key people who make decisions and ask them how you can support their goals.

2. Provide performance analysis assessment skills for the managers, supervisors, and lead people to distinguish between training and non-training issues. If the department personnel become adept at performance analysis, it is easier to provide the appropriate training. Learn as much as you can about the work of the business unit so subject matter experts begin to trust your suggestions and coaching.

3. Consider the possibility of having the business unit maintain the training budget for their unit.

Following are suggestions for the decentralized function to overcome the disadvantages listed in Table 1.

1. Work at finding a mentor who is more skilled, expert, and capable than you, whether or not the person is in your department. If no appropriate mentor exists in your organization, identify resources in professional associations who can help you with your development.

2. No generalist is equally adept at a variety of roles. Identify your strengths and weaknesses and develop a plan to grow each of these skills over time. Select the skills for development that make the greatest difference in supporting your business unit.

3. Seek opportunities for cross-training and attendance at training events and conferences outside your organization.

4. If you report to a business unit manager AND have dotted-line reporting to a corporate training manager, ask for clarification for which manager decides various issues. If you're not sure who makes what type of decision, look at who completes your performance and salary reviews.

Jean Barbazette *is the author of* Successful New Employee Orientation *(Pfeiffer, 2007),* The Trainer's Support Handbook *(McGraw-Hill, 2001),* Instant Case Studies *(Pfeiffer, 2003),* The Trainer's Journey to Competence *(Pfeiffer, 2005),* Training Needs Assessment *(Pfeiffer, 2006),* The Art of Great Training Delivery *(Pfeiffer, 2006), and* Managing the Training Function for Bottom-Line Results *(Pfeiffer, 2007).*

Does Informal Learning Make Business Sense?

Jay Cross

Summary

In this article, informal learning advocate Jay Cross discusses the ways in which management often makes business decisions, sometimes to the detriment of the organization's long-term health, and provides a series of examples to show what can be accomplished with more expansive thinking.

Informal learning is the path to organizational capability, agility, and profits. It also respects workers and challenges them to be all they can be. Yet some executives shy away from projects whose outcomes are difficult to measure; many have their heads in the sand.

Successful, observant businesspeople make decisions based on reasonable expectations of future returns. In general, the more senior the leader is, the further out the time horizon. The further in the future, the less precise is the expectation. Great leaders have vision, not exactitude.

The investment community is, misguidedly in my opinion, fixated on quarterly results. But wisdom tells us that perpetually focusing on short-term numbers is not a prescription for long-term success. Given a choice of now or later, senior managers want both. How can we deal with this conundrum? I suggest that we adopt the perspective of a supremely successful businessperson, someone like Andrew Carnegie.

Carnegie rose from abject poverty to unimaginable riches through enlightened management and sound investments. He quit at the peak of his game, sold his holdings to J.P. Morgan, built himself a castle in his home town in Scotland, and spent the rest of his days giving his fortune to good causes. As a businessman, he did not put up with foolishness.

When you're evaluating an investment of time or money or a new approach such as informal learning, ask yourself, "What would Andrew Carnegie do?" Ask yourself the questions he'd ask. Get to the heart of it: Does this project feel right? Is this the best use of your hard-earned money? Will this pay us back for taking a risk on it?

If a learning project—make that any project—does not make business sense, don't do it. If the return on investment is not so obvious that you can sketch it out on the back of a napkin, do something with a higher return.

Here are ten cases in which it's tough to measure precise outcomes. Each, however, provides an example of what can be accomplished by allowing an organization's systems and employees to stretch beyond what's considered standard or "safe."

Sales Force Readiness

A global technology leader is moving at a fever pitch, acquiring a new company on average once a month. The company maintains its competitive advantage by providing its sales force and customers with instant access to case studies, product specs, sales tools, and insight into future trends. Company thought leaders in twelve strategically important areas meet regularly in person to update one another, talk with customers, and discuss what's new in their field. The firm says they "Google-ize" this content, making it as easy to search as with Google but also retrievable as video-on-demand, podcast, presentation, or text. The result is a better-informed sales force, more competence on sales calls, more cross-selling, better presentations, and ease in bringing partners up to speed.

Access to Expertise

Knowledge workers waste one-third of their time looking for information and finding the right people to talk with. Frequently, they spend more time re-creating existing information they were unaware of than creating original material. Expertise locators direct workers to people with the right answers. Organizational network analysis pinpoints bottlenecks and poor connections. Bottom-up systems provide exception-handling workarounds and rules of thumb. Instant messaging accelerates information flow. Reduced search times, streamlined organizational processes, and finding people faster can increase worker productivity 20 to 30 percent.

Innovation

Times of change require new approaches, and conversation is the parent of innovation. Organizations are redesigning the work space to encourage meaningful conversation. Mind maps and visualization tools accelerate discussion. Concept prototyping multiplies the volume of new ideas generated by work groups. Online collaboration and discussion software spark innovation among far-flung groups that share common interests. Formal learning promotes a curriculum; informal learning encourages thinking about opportunities.

Increase Information Technology Flexibility

An organization that brings Internet technology and Internet culture inside the firewall reduces total cost of ownership. Workers do not need to learn a new interface to participate. They already know how to search, blog, navigate, and add features. Software improves incrementally instead of in disruptive new editions. Modular web services replace brittle, hard-coded monolithic systems and flex with change.

Reduce Stress

Job stress has been implicated as a factor in heart disease, stroke, diabetes, ulcers, depression, serious accidents, alcoholism, and hypertension. It also devastates work performance. Three out of four American workers report stress on the job. Health care expenditures are nearly 50 percent higher for workers who report high levels of stress. Attacking the problems associated with stress head-on and giving workers more control over decision making yield dramatic improvements.

Increase Professionalism

Workers develop professional expertise in loose confederations of like-minded individuals. For example, engineers with an interest in optical computing might meet for beer after work to swap stories about breakthroughs and what's on the horizon. Security experts come together when facing a common threat. Corporations that support these communities of practice by providing workers time to participate and technical support to capture and distribute their conversations stay on top of new developments, foster camaraderie, and avoid the unnecessary step of requiring subject-matter experts to explain things to instructional designers.

Improve Morale

Knowledge workers balk at being told how to do their work; they see it as micromanagement and an insult to their abilities. People enjoy conversation and learning; they do not relish listening to pontification from the podium. Formal training is top-down. By contrast, informal learning trusts the worker with the decision of how to master new knowledge and skills, which increases morale while lowering turnover.

Impromptu Meetings

Companies invest heavily in annual sales meetings and other galas under the big tent. Lead time for large events is six months or more. Often 90 percent or more of the airtime is devoted to presentations. I'm not one to complain about occasional celebrations or parties, but they are a poor way for people to learn anything. Participatory sessions, conducted as needed and often impromptu, cost less and get more across.

Conversations

Conversation is the most powerful learning technology ever invented. Conversations carry news, create meaning, foster cooperation, and spark innovation. Encouraging open, honest conversation through work space design, setting ground rules for conversing productively, and baking conversation into the corporate culture spread intellectual capital, improve cooperation, and strengthen personal relationships.

Keeping Up

San Franciscans know that when the ground shakes, rigid structures crumble and flexible ones roll with the punches. The acceleration of time, globalization, outsourcing, software interoperability, open sourcing, supply chains, and more are rattling the foundations of business. Business is going from push (rigid, conforming, monoliths) to pull (flexible, innovative, small pieces). Training programs are push; they are top-down, teach the standard, and are difficult to revise. A learning platform is pull—dynamic, always responding to change.

Trainers and facilitators must ask themselves, "What is the return on investment of survival?"

Jay Cross *is a champion of informal learning, web 2.0, and systems thinking. His calling is to change the world by helping people improve their performance on the job and satisfaction in life. Jay served as CEO of eLearning Forum for its first five years, was the first to use the term e-learning on the web, and has keynoted major conferences in the United and Europe. He is a graduate of Princeton University and the Harvard Business School.*

Making the Training Content Come Alive
Ten Types of Training Activities
Sivasailam "Thiagi" Thiagarajan

Summary

Training requires an effective blend of content and activities. This article discusses (and provides examples of) ten types of training activities that reinforce different sources of content: textra games that incorporate printed text, item processing activities that incorporate unorganized bits of information, on-the-table activities that incorporate reference tables, application games that incorporate job aids, assessment-based learning activities that incorporate tests and instruments, graphic games that incorporate pictures and images, online games that incorporate content on the Internet, audio games that incorporate audio recordings, double exposure activities that incorporate video recordings, and interactive lectures that incorporate presentations by subject-matter experts.

Effective training involves two critical activities: presenting *content* and facilitating learning *activities*. Traditionally, instructional designers focused their efforts and resources on analyzing, outlining, and rewriting the content and presenting it through a variety of media. In contrast, designing activities was either completely ignored or relegated to asking participants to talk to each other.

Unlike the previous decades during which instructional design models were created, content is abundantly available nowadays in various formats and media. Once the training content is presented, we can then use different types of learning activities to review this content and provide practice opportunities for applying them.

There are several different types of review and practice activities, depending on different types of content resources. In this chapter, we discuss ten of the types of activities that reinforce the presentation of training content.

Text Materials

Printed text, ranging all the way from fortune-cookie messages to multivolume encyclopedias, is a major source of training content. More than half a million English-language books were published last year. Most training sessions are supported by training manuals, reference manuals, articles, and handouts. However, there is consensus among trainers that the typical participant is a reluctant reader. Textra games (a brilliant portmanteau word coined by my friend Roger Greenaway to combine *text* and *extra)* involve participants in completing a reading assignment and working through a structured activity to review the content and apply it to a suitable task.

Here are a couple of examples of textra games:

Leadership Library

During the first round of this textra game, ask each participant to pick a different book on leadership and spend some time scanning, skimming, and highlighting six practical guidelines that can be immediately applied back on the job. During the second round, ask each participant to pair up with another and take turns to share the practical ideas gleaned from the book, listening carefully to each other, and taking notes of the guidelines. During the third round, ask each pair of participants to join another pair. In the group of four, participants take turns presenting one of the guidelines that they learned from the partner during the previous round. After all guidelines have been shared, the group selects the one best idea. During the final round, a representative from each group presents the best idea to the entire group.

Epigrams on Change

Begin this textra game by distributing a dozen or so pithy sayings related to change to the participants in such a way that each participant receives two different sayings and each saying is given to two different participants. During the first round, participants reflect on the two pithy sayings and come up with their own interpretations and explanations. During the second round, select a pithy saying. The two participants who received this pithy saying take turns to present their personal analysis to the entire group. Repeat this process until all pithy sayings are explored.

Unorganized Information

Sometimes authentic content that is relevant to the training objectives could be in an unorganized form (for example, *complaints from customers* or *frequently asked questions about a product*). As an instructional designer, your immediate reaction will be to analyze and organize the content and make it easy for the learners to recall it.

In this analysis and organization process, you acquire a deeper understanding of the content. A more effective approach for handling this type of content is to provide the raw information to participants and have them analyze and organize it. Item processing activities do exactly that.

Here are a couple of item processing activities:

Complaint Clusters

The training objective for this item-processing activity is to identify major categories of customer complaints and to come up with examples of each. To prepare for the activity, collect several customer complaints and print each complaint on a separate card. Lay out the cards on a table in a random order. Ask participants to silently study the complaints and sort them into categories by moving the cards around. Ask participants to study each cluster of cards and discuss suitable labels for the category. Finally, ask participants to study different categories and discuss similarities and differences among them.

Top Suggestions

To prepare for this activity, collect different ideas from a suggestion box and print each suggestion on a card. Give a single card to each participant. Ask participants to turn their cards over, walk around, and exchange the cards with each other. Blow a whistle to stop the exchange process. Ask participants to pair up. Ask each pair to review the two items they have and distribute seven points between these two items to reflect their relative merit. Participants should write these points on the back of the cards. Repeat the process (of exchanging suggestion cards, pairing up with another participant, and distributing seven points) four more times. At the end of the fifth round, ask participants to add the five score points and write the total. Finally, identify the highest-scoring suggestion cards. Read and discuss the suggestions.

Reference Tables

Tables effectively organize complex information and enable users to understand the similarities and differences among related items. On-the-table games help participants to extract maximum information from tables, identify key trends, and recall useful facts and data.

Here are a couple of examples of on-the-table games:

Asian Nations

This activity involves a table that provides information on the area, population, languages, religion, government, and political leaders of five Asian nations.

To prepare for the activity, print sections of the table that show only one column or one row. Give one of these sections to each participant. Ask participants to study their sections carefully to discover the relationship among the items. Later ask all participants to get together and create the complete table.

Development Stages

Prepare a table showing different aspects of a team's development during the four stages of forming, storming, norming, and performing. However, do not give this table to the participants. Give a mini lecture on the developmental stages of a team, encouraging participants to take ample notes. Organize participants into teams and ask them to summarize key pieces of information from the lecture in the form of a reference table. After participants prepare their tables, give them copies of your table for comparison purposes.

Job Aids

Job aids are documents that provide just-in-time support to professional performance. An effective approach to rapid training involves designing job aids and training participants to use them. Application games incorporate job aids as a strategy for improving performance.

Here are a couple of examples of application games:

ROI

This application game uses a step-by-step job aid on how to calculate the return on investment (ROI) for a project. Begin the activity by dividing participants into as many teams as there are steps in the calculation procedure. Distribute different sections of the job aid to participants so that members of each team learn how to complete one of the steps. Reorganize participants into mixed teams so that each person in this new team knows how to perform a different step and the team as a whole can perform all the steps. Give sets of information about different projects to each team. Ask team members to work collaboratively and compute the ROI for each project. Encourage participants to teach their step to the other participants and to learn the other steps. Give a final assignment to each participant for working independently to compute the ROI for a new project.

Feedback, Feedback

This application game uses a checklist for giving constructive feedback to employees. Distribute copies of the checklist to teams of participants. Ask each team to prepare a skit featuring a feedback conversation between a manager and an employee. After a suitable pause, ask each team to present its skit. After each skit, ask members of the other teams to evaluate the skit using the job aid as the rating scale. Repeat the procedure until all teams have had a chance to present their skits.

Tests and Other Assessment Instruments

Inventories, questionnaires, and surveys of the type found in this *Annual* (and other resources) along with information on how to interpret participants' responses contain valuable training content. Similarly, written and performance tests along with their scoring keys provide content related to technical topics. All of these materials can be incorporated into review and practice exercises called assessment-based learning activities.

Here are a couple of assessment-based learning activities:

Logic or Intuition?

This assessment-based activity uses cards with individual items from a thinking-styles inventory. Each card contains a number and a statement. Distribute eight randomly selected cards to each participant. Ask everyone to exchange cards so that each participant ends up with eight statements that best reflect his or her personal preferences. After a suitable time for these exchanges, ask everyone to choose the six best cards and discard the rest. Explain that the cards with odd numbers are associated with intuitive thinking, while those with even numbers are associated with logical thinking. Divide participants into three groups (logical, intuitive, and mixed). Ask each group to discuss the advantages of their preferred thinking style and list them on a flip chart. Finally, encourage participants to study the different lists and figure out strategies for working in a team with diverse thinking styles.

True or False?

This activity uses a true/false test related to customer service. Begin the session by distributing copies of the test and asking participants to independently decide whether each item is true or false. After a suitable pause, read the first item and ask participants to indicate their choices. Randomly select a few participants and ask them to justify their *true* or *false* choice. Present information related to the item so participants can make the correct response. Repeat the process with each item until the training topic is thoroughly explored.

Graphics and Images

If a picture is worth a thousand words, it could be used as an efficient resource for presenting training content. Graphic games reward participants for carefully analyzing and interpreting key ideas that are presented visually.

Here are a couple of examples of graphic games:

What's Wrong?

Let's imagine that you are using a discovery approach to safety training. Ask teams of participants to examine a portfolio of photographs of workplace situations. Participants attempt to identify violations of safety procedures. After a suitable pause, distribute a list of violations identified by a panel of safety experts. Ask teams compare their list with the experts' lists and prepare a generic checklist of safety rules. Finally, ask participants to apply the checklist for analyzing another set of photographs.

Graphic Details

Begin this activity by giving teams of participants a graphical flow chart of different stages in a process. In addition, give each team a close-up diagram of one of these stages that provides additional details. Ask teams to study the overall graphic and the detailed close-up. Later, teams take turns to explain details of what happens during different stages in the correct sequence.

The Internet

The Internet is the major source of information, especially among the younger generation. Google has become the most important e-learning tool, and Wikipedia contains over seven million articles on diverse topics. Several online games and activities help participants to effectively interact with these content sources.

Here are a couple of examples of online activities:

The Four-Door Approach

The training objective for this e-learning activity is to prepare a business proposal for a client. Ask participants to visit the online *library* and read articles about business proposals, review different sample proposals, and learn to use proposal templates. Ask participants to visit the *playground* and play Flash-based games that test and improve their mastery of the principles and procedures they learned from the library. Ask participants to visit the *café* and discuss open-ended questions related to the content of the library. Encourage participants to visit these three different locations (library, playground, and café) any number of times and in any sequence. Finally, ask participants to visit the *assessment center* and take a performance test to demonstrate their ability to write a business proposal for a real-world client.

Outsourcing WebQuest

The WebQuest method was originally created by Bernie Dodge at San Diego State University. Let's present this WebQuest with you playing the role of a participant. On the WebQuest, you are given a task in two parts: research the advantages and disadvantages of *outsourcing* and create a PowerPoint presentation to persuade others to agree with your conclusions. The WebQuest also suggests a procedure for completing the task, along with links to relevant websites. After you complete the task, you evaluate your presentation by using an assessment checklist ("rubric") that identifies key elements and suggests appropriate ratings.

Audio Recordings

In these days of MP3 players and podcasting, audio recordings provide a useful content resource. Audio games require participants to listen to authentic recordings of on-the-job conversations (for example, *handling customer complaints* or *conducting exit interviews*) and learn from them. A different type of audio games uses recorded lectures as the content source.

Here are a couple of examples of audio games:

Audio Analysis

You start this audio game by assigning teams of participants to three or four listening stations where different audio recordings of conversations with irate customers are replayed. After carefully listening to these recordings and taking notes, each team comes up with a checklist of empathic listening behaviors demonstrated by the customer service representative. During the next round, teams are reorganized in such a way that each new team includes one member of each of the different original teams. Members of the new teams discuss the earlier checklist items and develop an improved checklist. During the final round, participants plan for personal application of selected checklist items.

Words into Pictures

In this audio game, participants listen carefully to a recorded lecture. Later, participants work as teams and prepare posters that graphically summarize the key ideas they heard in the lecture. When all posters are completed, teams move from one poster to another and identify different interpretations of same ideas.

Video Recording

Video recordings permit dramatic presentation of the training content. Unfortunately, these recordings sometimes tend to lull participants into a passive mode. A double exposure game (a memorable label coined by my friend Bill Matthews) involves viewing a videotape and working through a structured activity that requires review and application of the content.

Here are a couple of double exposure games:

Surprise Ending

In this double exposure game, participants watch a video documentary about the stages of team development. The video begins with a brief explanation of the four stages of forming, storming, norming, and performing stages in the growth of a work team. The video proceeds through a dramatized documentary of a team engaged in building a sailboat. Participants watch the documentary as the team goes through the three stages of forming, storming, and norming. Pause the video at this stage, even though there is a five-minute segment that deals with the *performing* stage. Participants now work in teams to come up with an outline of the concluding segment of the documentary. The teams take turns presenting their version of the final segment. Play the rest of the video recording and ask participants to discuss the relative merit of their concluding segments and the official one.

Essence

In this double exposure game, forewarn participants to pay careful attention to important points in a video recording. After watching the presentation, ask participants to work in teams and come up with a summary of the key points in exactly sixteen words. Listen to summaries from different teams and select the best one. Continue with teams shrinking the summaries to exactly eight words, borrowing memorable phrases and key points from each other. As before, listen to these shortened summaries and select the best one. During the final round, ask teams to produce four-word summaries (in the form of a slogan or bumper sticker) and present them to the entire group.

Subject–Matter Experts

Some subject-matter experts claim that there are no books or mediated materials that contain information about their specialized topics. In this situation, we fall back on the time-honored lecture method and request the expert to present the relevant content. Lacking from traditional lectures are interaction and two-way communication. A special type of activity called an *interactive lecture* provides basic content through a lecture and then uses a structured activity to encourage participants to interact with the content, with each other, and with the facilitator.

Here are a couple of interactive lectures:

Multilevel Coaching

During the first round of Multilevel Coaching, give a demonstration of the Heimlich maneuver to a small group of participants (for example, *four*). Organize the participants into two teams (*Red* and *Blue*) of two people each. During the second round, instruct members of these teams to individually recruit, demonstrate, and train a new participant. Once a member of the Red team has taught a new participant, she takes the learner to a member of the Blue team for performance assessment. The Blue Team member observes the participant demonstrate the newly learned skill and either awards a passing certificate or provides constructive feedback for remedial learning. When the new participant passes the assessment, she becomes a certified member of the Red team (the team whose member taught her). (At the same time, recruits of the Blue team are assessed by members of the Red team.) Ask teams to repeat the process of recruiting additional participants and training them until all participants master the skill and pass the performance assessment.

Best Answers

During the first round of this interactive lecture, make a short presentation. Divide the participants into groups of five. Give an open-ended question to each group. Ask each participant to independently write an answer to the question. Collect answers from each group and give them to another group. During the second round, ask the groups to work as teams and jointly review different answers and select the best one. During the third round, ask each team to read the best answer. Identify the author of the best answer, and lead a round of applause.

What's the Point?

Here are some main points about different types of review and practice games based on the source of the training content:

- The purpose of training is to enable participants to recall and apply new skills, knowledge, and attitudes.

- In designing training, we should set aside ample time for structured review-and-practice activities.

- Most training content is readily available in different forms such as lectures, text materials, audio recordings, video recording, and pictures.

- We can design activities that require participants to recall, process, and apply the content they learned from different resources.

- Practice opportunities contribute more to effective learning than the presentation of additional content.

- We should hold participants accountable for recall and practice.

- Participants can assess one another's performance and provide useful feedback. This act of assessment works as an excellent learning tool.

Here is another important point that I did not emphasize earlier because I felt that you would have figured it out for yourself:

- Although the review-and-practice activities are organized according to different sources of content, with suitable modifications, you can apply most of these activities with content presented through any source.

Closing Assignment

This article probably presented some new content to you. In the true spirit of practicing what we preach, let's transform you from being a passive reader into an active collaborator. Here's a list of practice-and-review activities for you to complete:

- Summarize the key points of this chapter in exactly sixteen words. Once you have done that, shrink your summary to exactly eight words. Finally create a tag line for this chapter in exactly four words.

- Create a tag line for each one of the ten types of activities. Example: *Textra: They add something extra to your text materials.*

- Organize the ten types of activities into logical categories. Once you have completed this task, begin from scratch and organize them into another set of logical categories.

- Select the two types of review-and-practice activities that you think will be of most use to most corporate trainers.

- Prepare a reference table with the ten types of activities as rows. Select your own headings for the columns.

- Prepare a job aid on how to use one of the ten types of activities with any new content.

- Prepare a set of closed questions, open questions, and true/false questions on the content of this chapter.

- Surf the Internet to track down additional information on the WebQuest.

- Prepare a short audio or video recording that summarizes the key points of this chapter.

Sivasailam "Thiagi" Thiagarajan *is currently the Resident Mad Scientist at The Thiagi Group, an organization that is dedicated to improving human performance effectively and enjoyably. Thiagi's younger co-workers keep him supplied with food, books, and mortgage money and make him design a new training activity each day.*

Linking Learning Strategy to the Balanced Scorecard

Ajay M. Pangarkar and Teresa Kirkwood

Summary

It appears that implementing the Balanced Scorecard (BSC) as the strategic management tool of choice is a trend that is well on its way in many organizations worldwide. Initially introduced in the early 1990s as a tool to help companies translate their corporate mission to all levels organization, the BSC is widely acknowledged to have moved beyond this ideology (Kaplan & Norton, 2006). It is now becoming a strategic change management and performance measurement process.

According to surveys by the Institute of Management Accountants (IMA), more than 50 percent of the large companies in the United States are using some form of Balanced Scorecard. This is reflective of the power and simplicity of the BSC to provide direction for all levels and areas of the organization. The Balanced Scorecard, developed by Robert Kaplan and David Norton (1996), is a management system that gives business people a comprehensive understanding of business operations. After more than fifteen years, it is surprising that there are still many business people unconvinced about the utility and effectiveness of the Balanced Scorecard. And even more surprising is the number of organizations giving up on it through their own misapplication or misuse of the tool.

At its roots, the BSC is designed to give companies the information they need to effectively manage their business strategy. The scorecard is similar to a dashboard in a car. As you drive you can glance at the dashboard to obtain real-time information, such as how much fuel remains, the speed you are traveling, the distance you've traveled, and so forth. The BSC provides similar information to all levels of the organization through performance measures connected to specific business areas. The scorecard communicates to managers in clearly defined terms how well the business is meeting its strategies and goals.

Fundamentally, the BSC is about performance measures. Coincidentally, this is also what our role as learning professionals has become as well (hence, workplace learning and performance). The BSC incorporates traditional financial performance metrics, familiar to financially oriented stakeholders and management of the organization, into a broader report of performance indicators. In the past this financial information would have been sufficient; however, the current reality dictates something more comprehensive.

The appeal of the BSC is its ability to include both traditional financial metrics and non-financial performance measures in its reporting capacity, thus the term "balanced." Therefore, managers can obtain information on a variety of intangible and non-financial metrics—such as customer satisfaction, cost per new hire, percent of jobs that meet schedule, percent of errors in budget predictions—essential to capturing information about the performance of an enterprise.

The BSC Measures

The attractions of the BSC are its simple structure and function and its ability to bring together leading and lagging performance indicators. The BSC is divided into four primary business and strategic areas (as shown in Figure 1) on which an organization must focus in order to receive a complete picture of how the enterprise is performing:

- *Financial Perspective:* The question asked here is, "How do we look to our stakeholders?" The objective of every organization is to deliver maximum value to stakeholders. For profit-oriented companies, these are the shareholders and customers; for non-profit it many be government, taxpayers, or community.

- *Customer Perspective:* The question to ask is, "How do we look to our customers?" All organizations, profit and non-profit, have customers. To survive and grow, an organization must be able to deliver quality goods and/or services providing for overall customer satisfaction.

- *Internal Business Processes:* The question here is, "What must we excel at?" The reason for an organization's existence is what it produces or delivers. Identifying the key business processes at which an organization must excel is essential if it is to meet strategic goals and customer expectations.

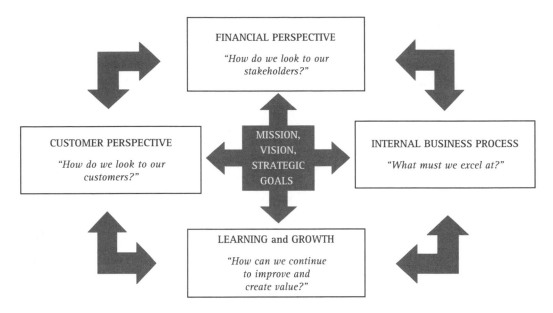

Figure 1. BSC Interdependency Diagram

Adapted from Norton and Kaplan, 1996.

- *Learning and Growth Perspective:* The question to ask is, "How can we continue to improve and create value?" This is the perspective management recognizes as the root of competitive sustainability. This is also where WLP can deliver significant results, connect with strategy, and move past Kirkpatrick's Level 4, business impact, and Phillips' Level 5, return on investment of training.

The current business climate requires managers to have a balance between financial and non-financial measures from which to make decisions and develop effective solutions. Financial measures provide historical results; non-financial measures usually indicate the positive outcomes of a particular decision. This is where our role as learning professionals comes into play. Our efforts are directly correlated to non-financial performance metrics. These metrics support, for example, why developing a specific skill set for a group of employees increases productivity leading to strong growth, helping to build credibility for WLP and our role within the organization. Non-financial measures are essential to helping companies succeed. If used effectively, they can drive an organization—using its performance measurement system—to higher and higher levels of achievement.

Connecting the BSC and WLP

To truly understand the reason for the growing need for the BSC, one must understand the significance of organizational strategy. Most business professionals recognize that strategy is at the center of every business process. Successful business managers have a laser-like focus on it. Although this may be common sense for business people, many are unable to connect their business objectives and the organization's mission, resulting in many companies not meeting their strategic goals. This is not necessarily a result of managerial incompetence, although this may be the case in some instances, but results more from not knowing how to develop or connect short- and mid-term objectives to the proposed strategy.

Go and read the organizational mission statement in the lobby of your company and asked yourself, "How does my role or what I do fit into this objective?" In a simple framework, the BSC helps senior managers translate and effectively communicate performance objectives and measure in tactical terms how their roles contribute to the strategic vision of the organization.

For those responsible for talent management and employee development, strategy has never been at the forefront of their mandate or learning plans. Again, the failure may be more with senior management not effectively communicating the importance of strategic alignment with the "softer side" of the business, such as workplace learning and performance. This was the case in less turbulent economic times. As a result of increasingly hyper-competitive and global markets, management's performance, specifically the C-level suite (CEO, COO, CFO, etc.), is tied directly to executing successful strategic outcomes for their organizations. Expectations are not just from the traditional "shareholders" anymore, who may be satisfied simply with reporting of financial performance, but now include non-traditional "stakeholders," such as customers, suppliers, and employees as well as specific business processes and innovative capability.

So why is this relevant for those responsible for employee development and workplace learning? It is relevant for a few reasons:

First, achieving strategic objectives requires organizational decision-makers to answer the questions "Where do we want to be?" and "What do we want to be?" In both instances this necessitates building on existing organizational knowledge (human capital). In simpler terms, "What you know now brought you here, but will not take you to where you want or need to be." Learning professionals must acquire the strategic skills and understanding to better align employee skills and abilities with strategic objectives.

Second, contrary to what we are told by the "training ROI" movement in recent years, C-level managers are less concerned about financial outcomes of learning investments and more preoccupied about obtaining non-financial performance outcomes (Kaplan & Norton, 1996). In more direct terms, they want to see how T&D delivers results in relation to organizational objectives, rather than just knowing whether the training solution made more money than it cost. Again, this is because financial measures are lagging indicators of performance and, in the end, if training costs exceeded its benefits, then it is too late to do anything about it. The results have "already happened," and, when you are concerned about what is going to happen tomorrow, you don't really want to know what occurred yesterday. Time and again many C-level directors indicate to us the importance of having some type of forward-looking indicators, because they already possess sufficient financial data.

Although anecdotal, the same decision-makers also indicated that "We [T&D] are not good at applying financial measures." They are unconvinced about the objectivity of training ROI measurement results. As learning consultants, we are told to do what we are good at—helping management obtain and connect to leading, non-financial performance indicators, something they desperately require. This may sound repetitive, but corporate leaders are concerned about strategic outcomes and the BSC effectively facilitates this process.

Third, for many years, companies preached that their employees are their greatest asset, but only in recent times have senior managers truly recognized this truth. Not to slight business leaders of the past, but it is evident from the authors' discussions with many organizational leaders that the marketplace leaders are the same ones investing a significant percentage of their payroll in learning solutions, connecting employee development to strategic objectives, and effectively leveraging employee knowledge to innovate in a variety of ways. C-level managers realize that true competitive advantage comes not through physical assets or products but through their people. Everything else is simply the result or benefit of employee skill development and creativity. One concern some clients voice is that their employees may leave after the organization has invested in training. We respond by asking: "What if you don't train them and they stay?"

An Opportunity to Sit at the Table: Connecting Learning to Strategy

Astrologers would say the planets are lined up for the professional learning sector. Externally, economic and market factors call for organizations to adapt instantaneously, and technological evolution is accepted now as a constant. Internally, organizations need to change and evolve quickly, resulting in the need to build employee knowledge, competencies, and skills for the future. The common thread in all of these factors is the need for continuous learning leading to improved performance. Add to the mix management's need to reconcile and integrate all of these issues to achieve their strategy (the Balanced Scorecard), and that places workplace learning performance at the top of many CEOs' priority lists.

Accountability does not solely rest with senior management when it comes to incorporating workplace learning in organizational strategy. Senior managers may shoulder the responsibility to include it in their strategy development discussions (the coveted seat at the table), but learning professionals must also be held accountable as well. Until recently, those responsible for employee development did not see the relevance of connecting to organizational objectives. This is highly evident with the types of performance measures used in the past, such as number of employees trained or testing scores. Add the learning profession's disdain for business and you quickly have a learning environment very much disconnected from corporate and market reality.

Take a look back at Figure 1 (the BSC Interdependency Diagram). You will notice two important items. The first is that the BSC accounts for "learning and growth." Not impressed? You should be. Never before has any business trend elevated the importance of "learning" in the discussion about, let alone the development of, strategy. The second noticeable item is that it sits at the bottom of the diagram. Many business people state that the positioning clearly minimizes the importance of this perspective. Kaplan and Norton rebut this notion, stating that, "It's at the bottom because it acts as the foundation for everything else above it" (Niven, 2006, p. 125). Dr. Kaplan once described the employee learning and growth perspective

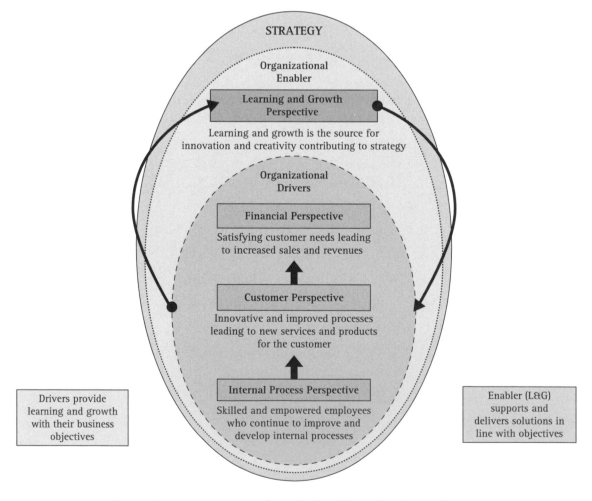

Figure 2. Learning and Growth Enabling Strategic Drivers

"as the roots of a powerful tree, which are the sources of support and nourishment leading to the blossoms of financial returns" (Niven, 2006, p. 125).

Figure 2 illustrates more literally the relevance and importance or learning as described by the creators of the BSC.

Making the Connections: Linking Learning to the BSC

Like a well-oiled machine, every organization functions best when the sum of its parts (departments and divisions) work toward a common goal. The driving perspectives of the BSC (financial, internal processes, and customer) work interdependently through very tangible objectives, targets, measure, and initiatives. But how does learning tangibly connect with the other business areas through the BSC? A simple example demonstrates the process more clearly.

Let's say company ABC's primary strategic objective is to increase revenue in the next three years (see Figure 3). To increase revenue, the company will have to increase production and sales by introducing and producing new products and repositioning current products. In this case, the financial perspective is the primary driver of strategy for the other three perspectives. We can derive the customer perspective by looking to increase customer loyalty and develop customer relationships, enticing repeat purchases. This in turn requires internal processes to support new product development through R&D, ramp up production for the increasing sales, ensure adequate inventory, and ensure purchasing processes are functioning properly. These three perspectives are the drivers for the strategy. The role for learning and growth is to enable and support the needs of the first three perspectives—similar to how internal processes support sales. By partnering with the other business areas, workplace learning is better positioned to understand their needs. For company ABC, workplace learning would collaborate with the sales and marketing department to train and coach the sales staff, work closely with customer relations through a customer service and new product training program, and even look at developing production efficiency and new equipment training courses for manufacturing. Wrapped around all of the perspectives would be specific objectives (the expected results), targets (tangible metrics), measures (the reports to obtain the metrics), and initiatives (what you will actually do). WLP solutions are the vehicle to help other business units achieve these critical metrics.

So how do you begin? The following steps will help you to contribute to these critical business areas, become more strategic in your learning solutions, and be more tactical in your approach with your customers in the organization.

The first step is to clearly understand your organization's corporate strategy. Analyze the mission and vision statements as they provide succinct insight into senior management's objectives. When done well, these statements outline the

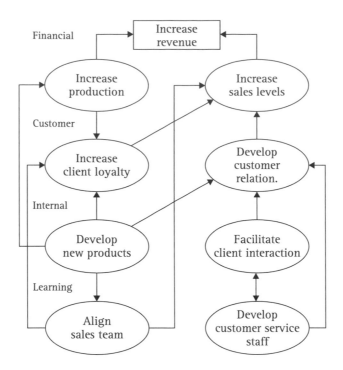

Figure 3. Company ABC: Mapping Learning to Strategy Example

critical areas requiring the support of an enabling perspective. If you are a public company, review the annual reports to gain further insight into management's message and an appreciation of stakeholder expectations.

Next, find a copy of the corporate Balanced Scorecard. If one is being developed, become involved. The BSC will provide you with the "tactical" information of what is expected from each of the business units under each perspective. Review the BSC and learn about the relationships among the driving perspectives. If you are fortunate, your organization will have cascaded the scorecard through each business unit. This will allow you to work closely with every level of the organization to develop more targeted learning solutions.

Conduct interviews with management and stakeholders. Meet with the C-level decision-makers in your organization. Determine their expectations from workplace learning and performance and the role that it will play in the strategy. They will provide significant amounts of information, a clear direction for the organization as a whole, and how the strategy flows through the organization. Meet with business unit stakeholders and process-critical staff. Building partnerships with these groups helps to create synergy between their knowledge of what they require and your learning expertise to develop effective and targeted solutions.

Determine the measures and metrics for the objectives set forth by the BSC for each perspective. When working with other business units within the BSC, be aware of the objectives and metrics they're expected to meet.

Develop a BSC for learning and performance. Traditionally, training and development is viewed as a functional, supportive unit. In the evolved strategic context, learning and performance must become operational and interactive with the other units. This means that, as a strategic business unit, WLP should develop its own scorecard. This is not solely about training ROI. When developing a WLP scorecard, your performance measures should be forward-looking and make a strategic contribution.

Conclusion

The role of learning in the workplace is increasingly critical and demanding. It is more than measuring business impact. It is also more than simply measuring return on investment of training. It is about connecting to strategy. More than ever before, the sole competitive advantage for every organization is ensuring that employees not only understand strategic objectives but are able to attain them. This is where WLP must take on a strategic capacity. This is the driving message of the Balanced Scorecard and senior management's new paradigm. Your role is to value workplace learning and performance in this context, rather than simply the traditional functional role. There are many ways to measure the impact any learning initiative has on an organization. Begin with the strategic objectives of the organization and work back, linking learning objectives with immediate business objectives as stated by the BSC. By doing this, you will easily determine the relevant performance measures and metrics and satisfy senior management's concerns about such elements as operational performance and efficiency, compliance issues, organizational effectiveness, and workforce capacity and proficiency, as well as more intangible dimensions such as motivation, innovation, and adaptability.

It's time to start thinking "outside of the course" and inside the BSC to develop learning solutions that directly connect with the business concerns and strategic objectives or the organization.

References

Kaplan, R.S., & Norton, D.P. (1996). *The balanced scorecard: Translating strategy into action.* Boston, MA: Harvard Business School Press.

Kaplan, R.S., & Norton, D.P. (2006). *Alignment: Using the balanced scorecard to create corporate synergies.* Boston, MA: Harvard Business School Press.

Niven, P. (2006). *Balanced scorecard step-by-step.* Hoboken, NJ: John Wiley & Sons.

Ajay Pangarkar, CTDP, *and* **Teresa Kirkwood, CTDP,** *are partners at CentralKnowledge.com. At CentralKnowledge, they align learning strategy and performance with business and strategic objectives. They are the authors of* The Trainer's Balanced Scorecard *(in press, Pfeiffer) and* Building Business Acumen for Trainers *(Pfeiffer).*

How Leaders Think: Developing Effective Leadership

Homer Johnson

Summary

Effective leaders are effective not because they have more knowledge, experience, or training, per se, but rather because of how they think. That is, effective leaders have more valid and inclusive mental models that allow them to successfully handle the complex issues they face. Therefore, the strategy (as described in this article) for developing leaders should put less emphasis on informational input, and should focus more on experiences that challenge existing mental models and that force the leader to acquire new, and more valid, mental models.

How Do Leaders Learn to Lead?

If one looks at the leadership development activities in most organizations, it appears that the assumption is that leaders learn to lead via informational input. That is, the primary strategy for developing leaders is via company training programs, workshops, conferences, and university programs. In a sense, this is the "knowledge creates leaders" strategy for developing leaders. However, when successful leaders are asked to identify their most significant leadership learning experiences, these informational inputs are rarely mentioned.

The major premise put forward here is that effective leaders are not effective because they have more information or knowledge, nor is it because they have more experience. Rather effective leaders are effective because they have more valid and inclusive mental models that allow them to successfully handle the difficult and complex issues of leadership.

Thus, the key task of leadership development is the acquisition of effective mental models or meaning structures, that is, ways of thinking and structuring the myriad and often complex and novel issues leaders face. Further, the strategy for developing effective mental models is through transformative learning, not informational learning. More specifically, mental models are best transformed through context-specific experiences that challenge the adequacy of one's current mental models, and additionally force the leader to create models that are more successful in both understanding and acting on the issues being faced.

To illustrate this point, consider the case of Peter.

The Case of Peter

In his introduction to transformative learning and adult development, Kegan (2000) describes the case of Peter, the forty-two-year-old president of SafeSleep Products, a newly formed division of Best Rest, Incorporated, a major bedding manufacturer. As Kegan tells the story (which is altered somewhat here), Peter joined Best Rest immediately on graduation from college. As a bright and dedicated employee, he caught the eye of his then plant manager, Anderson Wade, who was impressed with Peter and became his mentor. As Anderson moved up the ranks, Peter was close behind and demonstrated effectiveness at each step. Along the way, Peter completed his MBA at the company expense and participated in several company leadership training programs.

When Anderson became a corporate vice president, Peter was put in charge of a product line. And when a decision was made to make this product line a division of Best Rest, Anderson very proudly and excitedly offered Peter the position as president of the new division called SafeSleep, a manufacturer of fire-retardant products for the bedroom. As Anderson put it, this was Peter's golden opportunity to lead.

Division presidents have considerably more responsibility and autonomy than do product managers. Division presidents have profit and loss responsibility, as well as responsibility for division strategy, annual plans, budgets, the allocation of resources, hiring and firing, and a myriad of other duties. Where Peter previously could turn to his close friend and mentor Anderson for advice and direction, he was now on his own. When Peter was head of the product line, Anderson made the tough decisions and took the credit or blame for the outcomes. Now it was on Peter's shoulders. He must submit his plans and budgets to Anderson, receive the same treatment any division president would receive, and take the blame or credit for the division's performance.

Peter has (very accurately) perceived that his relationship with Anderson has changed substantially, and he feels very uncomfortable as a result. Their once close relationship seems to have turned into something more distant. In the past Peter frequently turned to Anderson for advice and direction and spent a lot of time in Anderson's office. However, when he attempted to do the same as president of SafeSleep, Anderson was not forthcoming with advice and counsel. He would tell Peter that as the president of a division Peter had to stand on his own two feet. More recently, Peter has limited his contact with Anderson because he thinks the meetings between the two are unproductive. Peter has observed that most of the time when he asks Anderson a question, Anderson throws the ball back in his court and replies that Peter should figure it out. Consequently, Peter usually leaves these meetings feeling very frustrated.

In addition to handling many big and little business problems that are wearing him down, Peter is also having difficulty dealing with more personal issues. His best friend of ten years is Ted, one of the best salespeople at Best Rest. Ted's specialty is selling mattresses to furniture stores and to the furniture departments in a couple of the large department stores. His contacts in those areas are extensive. When SafeSleep was a product line, Ted also picked up some limited sales of those products from his furniture store contacts.

However, a major reason for making SafeSleep a separate division was to move the product beyond the limits of furniture stores. Anderson thought that there may be huge untapped market for flame-retardant products, such as bed pads, bed clothes, sheets and drapes, and so forth, in stores that handle bed linens, baby clothes, and other products. In order to exploit these market opportunities, Peter's first hire at SafeSleep was a sales manager, Harold, whose sales experience was with soft goods, not mattresses. Harold turned out to be a take-charge guy, full of energy and ideas, and he has produced great sales numbers for SafeSleep.

Harold recently submitted a sales strategy for the division, which argued that if SafeSleep was to meet its potential, it had to develop its own identity and vision, focus on its own market segments, and develop its own sales force independent of Best Rest. In fact, Harold thought that Best Rest's sales force, with their narrow view of the market, was a serious barrier to SafeSleep's growth and recommended severing the relationship at once. Peter thought Harold's logic and ideas were pretty solid. But once Ted heard about the plan, he became very angry and accused Harold of trying to cut him out of his profits (he didn't make his bonus this year and blames Harold for stealing some of his sales). In conversation with Peter, Ted has repeatedly referred to his close friendship with Peter and asks why Peter lets Harold, a relative stranger, take bread off his (Ted's) table. Peter is starting to feel guilty over what is happening to Ted and wonders whether his position as president is going to cost him the loss of his closest friend.

While Kegan only gives us a snippet of Peter's life at SafeSleep (which additionally has been edited here), it is obvious that Peter has been going through some sleepless nights, even on his Best Rest mattress. Here is a bright, hard-working manager who has moved up steadily in the organization. However, the initial excitement of a presidency, the "golden opportunity to lead," as Anderson put it, has turned out more like a bad dream. He is confused by his changed relationship with Anderson, and doesn't know how to handle his friendship with Ted. Harold's plan has some strong points as well as some questionable points (flame-retardant pajamas for people who like to smoke in bed?). Moreover, Harold is really pressing him to implement the plan immediately and is getting frustrated with Peter's lack of action. Peter doesn't know what to do. Should he let Harold run with the plan as is? But what about Ted? When Peter asked for Anderson's opinion on the plan, he just shrugged. Maybe Anderson doesn't think it is a good plan? At this point, Peter is struggling with indecision and is not functioning very well as a president.

How Doctors and Leaders Think

In order to better understand Peter's dilemma, and perhaps determine what he should do about it, we have to first understand how leaders think.

In his recent book, *How Doctors Think*, Gropman (2007) provided some insight into the thinking process used by medical doctors. As Gropman points out, medical doctors typically make a diagnosis on a new patient within twenty or thirty seconds. This usually occurs without any conscious analysis, and the doctor would probably be hard-pressed to tell anyone what occurred in her or his mind while making that decision. It certainly is not the lengthy, rational, and linear process that we are so fond of teaching. Rather, the decision making is instantaneous, quickly integrating complex information in a search for patterns. Moreover, the diagnosis is usually accurate, although (as Gropman illustrates) some of these thinking short-cuts can be the cause of medical errors.

The reason medical doctors respond so quickly in making a diagnosis is that they think via their mental models. They look for patterns. Not just any pattern, but patterns that *fit their mental models*. This point is critical—the environment does not impose a structure on the doctor's thinking; rather, the doctor's mental models impose a structure on the environment. It is the mental model that makes "sense" out of the patient's symptoms. Moreover, it is assumed that the extent to which the doctors have developed valid and useful models is indicative of the extent to which their diagnosis (and treatment) is accurate.

The way business leaders think is no different than how doctors think. The thinking process and structure are the same, but the content and context are different. Effective leaders acquire mental models that they impose on the enormous amount of information with which they are continually faced and that allow them to make sense out of the inputs. Peter hasn't acquired these models to impose on his inputs. He is loaded with information, but he can't make a decision because he doesn't have the mental models that would "tell" him how to make the decision or what decision to make. Had he acquired the models appropriate to his position, he would have quickly sorted out what would work in Harold's plan and what would not work and then acted on it! He also would have (diplomatically) explained to Ted that business is business, and friendship is friendship, and sometimes they don't fit the way we would like.

Informational and Transformative Learning

Before going into Peter's problem, we also have to understand the difference between informational learning and transformative learning. Informational learning is the more common type of learning. We are constantly exposed to information from a variety of sources, whether it is newspapers, books, workshops, television, or colleagues. Much of this information is very valuable and helps us become more effective in life and work.

This information is given meaning only in the context of relatively stable mental models or meaning structures. These mental models enable us to make sense out of the information we receive. For example, consider the medical doctor who questions a patient. The information provided by the patient has meaning in context with the doctor's diagnostic mental models. The doctor is able to make a reasonable diagnosis and prescribe treatment because of the mental models he or she developed during both medical training and medical practice. These same mental models also enable the doctor to become a better doctor. As the doctor becomes aware of new medical information through conferences, medical journals, and colleagues, the mental models allow him or her to interpret and understand and then perhaps use the information. Without any such models, the new information would have no meaning.

In defining informational learning, Kegan notes that "Learning aimed at increasing our fund of knowledge, increasing our repertoire of skills, or extending already established cognitive capabilities into new terrain serves the absolutely critical purpose of deepening the resources available to the existing frame of reference" (2000, pp. 48–49). The medical doctor cited above may learn about a new diagnostic procedure, or learn of a new medication, and use them. This new information, in Kegan's terms, deepens the resources available to the existing frame of reference and increases the doctor's effectiveness. However, the information probably would not significantly change the doctor's way of deciding diagnosis and treatment. That is, the information would add resources to the existing mental models, but not radically change them.

While *informational learning* is incorporated into one's meaning structure, *transformative learning*, on the other hand, is learning that changes one's mental models or meaning structures. In his initial discussion of transformative learning, Mezirow (1978) described the case of a woman who found her beliefs in the traditional role of women challenged when she returned to school and came into contact with other women who did not hold these beliefs. The mental models that had served her well over many years now were being questioned. Over time her mental models changed, which, in turn, triggered a different interpretation of incoming information as well as a change in her behavior.

In Kegan's (2000) terms, informational learning is literally in-form-ative because it brings valuable new content into the current forms of meaning. Transformative learning is truly trans-form-ative in that it changes the forms by which we derive meaning.

It is not surprising that our meaning structures are stable. With frequent and dramatic changes to our mental models, we would have difficulty making sense out of the world. Mental models make the world very predictable, at least in our eyes (although another person may see a different order in the world than we do). However, they do change, sometimes intentionally and sometimes incidentally. They usually change fairly slowly, although occasionally there are some dramatic examples of rapid change in meaning structures, for example, as in religious conversion.

Understanding Peter's Problem

What does this all have to do with Peter? Quite a bit, actually. He is receiving plenty of informational input about his situation from Anderson, who has told him that he has to stand on this own feet and make the tough decisions a president has to make. In fact, Anderson appears to be getting a bit frustrated with Peter. How many times does he have to repeat the message? But Peter "just doesn't get it," because Peter's dilemma has more to do with his mental models, not with the information he is receiving.

Most probably Peter could explain Anderson's motives in this situation, at least at an intellectual level. He probably would tell you that Anderson wants him to stand on his own as any effective division president should; to learn to make his own (sometimes tough) decisions; and to learn to live with them. However, at another level, Peter is not able to understand his relationship with Anderson and finds Anderson's behavior very confusing. And Peter may well be able to explain the issue with Ted, again at an intellectual level, that they really are involved in two separate relationships, one business and one social. However, neither Peter nor Ted is able to make the separation or even see the need for a separation.

The point is that additional information will not help Peter. We could explain to Peter what Anderson is trying to do, or what Peter needs to do, or alternatively we could send Peter to a workshop on "managing your boss," or "taking control of your life and work," or "learning how to lead." Or we could ask him to read several of the more than two hundred books that are published each month on leadership, rendering advice from such diverse sources as Jesus, Attila the Hun, Jack Welch, and Dilbert. However, it probably would not do any good.

Peter's problem is not with the information he is receiving, it is what he is doing with it. If Peter is going to move on and truly lead his division, his mental models are going to have to change. He is bright and knowledgeable. However, the models he is using to make sense of the world are not valid for his leadership position. Peter needs to change his mental models. And that is the role of transformative learning.

How Transformative Learning Transforms

Perspective transformation, as defined by Mezirow (1991), "is the process of becoming critically aware of how and why our assumptions have come to constrain the way we perceive, understand, and feel about our world, changing these structures of habitual expectation to make possible a more inclusive, discriminating, and integrating perspective, and, finally, making choices or otherwise acting upon these new understandings" (p. 167). The outcome of transformative learning is a more valid view of the world, to better cope with one's experience, to become more self-sufficient, to gain greater control over one's life, and to be less dependent on the views of others in directing one's behavior.

Mezirow (2000) has outlined a ten-step process by which meaning structures typically change. The process begins with a disorienting event, followed by an examination of feelings, then a critical assessment of one's assumptions, and continues through a trying of new roles and ending with a reintegration into one's life based on the new meaning. All ten steps will not be detailed here. However, two of the steps, a *disorienting event* and a *critical reflection*, have received the bulk of the attention in the transformative process, and will be covered in more detail here.

In the initial formulation of transformative learning, a disorienting event was seen as a necessary condition for this type of learning to occur. In the example cited above, the woman with a traditional view of the role of women found her beliefs challenged by other women in the class. Disorienting events of this type put one's mental models in question and, in turn, trigger a reexamination of the structures. Given the absence of a disorienting event, for example, had the woman not returned to school, her mental models would not have been questioned and would have stayed the same.

A second important component in transformative learning is critical reflection, defined as the process by which an individual critically examines his or her beliefs or values or attitudes. This often follows a disorienting event. For example, consider the above example of the woman with traditional values who returned to school and found herself in a class with women who didn't hold these values. This experience triggered a reexamination of not only her values, but perhaps more importantly, why she held these values. What emerged from this apparently somewhat painful examination were new mental models that not only redefined her role in her household but also reformulated her views of the role of women in society.

Certainly, one option for this woman would have been to refuse to reexamine her original beliefs and values and become more solidified in those values, perhaps by dismissing the credibility of her classmates and by seeking confirmation of the validity of her values from like-minded friends. Or perhaps she could have critically examined her current beliefs and concluded that they were valid for her. Given either scenario, her mental models would have remained intact. Certainly this would have been a more likely occurrence. People don't change their mental models each time their beliefs are challenged. What is evident from the description of the case, however, is that the woman was willing to engage in dialogue regarding her beliefs and to critically reflect on the underlying basis of her thinking.

How Do Leaders Learn to Lead?

Our discussion on the role of mental models and transformative learning has important implications for the development of effective leaders. For example, in a study conducted at the Center for Creative Leadership (Lindsey, Holmes, & McCall, 1987; McCall, Lombardo, & Morrison, 1998), successful executives were asked to list their most significant learning experiences. The two highest-ranking categories of learning experiences were "hardships" and "challenging experiences." Examples of "hardships" included business failures, failure to obtain an expected promotion, and being fired. Interestingly enough, also included in this category were personal traumas such as divorce and a death in the family. The other high-ranking category, "challenging experiences," consisted of experiences such as building an operation from scratch, managing a turnaround operation, being part of a task force, and being given increased responsibility in terms of people or functions.

Both "hardships" and "challenges" would seem to be prime examples of disorienting events that would call into question a person's mental models, albeit in somewhat different ways. The key would be how one handles that experience. Given that these experiences lead the person to critically reflect on his or her mental models, one might expect a new model to emerge that would more effectively handle the current challenge and position the person to better handle future challenges. It is through this process that "hardships" and "challenging experiences" become the significant learning experiences for managers.

Based on the above data, one could assume that there may be several variations of the critical reflection process. For example, consider a person who has been fired from his or her job (a "hardship," as listed above). One would suspect that a typical response might be shock followed by anger followed by "blaming." But someplace in the process the person might get around to reflecting on what behaviors led to the firing and what one might do differently in the future. In contrast, being given responsibility for a turnaround project (a "challenge") probably would force one not to look so much at past behavior but rather to search for (new) mental models to help handle this new and complex experience. When managers talk of trying to "get their arms around" a difficult project, they are really talking about searching for more inclusive and valid mental models that will enable them to effectively deal with the complexities of a project, which is something beyond the scope of their current structures.

Another interesting finding of this study was the low rank that executives gave to those types of experiences that were specifically designed to assist people become better leaders through informational learning, such as conferences, workshops, in-house training programs, and graduate degree programs. Given the ubiquity and volume of these educational activities, it seems important to ask the question: When in the leadership development process would these activities would have the greatest impact on development?

It may well be that educational activities are important in mapping out the mental landscape and in developing the appropriate terminology and concepts to operate in that landscape. In this sense, informational activities may be "formative" as well as "informative," in that they help form the mental models that will allow a person to operate in, say, a business organization. This may be critical early in one's career, but be of limited value for the more experienced manager.

Other studies on the development of leaders support the above results. For example, Ready (1994) asked leaders to identify their top learning experiences. Job assignments, projects, and task forces ranked number one. These experiences look very similar to the "challenging experiences" reported earlier. The category that ranked second was "coaching and performance feedback," which could also challenge a leader's ways of operating, as well as encourage a critical reflection of one's meaning structure. Traditional management education programs did not score very high on the list of important learning experiences. For example, university executive education programs ranked very low as important learning experiences, and in-company programs were reported to have little usefulness except in developing an understanding of the company's strategic vision.

Ready concluded that "to develop leadership capacity, one must be presented with challenging opportunity and must be ready and capable of acting on it. The lessons gained from this opportunity will be leveraged considerably when the individual is offered honest, thoughtful, and timely feedback on his or her performance. In addition to opportunity and feedback, the person must have the time and capacity to reflect on this feedback, to internalize it, and to transfer the lessons learned to day-to-day behaviors" (1994, p. 27). This recommendation sounds very similar to the steps in the transformative learning process: challenging opportunity (or disorienting event), honest feedback, critical reflection, and trying out new approaches and behaviors.

An interesting variation on determining the important learning experiences of leaders appeared in two studies reported in Gilber, Carter, and Goldsmith (2000). In one study leaders were asked what formal leadership development programs were influential in their development as leaders. In the second study, those individuals who were in charge of developing leaders were asked which formal leadership development programs they thought were most successful in developing leaders in their organizations. The results were similar in both studies. The activity that clearly ranked highest was action learning, which typically consists of a group of managers working as a task force on a change project that is of considerable value to the organization. This, again, sounds very much like the "challenging experiences" of the studies cited above. The formal activity that ranked second was the 360-degree review, which fits well with the "coaching and performance feedback" category that ranked second in the Ready study. And, as with the other studies cited above, the traditional information-based methods, such as university courses, ranked quite low.

Finally, in a study that looked at why executives derail, Leslie and Velsor (1996) found that the leading cause of executive derailment was the failure to adapt and change one's management style. Conversely, these researchers found that the number one factor for successful executives was the ability to adapt and develop. Respondents talked of successful leaders "growing" and "maturing over time" as the job or the organization expanded. Successful leaders were also characterized as "learning from mistakes" and "learning from direct feedback," in contrast to unsuccessful leaders who seemed unable to learn and adapt (p. 7). These results fit nicely within the context of transformative theory. The old mental models, which probably served the unsuccessful leaders well in the past, were inadequate to effectively handle the new situation, and the failure to transform these structures seems to be a critical cause of their derailment. This seems to nicely describe Peter's problem.

Developing Strategies to Develop Leaders

The evidence cited above, both on mental models and on leadership development, suggests that the focus for developing effective leaders should be on developing valid and inclusive mental models that allow the leader to effectively handle the increasing complexity of the leadership position. Furthermore, the key to developing these mental models is through transformative learning.

Broadly speaking, mental models change (and leadership develops) through a continuous process of facing new and challenging experiences involving increased responsibility, through receiving feedback on both performance and style, and critically reflecting on one's behavior and the assumptions underlying it. While input is valuable, the critical process in successful leadership is the transformation of one's mental models or meaning structures (Johnson, in press).

To implement such a process, several steps seem critical:

First, there has to be the provision of challenging opportunities of increased scope and responsibility, opportunities that challenge current meaning structures. These challenges should be real on-the-job experiences with important consequences, in contrast to simulated activities that are unrelated to the job (such as outdoor experience programs) that are of questionable value. These on-the-job challenges may be in the form of task forces, job rotation, jobs with increased responsibility, global assignments, action learning projects, and the like.

Second, to maximize development, the leader must face challenging experiences early in his or her career, and these should continue throughout his or her career. Unfortunately, this seems to rarely occur. For example, the most common leadership career pattern identified by Kotter (1990) is that one's career path is a succession of jobs that are narrow in scope, tactical in focus, and within the same functional area. However, at some point in the career progression, the leader is moved into a position that entails broader cross-functional and strategic responsibility. Unfortunately, it may be too late at this point to become an effective leader. On the other hand, Kotter found that the successful leaders that he studied benefited from a variety of on-the-job challenges early, and throughout, their careers.

From the perspective of transformative theory, the common managerial career pattern that Kotter describes provides very limited opportunity for a person to grow, to mature, to develop, and to adapt. Under these conditions, the manager's meaning structures become almost "fossilized." One simply can't grow by doing the same things year after year. While these structures may be well suited for the very limited managerial role for which they were developed, they become more difficult to change as time goes on. The consequence is a "failure to adapt," which Leslie and Velsor (1996) found was the leading cause of executive failure and derailment.

Third, the provision of honest and constructive feedback on one's individual performance, or one's unit performance, is critical. Very often no feedback is given. For example, during or after a project is completed, there may be no evaluation as to the outcome of the project, nor of the process leading to the outcome. Even if some evaluation is available, most people find feedback difficult to give and even more difficult to receive. Often what is given is limited, "softened," and sugar-coated. As a consequence, honest and constructive feedback is rarely offered, is rarely asked for, and, even if asked for, is rarely given. The lack of feedback, or the lack of valid feedback, negates one of the most valuable parts of the learning experience.

Fourth, leaders and prospective leaders must learn to use critical reflection techniques. Providing challenging opportunities and feedback is not enough. Transformative learning is a cycle consisting of new and challenging experiences, valid feedback, critical reflection and examination, and the trying of new approaches. Then the cycle is repeated again and again.

Several approaches to the critical reflection process have been proposed. Some of the better known are those of Meizrow (1990) and Fisher, Rooke, and Tobert (2000) and that of action learning developed by Revans (1980).

Fifth, some sort of guidance would seem to be critical for the growth of leaders, particularly early in their careers. Discussions of transformative learning have tended to focus on how one can develop more effective, or more valid, meaning structures by using self-reflection. However, there is little discussion of when self-reflection fails to produce more effective mental models. Or for that matter, are there occasions in which self-reflection produces a meaning structure that is less valid or less able to handle the situation at hand? We know that there is a narrowing of focus and perspective under stressful conditions. One might conclude that facing highly challenging and stressful situations may not be the most opportune time for realizing the benefits of self-reflection.

The purpose of the guidance would be to assist the leader in moving in a productive direction. One mode of guidance might be through others—through coaching, mentoring, or group discussion (such as in action learning groups)—or similar activities in which the leaders can discuss and examine their perceptions of the situation they are facing and the action alternatives (Johnson, 2008).

Note the guidance needed here is not to tell the leader what to do, but rather to ask the tough questions about the leader's perception and behavior in the situation. Looking back on the case of Peter, Anderson was always there to tell Peter what to do as he moved up the ladder, and consequently Peter never developed the meaning structures to make the important decisions on his own. It would have been much more constructive if Anderson had asked of Peter the tough questions that Peter needed to ask, and let Peter struggle with the answers, as well as face the consequences (positive or negative) of his actions.

Moreover, this guidance might fit within the framework of a model that has demonstrated effectiveness. For example, Charan, Drotter, and Noel (2001) have provided a model of the transitions leaders must make as they move up the career ladder, as well as the requirements for effective leadership at each stage. For example, the move from being an individual performer to a manager of people seems one of the more difficult transitions for many leaders. However, these authors provide considerable data on the transition issues the new manager faces, as well as what types of behaviors are characteristic of the more successful new managers. Models such as these provide valuable frameworks for both leaders and coaches and mentors, and they can be used to structure both the discussions and self-reflection.

Finally, to be most effective, the transformative learning process should occur in real time. To reflect on, or discuss, an experience a year later at an annual performance review misses the opportunity for the maximum learning effect. While reflecting on an event some time after an event has occurred can be very helpful, a delayed reflection misses the richness and the immediacy of real-time learning. Most good leadership learning experiences (for example, a challenging project) consist of a series of mini-events, each of which requires an important decision. Reflection or guidance at each of these mini-events is probably the most effective way to constructively change meaning structures. Moreover, reflecting on decisions in real time should have the added advantage of producing more successful projects.

So, What About Peter?

We started this article with a discussion of Peter, the new president of a new division of Best Rest, who is failing as a leader. In fact, Peter seems immobilized and unable to do much of anything. He seemed to be doing well as he followed Anderson up the corporate ladder. So what happened to this promising executive?

To begin with, while Anderson has been a good friend and mentor to Peter, he also has been a major source of Peter's failure to develop as a leader. Peter's role in the organization, regardless of his title, was more of an administrative assistant to Anderson. Anderson gave him an assignment, told him what to do and how to do it, was there to help Peter over the bumps, and took credit or blame for the outcomes. Not a good way to develop leaders.

As suggested in the process outlined above, Anderson should have let Peter "stand on his own feet" from the beginning assignment. He should have given Peter the responsibility and authority to carry out the assignment, and let Peter struggle to figure out how to do it. Peter had it too easy. He never had to think. He never had to face the challenging experiences and hardships that McCall, Lombardo, and Morrison (1998) found so important in developing leaders. And he never had to reflect on his experiences because he had little of significance on which to reflect.

As a consequence, Peter never developed the mental models that would allow him to meet the challenges he is facing as a division president. Peter seems to be a classic case of what Kotter (1990) spoke of when he talked of people being stuck in narrow, functional roles for most of their careers, and then suddenly being called on at age forty-five or so to become a leader or executive, only to find themselves "in over their heads."

So, what's to become of Peter? Can his career be salvaged? It is doubtful whether Peter is going to make a miraculous recovery in his current position, but all is not lost. Certainly some leaders from the McCall study said that their most important leadership learning experience was "failing at an assignment" or even "getting fired." The question is whether Peter can learn from this experience, not in the sense of acquiring information or knowledge, but rather in the sense of acquiring more effective mental models. The point being made in this article is that the critical determinant of effective leaders is not what they know, but how they think.

References

Charan, R., Drotter, W., & Noel, J. (2001). *The leadership pipeline.* San Francisco, CA: Jossey-Bass.

Fisher, D., Rooke, D., & Tobert, W. (2000). *Personal and organizational transformations through action inquiry.* Boston, MA: Edge/Work Press.

Gilber, D., Carter, L., & Goldsmith, M. (2000). *Best practices in leadership development handbook.* San Francisco, CA: Jossey-Bass.

Gropman, J. (2007). *How doctors think.* Boston, MA: Houghton Mifflin.

Johnson, H.H. (2008). Helping leaders learn to lead. In E. Biech (Ed.), *The 2008 Pfeiffer annual: Training.* San Francisco, CA: Pfeiffer.

Johnson, H.H. (in press). Mental models and transformative learning: The key to leadership development? *Human Resource Development Quarterly.*

Kegan, R. (2000). What "form" transforms: A constructive-developmental approach to transformative learning. In J. Mezirow, *Learning as transformation* (pp. 35–70). San Francisco, CA: Jossey-Bass.

Kotter, J. (1990). *A force for change: How leadership differs from management.* New York: The Free Press.

Leslie, J., & Velsor, E. (1996). *A look at derailment today: North America and Europe.* Greensboro, NC: Center for Creative Leadership.

Lindsey, E.H., Holmes, V., & McCall, H.M., Jr. (1987). *Key events in executive lives.* Greensboro, NC: Center for Creative Leadership.

McCall, M.W., Jr., Lombardo, M.M., & Morrison, A.N. (1998). *Lessons from experience.* Lexington, MA: Lexington Books.

Mezirow, J. (1978). *Education for perspective transformation: Women's re-entry programs in community colleges.* New York: Teachers College at Columbia University.

Mezirow, J. (1991). *Transformative dimensions of adult learning.* San Francisco, CA: Jossey-Bass.

Mezirow, J. (2000). Learning to think like an adult: Core concepts of transformation theory. In J. Mezirow, *Learning as transformation* (pp. 3–34). San Francisco, CA: Jossey-Bass.

Mezirow, J., & Associates (Eds.), (1990). *Fostering critical reflection in adulthood.* San Francisco, CA: Jossey-Bass.

Ready, D. (1994). *Champions of change.* Lexington, MA: International Consortium for Executive Development Research.

Revans, R.W. (1980). *Action learning.* London: Bland and Briggs.

Homer H. Johnson, Ph.D., *is a professor in the School of Business Administration at Loyola University Chicago. He is the author of numerous books and articles and is the case editor of the* Organization Development Practitioner. *His most recent book (with Linda Stroh) is titled* Basic Essentials of Effective Consulting, *published by LEA Press in 2006.*

Leadership Development
The Value of Face-to-Face Training
Barbara Pate Glacel

Summary

As leaders are promoted up the organizational chain, they report that they spend significantly more time on people and less time on the content of their organization. Even in highly technical or specialized organizations in which leaders are promoted for their specialized skills, the people leadership becomes more time-consuming and important as one approaches higher levels.

In the past two decades, training of people in organizations has become much more computer-based and less focused on the seminar-style face-to-face training methodology. However, for leaders to learn more about leading people and dealing with people issues, training must involve people more than technology.

This article explores what senior leaders say they learn from face-to-face training that they could not learn as well, or perhaps learn at all, from reading or computer-based training. In an informal poll of senior leaders who use executive coaching services, ten takeaways emerged as significant leadership learning that can be demonstrated or practiced in face-to-face encounters.

Nearly two decades ago, many in the training industry warned that training companies would need to adopt computer-based training in order to survive into the 21st Century. Some companies invested heavily in developing computer-based surveys and courses, while others continued the face-to-face seminar-style training on which they had built their reputations. No one knew at that time whether either course of action would lead to organizational survival or organizational death as the world became even more "hooked up."

At this point, the evidence seems clear that, despite the world of instant communication, BlackBerries, iPhones, wireless networks, and YouTube, there continues to be a strong need for the kind of face-to-face leadership training and development that organizations have conducted for decades. Rather than making face-to-face training obsolete, the technological advances in communication have actually made face-to-face even more important in those areas for which leadership, communication, and interpersonal relationships are necessary.

In an informal poll conducted by the author, senior leaders from around the globe were asked what they learn from attending face-to-face leadership training and from working face-to-face with an executive coach. The leadership lessons they report all indicate the essential need for face-to-face training, interaction, and practice in communication. This is their advice.

Get Off the Computer

One cannot be an effective leader when spending most of the time behind the computer screen. Leading means interacting with people and influencing them to behave in ways that are in alignment with the organizational direction. This means getting to know people, seeing and being seen, and setting a visual example. It is impossible to practice and exhibit leadership behaviors in the privacy of one's own office. Leading requires one to be out front in public, where actions speak louder than words.

How long has the acronym MBWA appeared in management literature and training? Leaders know that it means "management by walking around," and they often report that it doesn't work well for them. Why? When they step out from behind the computer screen, they spend a few precious moments walking the halls and what do they find? Everyone else is also behind a computer screen. So these leaders conclude that MBWA is no longer relevant, and they go back into their offices.

A better decision would be to get everyone out from behind the computer screens for scheduled periods of time together. Talk to each other, get to know one another, make decisions together, solve problems jointly, and become a team that functions well in relationship to one another, not through the electronic medium.

Move to the Right

More often than not, communication today is by email. Even colleagues in adjacent offices or cubicles send each other emails instead of walking across the hall, leaning over the partition, or picking up the telephone. While email may be expedient and nearly instant (especially with the use of BlackBerries), it creates a depersonalization of communication and a huge opportunity for misunderstanding. Without tone of voice, emotional cues, and visual expressions, the intent and underlying meaning of email messages can be misconstrued. Emoticons just don't pass muster.

Consider a continuum of communication methods ranging from asynchronous and impersonal on the left (like sending a letter) to synchronous and personal on the right (like a face-to-face conversation). Methods might include, from left to right:

Letter—Fax—Email—Instant Message—Telephone—Video Conference—Face-to-Face

Whenever the conversation becomes troublesome, emotion is involved, or conflict is possible, then the preferred methodology of communication should move to the right. Email does as much to confuse communication as it does to ease communication. Using a methodology that is both synchronous and personal allows all those involved in a situation to ask questions, clarify confusion, and understand one another's intent.

Questions Are the Answers

A common misconception among new managers is that they need to have all the answers. They somehow believe that once ordained with the title and the position of manager on the organization chart, they can no longer profess, "I don't know" or even ask "What do you think?" On the contrary, with the rate of change today in almost every facet of life, the most correct answer on many occasions is, "I don't know."

When in doubt, the best answer to any situation is a question—and not just any question, but a good, open-ended question. Questions that can be answered with an easy "yes" or "no" often simply lead the witness to confirm or deny what the questioner thinks is the right answer. A better question would be one that is completely open-ended that requires the person answering to actually think, to express reasons and data, and to explore options, not to confirm whether a previous thought is right or wrong.

Questions allow one to elicit unknown information, to reach better understanding of a situation or of another's point of view, and to get inside the heads of others who may know more or at least different information. Action learning is a powerful technique for teaching questions. It is a process in which groups of people tackle problems together. During their conversations, each individual is only allowed to make a declarative statement when answering another person's open-ended question. This rule of engagement prevents fixed opinions from being expressed during both the problem-defining and problem-solving phases. The results are wider-ranging conversations that teach the technique of using open questions to guide the conversation, and often lead to solutions that are new and unique. This process is the accepted form of "action learning" as invented by Reg Revans and currently espoused by Michael Marquardt.

Seek First to Understand

Leaders are often in situations requiring answers, wisdom, pronouncements, and action, leading to the impression that listening to another's point of view implies a personal uncertainty. This misconception may cause leaders to speak first and listen poorly. The truth, however, is that listening to another's point of view or disagreement does not imply weakness. It merely leads to understanding.

Understanding does not necessarily imply agreement. Listening to others in order to understand their attitudes, opinions, and judgments allows a leader to consider all options, to look for common ground, and to consider in advance where disagreements may cause problems. Asynchronous communication often seeks the lowest common denominator of communicating brief facts and statements. It does not allow for expanded conversations during which participants build on each other's thoughts as they understand both similarities and differences.

Face-to-face interaction provides a forum for rich discussion during which people can learn that others have a right to their opinions, have a right to be heard, and that disagreement with understanding can lead to more creative results.

Fill in the Blanks

Understanding is built on information, not assumptions, which often are not fully informed. When one does not have complete information, the human tendency is to assume the worst. In the absence of information, one asks questions of concern such as, "Is she doing that because she wants my job?" or "Did he forget about the deadline and leave me without the required report?"

It is important when working in relationships with others to provide opportunities for people to fill in the blanks of available information—to answer those questions that sometimes one doesn't even know to ask, but which may lead one to make erroneous assumptions.

Training together in actual work groups provides the basis for understanding, asking questions, and filling in the blanks of information so assumptions are positive, not negative. It teaches people to value what others know and to see the results of synergistic thinking.

What's in It for Them?

People do things for their own reasons, not for the reasons of the boss, the organization, or the co-worker who may be half-way around the world. When the work is aligned with one's own values, when it supports one's own beliefs, and, even more importantly, when it builds on one's own good ideas, then it is carried out with more commitment and motivation.

The way people work today complicates their ability to figure out what another's motivation might be. Many companies work in virtual teams in which the members are literally located around the world. Their interactions are electronic, and their work is carried out in time zones that may overlap for only a few hours a day, if at all. When that is the case, how do workers who depend on each other get to know each other?

People must get to know one another to understand one another's values, beliefs, and good ideas. Face-to-face interaction provides this opportunity. Periodic and regular all-hands meetings that bring together participants from different departments or different parts of the globe lay the foundation for learning "What's in it for them?" and explaining to others "What's in it for me."

Focus on the Middle

Leaders report that they spend 80 percent of their time dealing with non-performance or interpersonal problems of the lowest-performing 10 percent of their people. The upper 10 percent who are fantastic performers lead the way without the need for attention. The 80 percent in the middle are those steady workers who could become great performers with a little help from the boss.

Overall, any group's performance could be greatly enhanced if leaders could spend 80 percent of their time dealing with the 80 percent of performers who are in the middle of the pack and who have the potential to improve. This means that the leader must know who these people are, their performance levels, and the skills and abilities that each individual must develop. That sounds like a daunting task.

Capturing time from the 80-percent focus on the nonperformers would provide ample time to set up a program of individual development plans for those who have the potential and the desire to improve. It requires face-to-face time spent to support the program, assess needs, and implement an individualized approach to employee development, not a one-size-fits-all approach.

Who Is in Charge?

Even so-called flat organizations have an organizational pyramid in which there are fewer leaders at the top and more implementers lower on the organization chart. This structure, however, does not mean that every leader at the top of the chart leads all the time. It is important for leaders to understand where and when they are in charge and where and when they need to follow others. This idea may not come naturally to those who have climbed the organizational ladder and have been rewarded for taking charge.

Leaders need to be good followers when someone else is in charge. In face-to-face leadership training, the realization becomes clear that not everyone can lead at one time when people are put into new and untested situations in which they must call on different skills than those that have made them successful in the past. Important learning comes from these experiences when a take-charge person must become a good follower in order for the exercise to succeed.

Group problem-solving exercises may be fun and entertaining by themselves, but learning comes in the debriefing of what really happened and what roles people performed in completing those exercises. Examining how people worked alone or together, leading from the front or facilitating the work of others, adding information or putting together the separate facts can impart powerful understanding for leaders who must assume a variety of roles in their work lives, sometimes leading and sometimes following.

Turn Up the Heat

A significant number of leaders receive personal feedback from 360-degree survey data that they are seen as "cold and aloof." Often that perception comes as a surprise. Those who are close to the leader may know the warm and personal side, but others who observe the leader in the typical busy workday frenzy are not so privileged.

Leadership requires forming relationships so that those who follow feel a connection and a reason to follow the person in charge. Relationships can be built on many things—mutual respect, expertise, feelings of affinity—but relationships with warmth generally create stronger bonds. The most obvious examples are those people who are in combat together who uniformly report that they put themselves in harm's way because of their strong feelings of kinship to their colleagues, not necessarily to support the mission alone.

Putting warmth into a relationship requires face-to-face contact in which individuals show interest in one another, communicate sincerely, learn about one another, and care for each other's welfare. Expressing these emotions takes practice and, like practicing leadership, it cannot be learned in private.

Stay in School

Leaders often find truth in the adage that "it is lonely at the top." Without many peers or superiors with whom one can discuss issues, leaders learn to rely on their own judgment, even when the input of others could be helpful. The scarcity of senior-level support, coupled with the rapid changes in markets, technologies, and motivation of employees, mean that leaders must find ways to continue learning.

Face-to-face interaction with leaders from other industries, other nations, and completely new disciplines provides the opportunity to continue learning and applying new and different concepts to work and productivity. An executive coach serves as a sounding board, an advisor, and a reality check for leaders who make decisions in a vacuum.

The reality of leading people is that there is no one best way, no final answer. Continuous learning and frequent practice at the leadership skills of relationship, communication, understanding, and motivation increase one's leadership abilities. One does not find that opportunity without interacting with others.

Conclusion

While new technical advances in delivering information have made it easier to communicate instantly at times when people most need information, this efficient method of delivery has not eliminated the need for face-to-face training in the people-based skills of management and leadership. There are some lessons that must be learned by experience and by interacting with others. While the ideas can be read or heard, they are most meaningful in the richness of conversation and shared experiences offered by face-to-face training and experience with others.

Barbara Pate Glacel, Ph.D., *is principal of The Glacel Group of Virginia and Brussels, Belgium. She is co-author of a business bestseller on teams. She works with individuals, teams, and organizations in the Fortune 500 and not-for-profit arenas. She has over thirty years of experience in executive coaching and leadership development at all levels of organizations. She is a well-known author and public speaker and has consulted and coached executives in Europe, Asia, and South Africa.*

The Importance of Organizational Culture in a World of Change
Building Your Leadership Team of the Future

Richard T. Rees, Allen C. Minor, and Paul S. Gionfriddo

Summary

In this article, the authors describe the challenges related to assessing and changing organizational culture. They first address the roles of those involved—particularly the importance of the leadership team, then go on to discuss the elements of a culture framework, how organization members can contribute to the definition of the desired culture, and how that culture can be assessed to determine if the current culture meets the future goals of the organization.

As the rate and volume of change in today's business environment continue to accelerate, organizations focus on new challenges in policies, procedures, reward structures, legal issues, employee relations, recruitment and retention of key personnel, and other critical factors to prepare to meet the demands of a changing world. These changes are brought about by new alliances, mergers, acquisitions, advances in technology, shifting market conditions, increased competition, financial constraints, labor demands, internal structures, international and environmental events, and other key issues that could have a significant impact on the very nature of the organization, its employees, customers, and constituents.

Whatever the reason or reasons for organizational change, often lost in the mix is the focus on the character of a new culture that must be established and nurtured to ensure success for the organization as it moves forward. The fact is that the new organizational culture is the fundamental element that will sustain the organization and enhance its ability to remain a viable entity in the future. A key point in all of this is that any organizational culture is dependent on the nature of the style, skills,

The 2009 Pfeiffer Annual: Training.

and passion of its leadership team. Therefore, it would seem logical to examine what the new leadership expectations should be for an organization in transition to a new culture and how the governing body, the senior executives, the middle management, and the supervisory teams can be developed to meet those expectations. It should be noted that this process is often time-consuming and requires a great deal of fortitude on the part of the organization. A quick fix is not effective in the long run. Also, it is critical that everyone in the organization be "on board" with the new culture and be aware of what their roles in it might be.

This is not to say that any given organization does not currently possess an effective organizational culture, but rather that it's necessary to examine that culture relative to future demands on the organization to be sure the culture is "right" to meet future demands. The organization must have a well-defined, understandable, and articulated culture that meets the needs of the organization. If this does not occur, there will be departmental culture(s) that will grow and develop on their own and may very well result in internal conflict and be in direct competition with organizational goals. This, of course, could lead to a dysfunctional organization.

It is equally important for the leadership team to be fully prepared to lead the organization in direct alignment with the demands of the organizational culture. This will require significant analysis of what the organization wants to be, where it currently is, and any interventions necessary to close the gap. It is important to include staff from the organization who have been historically resistant to change in the process. This effort must be led from the top, beginning with the governing body through the leadership team to the staff. A strong and well-defined organizational culture will go a long way to enhancing customer and employee satisfaction, loyalty, and economic prosperity.

This article addresses:

- The roles of the key players in the organizational culture and its leadership expectations

- A definition of the desired culture and leadership expectations

- The foundations for the new organizational culture and its leadership expectations

- How to analyze the current state of the organization

The Roles of the Key Players

Governing Body

It is imperative that the governing body set the direction for the organization, hold the CEO and the senior executives accountable for accomplishments, and determine the mission, vision, values, goals, and strategic initiatives. The board should be a policy-making body, not part of the operational arm of the business. The board charges the senior executive team to develop the guiding principles, the philosophy, the conceptual framework, and the operational strategy for a new culture. The board serves as the approval mechanism for the senior team to move forward. The senior team submits periodic reports to the board regarding progress. The board *must* be involved in and committed to the process.

Senior Executive Team

The role of the senior executive team is to develop, implement, and evaluate the plans and processes that will make the culture "come to life" and to ensure that the leadership team is behaving in a manner conducive to meeting the expectations of the culture. This means conducting a comprehensive analysis of the desired culture and how that relates to the existing culture and developing the appropriate interventions that will serve to close any gap. The senior executive team must conduct a comprehensive analysis of the leadership competencies that will be required compared with the existing competencies of the current senior leadership team, the middle managers, and the supervisory staff. Potential barriers, anticipated resistance, weaknesses, and strengths of the organization must be noted.

Middle Management and Supervisory Teams

Middle managers and supervisors become key partners in determining the requisite leadership competencies for the new culture. Based on those competencies, the middle managers and supervisors participate in learning interventions designed to close any gaps. It should be noted that this process should *not* be an evaluative one, but rather a diagnostic one.

Getting Started

We recommend that a five-to-nine member "Design Team" be established, drawn from members of several functional areas, to analyze the overall needs, design an operational process, develop a plan to move forward, oversee implementation of the plan, and evaluate the entire process. One important responsibility of the design team is to communicate effectively with the governing board and the organization at large. There should be significant training for the team about the nature of their task, time commitment, and expectations for outcome.

Moving Forward

Once the design team has been convened and trained, its first task should be to determine how the organization would like its culture to be defined. There are numerous ways to accomplish this, such as:

- Focus groups

- Nominal group analysis

- Delphi-type studies

We offer the following thoughts for each of these techniques.

Focus Groups

1. Develop your objectives for the focus group session. For example, your key objective might be to identify the core principles that will become the cornerstones of your organizational culture.

2. Choose participants. The list should include, if possible, members of your governing board, members of your senior leadership team, and key members of your management team. For additional diversity, you may want to identify members of the general staff who are well-respected and would give you good data.

3. Develop three to five questions, such as:

   - As you look to the future of this organization, what principles should be stressed as part of our organizational culture?

   - Why are these principles important to our organization?

   - What learning opportunities should be made available to staff in our organization to be sure that these principles are present in our organizational culture?

4. Based on the number of individuals you have identified, determine the number of meetings you will need (five to seven persons per meeting).

5. Choose a comfortable meeting place to conduct the sessions.

6. Invite the persons from your list, giving them a choice of the sessions you have identified.

7. As you conduct each focus group, be sure to accurately record the responses. You can ask the participants to review your notes (on flip charts) to be sure of their accuracy.

8. Once you have completed the sessions and have recorded the responses, send a summation to all participants asking for corrections or additions.

9. Create a final summation of all of the responses to your questions.

Nominal Group Analysis

To begin, convene a group of key stakeholders, including members of the governing board, members of the senior team, members of the management team, and perhaps well-respected members of the staff at large.

After the topic has been presented, participants should be given ample time for questions and comments so that they understand what the issue is. Then ask the participants to respond to questions around the topic. For example, you might ask: "What elements should be present in our organizational culture?" Note group responses on a flip chart, and eliminate any duplications. One or two more rounds of this process will usually give you well-refined data.

Delphi Analysis

The Delphi approach is also a mechanism to generate opinions from experts on a given topic. It involves the following steps:

1. Bring together key stakeholders from the governing board, members of the senior team, members of your management team, and well-respected members of the staff at large.

2. Ask the members of the group what they see as the most important principles that the organization should stress as part of its culture of the future and post these on flip charts for easy review.

3. After the first round, ask the members of the group to add additional principles to the list.

4. Adjourn the group and send the list out to another group representing a wider audience. Ask for their review and comments.

5. Based on the comments from Step 4, compile a new listing.

6. Continue this process for another round or two to be sure that you have a list of principles that is representative of the entire organization.

Regardless of the specific methodology that is chosen, it should be used consistently to enhance reliability of outcomes.

Foundation Elements

Guiding Principles

Next, identify the "guiding principles." Some examples might be

- The organizational culture is aligned with the mission, values, goals, and strategic initiatives of the organization.

- The organizational culture emphasizes the use of teamwork.

- The organizational culture recognizes and rewards human growth and development.

- The leadership style in the organization is based on the values of transformational leadership.

- The organization values staff input and participation.

It should be noted that the principles are just that, principles, and that they are not operational strategies. Those come later.

Once your guiding principles are agreed on (you should use the same process that you used earlier to generate the culture principles), you can develop your philosophy.

Philosophy

The philosophy is simply a set of belief statements that parallel the guiding principles. For example:

- We believe that the organizational culture should be aligned with the organization's mission, values, vision, goals, and strategic initiatives.

- We believe the organizational culture reflects the commitment of the organization to its long-term success.

- We believe that the organizational culture reflects the concept of teamwork.

The foundation is building from the guiding principles to the philosophy. This gives ample opportunity for course corrections as the process moves forward.

Conceptual Framework

The "conceptual framework" comes next. In essence, this is putting some "flesh" on the guiding principles and the philosophy you have just developed. It begins to give structure to the processes that you will implement as you move forward to close the gap between what your organizational culture is at the moment and what you want it to be for the future. Remember that the guiding principles, the philosophy, and the conceptual framework must be fully integrated before moving forward.

The conceptual framework is a structure for supporting the guiding principles and the philosophy for cultural development in your organization. It is a set of practices to be developed and implemented to achieve the desired outcomes. It represents the specific principles that will guide any learning interventions necessary to achieve your cultural goals.

The following are some sample conceptual framework statements:

- All elements of our organizational culture will relate directly to the organization's mission, vision, values, goals, and strategic initiatives.

- All elements of the organization's culture will emphasize the use of teamwork principles and practices.

- All elements of the organization's culture will reflect the importance of recognizing and rewarding human growth and development. Take care of the staff and they will take care of the organization.

- All elements of the organization's culture will value staff input and participation.

The guiding principles, philosophy, and conceptual framework mirror each other. This is a critically important concept so that, as you develop the operational strategies, there will be consistency throughout the organization.

Operational Strategy

The final piece of your foundation for your organizational culture is the "operational strategy." If the first three elements of your foundation are well-thought-out and accurately reflect what you want your organizational culture to be, developing the operational strategy will be a somewhat easier process. The operational strategy should include elements such as:

- An approach to developing diagnostic measures to determine the gaps between the existing organizational culture and what you wish to the culture to look like in the future

- An approach to identifying, measuring, and implementing the leadership behaviors that will be necessary to make your new culture successful

- An approach to how to maintain the organizational commitment to the new culture

- An approach to the identification, design, development, implementation, and evaluation of the organizational learning initiatives that will be necessary to your success

- An approach to the identification, design, development, implementation, and evaluation of the organizational behaviors that will be expected of all members of the organization to be sure that the culture, in fact, becomes your way of doing business.

The operational strategy is the "road map" that you can follow to create your culture of the future. But, as noted earlier, it must be fully integrated with all of the foundation elements.

Measuring the Current Situation Against the Desired Situation

Now that you have developed the fundamental foundation for your organizational culture of the future, you can measure how your current organizational culture measures up with what you expect the culture to look like in the future. This is the way you will develop data on which to base your learning interventions. Otherwise, you will be just "shooting in the dark."

One effective way to generate the requisite data is to administer a survey about the current culture. You will be able to compare what you find with what you think the culture should be and design your learning interventions from there.

It should not be too difficult to design your survey. You might want to consider a series of statements with Likert scale responses that will give respondents an opportunity to express their views. Of course, the data collection process should be anonymous to encourage honest responses. Once all of the responses have been collected, you can generate means for each statement or means for groups of statements that represent a common factor. Some samples of statements for your survey tool might include:

- Everything we do around here is tied directly to our organization's mission, values, vision, goals, and strategic initiative.

- Our organization emphasizes that is important for me to be able to grow and develop personally and professionally.

- My organization values my opinion on matters that are important to me.

- My organization values and rewards teamwork in carrying out our everyday tasks.

Each item would be followed by the same scale, for example, Strongly Agree, Agree, Undecided, Disagree, Strongly Disagree.

Once you have developed the survey, it should go through the same evaluative processes that were outlined earlier to validate it and generate buy-in from the various stakeholders. Use any feedback you receive to refine the survey before administering it.

Give some consideration as to the sort of demographic data you might want to collect when you administer the tool. For example, would it be important to you to know any differences in perception among various levels of staff, types of jobs, and the like? But remember that the more demographic information we ask for, the more likely it is that respondents will feel that they might be identified. This might affect the quality of responses you receive. It is important that you obtain the most candid responses possible.

Once you have determined the content of the survey and have designed the data collection process, you are ready to administer the survey. Collect and score all responses according to the method you have chosen and compile aggregate data. The aggregate data will tell you how the respondents see the organizational culture at the moment. That can be compared with the ideal culture you have envisioned.

After any differences between what you want the culture to be and how it is seen at the moment are determined, you can plan your learning interventions to change the experiences and perceptions of respondents. To get a sense of whether or not your interventions have an impact, administer the same survey at six-month intervals after each intervention.

Summary

Creating a new organizational culture and/or changing an existing culture is a very rigorous and time-consuming process that will require a tremendous amount of organizational commitment, patience, and fortitude. In fact, many organizations may opt out of the process for these very reasons. But for organizations that meet the challenge, the results should be positive and far-reaching.

While challenging, addressing the issue of organizational culture so that the culture can be better aligned with organizational goals can lead to a more productive, competitive, and successful organization.

---

*The late **Richard T. Rees, Ed.D., FHCE,** held a master's and doctorate in educational administration from Rutgers University. After a ten-year stint as a university professor at Montclair State University and Wilkes University, Dr. Rees joined Mercy Hospital as the director of hospital education at Lakeland. He retired in 2002 to open his private firm, Rees and Associates, Inc. Dr. Rees presented at numerous national* *organizations, including the American Society for Health Care Education and Training, the Alliance for Continuing Medical Education, and ASTD, among others. He held the distinction of Fellow, Health Care Education through the Action for Professional Excellence Program of the American Hospital Association.*

Allan C. Minor, DBA, *is an assistant professor at Misericordia University and an adjunct professor at the University of Scranton in the Department of Health Administration and Human Resources. He has over thirty years' experience in health care management, serving as the chief financial officer at two hospitals and, more recently, as the vice president of operations of a three-hundred-bed hospital in Pennsylvania. Dr. Minor received his doctorate in business administration from Nova Southeastern University and his master of science in finance from the University of South Carolina.*

Paul S. Gionfriddo, MS, SPHR, *has over twenty years of experience in health care human resources management and leadership. He has co-authored and presented various management and leadership development courses and has successfully led coaching and mentoring programs in several health care institutions. He has a master's of science degree in organizational management from College of Misericordia. Mr. Gionfriddo is certified as a Senior Professional in Human Resources from the Society for Human Resources Management. He has been a presenter and human resources consultant to numerous boards and community organizations and is an adjunct faculty member in the Organizational Management graduate program at Misericordia University. He is the vice president of human resources at Moses Taylor Hospital in Scranton, Pennsylvania.*

Contributors

Mark Allen, Ph.D.
Pepperdine University
6100 Center Drive
Los Angeles, CA 90045
  (310) 568-5593
  email: mallen@pepperdine.edu

Dave Arch
President
Dave Arch and Associates, Inc.
603 S. Washington Street, Suite 10
Papillion, NE 68046
  (402) 871-8108
  fax: (402) 593-7655
  email: dave@sandler.com

Jean Barbazette
President, The Training Clinic
645 Seabreeze Drive
Seal Beach, CA 90740
  (800) 937-4698
  email: jean@thetrainingclinic.com
  URL: www.thetrainingclinic.com

Christopher A. Chaves
Program Coordinator/Visiting Assistant
  Professor
Southern Illinois University Carbondale
College of Education
Department of Workforce Education
  and Development
851 Lincoln Boulevard, Suite 343
McChord AFB, WA 98438
  (253) 582-6561
  email: learnapplychange@yahoo.com

Jay Cross
30 Poppy Lane
Berkeley, CA 94708
  (510) 528-3105
  email: jaycross@internettime.com

Peter R. Garber
PPG Industries, Inc.
One PPG Place
Pittsburgh, PA 15272
  (412) 434-2009
  email: garber@ppg.com

Dennis E. Gilbert
Appreciative Strategies, LLC
P.O. Box 164
Montoursville, PA 17754
  (570) 433-8286
  fax: (570) 371-4754
  email: dennis@appreciative
  strategies.com

Paul S. Gionfriddo, MS, SPHR
Vice President, Human Resources
Moses Taylor Hospital
700 Quincy Avenue
Scranton, PA 18510
  (570) 340-2030
  email: pgionfriddo@mth.org

Barbara Pate Glacel, Ph.D.
12103 Richland Lane
Oak Hill, VA 20171
  (703) 262-9120
  email: bpglacel@glacel.com
  URL: www.glacel.com

Marshall Goldsmith, Ph.D.
16770 Via de los Rosales
Rancho Santa Fe, CA 92067
  email: Marshall@marshall
  goldsmith.com

Homer H. Johnson, Ph.D.
Professor
Department of Management
School of Business Administration
Loyola University Chicago
820 N. Michigan Avenue
Chicago, IL 60611
  email: hjohnso@luc.edu

H.B. Karp, Ph.D.
Associate Professor
Hampton University
Hampton, VA 23668
  (757) 488-3539
  email: pgshank@aol.com

M.K. Key, Ph.D.
Key Associates
1857 Laurel Ridge Drive
Nashville, TN 37215
  (615) 665-1622
  fax: (615) 665-8902
  email: keyassocs@mindspring.com
  URL: www.mkkey.com

Teresa Kirkwood, CTDP
CentralKnowledge
214 Lamarche
Laval, Quebec H7X 3M7
Canada
  (450) 689-3895
  fax: (450) 689-3895
  email: teresa@centralknowledge.com

Michael Kroth, Ph.D.
Assistant Professor
University of Idaho
322 E. Front Street, Suite 440
Boise, ID 83702
  (208) 364-4024
  email: mkroth@uidaho.edu

Dawn J. Mahoney
Humana One
N2827 N. Lake Point Drive
Lodi, WI 53555
  (608) 219-5785
  email: dawnjmahoney@charter.net

Marilyn Martin
Owner/Principal Consultant
Marilyn Martin Consulting
1905 Old Marble Falls Road
Round Mountain, TX 78663
  (830) 825-3521
  email: Marilyn@marilynmartin
  consulting.com

Linda S. Eck Mills, MBA
Dynamic Communication Services
20 Worman Lane
Bernville, PA 19506
  (610) 488-7010
  email: LSMillsRD@aol.com

Nanette Miner, Ed.D.
The Training Doctor, LLC
P.O. Box 1819
Bristol, CT 06011
  (800) 282-5474
  email: nanette@trainingdr.com
  URL: www.trainingdr.com

Allen C. Minor, DBA
Assistant Professor
Misericordia University
301 Lake Street
Dallas, PA 18612
  (570) 674-8059
  email: AMinor@Misericordia.edu

Mohandas Nair
HRD Consultant and Trainer
A2 Kamdar Building
607 Gokhale Road
Dadar, Mumbai, Maharashtra 400028
India
  91.22.24226307
  email: mknair@vsnl.net
  email: nair_mohandas@
    hotmail.com

Ajay Pangarkar, CTDP
CentralKnowledge
214 Lamarche
Laval, Quebec H7X 3M7
Canada
  (450) 689-3895
  fax: (450) 689-3895
  email: info@centralknowledge.com

Alan Richter, Ph.D.
President
QED Consulting, LLC
41 Central Park West
New York, NY 10023
  (212) 724-3335
  e-mail: alanrichter@
  qedconsulting.com

Ronald Roberts
President
Action Centered Training Inc. and ACT
  Games, LLC
528 Elizabeth Drive
Eagleville, PA 19403
  (610) 630-3325
  fax: 610-630-3326
  email: SwimmerRR@aol.com
  URL: www.corporateteambuilding.com

Travis L. Russ, Ph.D.
Assistant Professor
School of Business Administration
Fordham University
1790 Broadway, Office Number 1304
New York, NY 10019
  (212) 636-6354
  fax: (212) 586-0575
  email: russ@fordham.edu
  URL: www.travisruss.com

William J. Shirey, Ph.D.
110 Tuckahoe Trace
Yorktown, VA 23693
  (757) 329-6537
  email: iseconsulting@cox.net

Avinash Kumar Srivastav, Ph.D.
Dean (Research)
Icfai Business School
19/3, Srinivasa Industrial Estate
Near Metro
Kanakapura Road
Bangalore 560062
India
  Phone: 91.26668059
  email: aksrivastav@ibsindia.org

Jonathan D. Taylor, Ph.D.
Associate Professor of Finance
Hampton University
Hampton, VA 23668
(757) 727-5166
Fax: (757) 727-5048
email: Jonathan.taylor@hamptonu.edu

Sivasailam "Thiagi" Thiagarajan
4423 East Trailridge Road
Bloomington, IN 47408
(812) 332-1478
email: Thiagi@thiagi.com
URL: thiagi.com

Lorraine L. Ukens
Team-ing With Success
25252 Quail Croft Place
Leesburg, FL 34748-1860
(352) 365-0378
email: ukens@team-ing.com

Yusra Laila Visser, Ph.D.
Florida Atlantic University
Instructional Technology and Research
  Department
777 Glades Road
Boca Raton, FL 33431
(561) 297-3000
email: yusravisser@gmail.com

Ryan Watkins, Ph.D.
Educational Technology Leadership
George Washington University
2134 G Street NW, Suite 103
Washington, DC 20052
(202) 994-2263
email: rwatkins@gwu.edu
URL: www.ryanrwatkins.com

Richard T. Whelan
Chesney Row Consortium for Learning
  and Development
520 Collings Avenue, Suite B823
Collingswood, NJ 08107
(856) 858-9496
email: MrPerker@aol.com

Marty C. Yopp, Ed.D.
Professor
University of Idaho
322 E. Front Street, Suite 440
Boise, ID 83702
(208) 364-9918
email: myopp@uidaho.edu

Devora Zack
President, Only Connect Consulting, Inc.
7806 Ivymount Terrace
Potomac, MD 20854
(301) 765-6262
fax: (301) 765-2182
email: dzack@onlyconnect
consulting.com

Sherene Zolno
President
Proaction Associates
25900 Pillsbury Road SW
Vashon, WA 98070
(206) 463-6374
email: coachpb@comcast.net

Contents of the Companion Volume, *The 2009 Pfeiffer Annual: Consulting*

Experiential Learning Activities

** Talent Management Topics

Editor's Choice

Inventories, Questionnaires, and Surveys

** Talent Management Topics

Articles and Discussion Resources

** Talent Management Topics

** Talent Management Topics

How to Use the CD-ROM

System Requirements

PC with Microsoft Windows 98SE or later
Mac with Apple OS version 8.6 or later

Using the CD with Windows

To view the items located on the CD, follow these steps:

1. Insert the CD into your computer's CD-ROM drive.

2. A window appears with the following options:

   Contents: Allows you to view the files included on the CD-ROM.

   Software: Allows you to install useful software from the CD-ROM.

   Links: Displays a hyperlinked page of websites.

   Author: Displays a page with information about the Author(s).

   Contact Us: Displays a page with information on contacting the publisher or author.

   Help: Displays a page with information on using the CD.

   Exit: Closes the interface window.

If you do not have autorun enabled, or if the autorun window does not appear, follow these steps to access the CD:

1. Click Start → Run.

2. In the dialog box that appears, type d:<\\>start.exe, where d is the letter of your CD-ROM drive. This brings up the autorun window described in the preceding set of steps.

3. Choose the desired option from the menu. (See Step 2 in the preceding list for a description of these options.)

In Case of Trouble

If you experience difficulty using the CD-ROM, please follow these steps:

1. Make sure your hardware and systems configurations conform to the systems requirements noted under "System Requirements" above.

2. Review the installation procedure for your type of hardware and operating system.

It is possible to reinstall the software if necessary.

To speak with someone in Product Technical Support, call 800–762–2974 or 317–572–3994 M–F 8:30 A.M.–5:00 P.M. EST. You can also get support and contact Product Technical Support through our website at www.wiley.com/techsupport.

Before calling or writing, please have the following information available:

- Type of computer and operating system

- Any error messages displayed

- Complete description of the problem.

It is best if you are sitting at your computer when making the call.